SignalR Programming in Microsoft® ASP.NET

José M. Aguilar

PUBLISHED BY
Microsoft Press
A Division of Microsoft Corporation
One Microsoft Way
Redmond, Washington 98052-6399

Library of Congress Control Number: 2014930486
ISBN: 978-0-7356-8388-4

Printed and bound in the United States of America.

Second Printing: May 2014

Microsoft Press books are available through booksellers and distributors worldwide. If you need support related to this book, email Microsoft Press Book Support at mspinput@microsoft.com. Please tell us what you think of this book at http://www.microsoft.com/learning/booksurvey.

Microsoft and the trademarks listed at http://www.microsoft.com/about/legal/en/us/IntellectualProperty /Trademarks/EN-US.aspx are trademarks of the Microsoft group of companies. All other marks are property of their respective owners.

The example companies, organizations, products, domain names, email addresses, logos, people, places, and events depicted herein are fictitious. No association with any real company, organization, product, domain name, email address, logo, person, place, or event is intended or should be inferred.

This book expresses the author's views and opinions. The information contained in this book is provided without any express, statutory, or implied warranties. Neither the authors, Microsoft Corporation, nor its resellers, or distributors will be held liable for any damages caused or alleged to be caused either directly or indirectly by this book.

Acquisitions Editor: Devon Musgrave
Developmental Editor: Devon Musgrave
Project Editor: Carol Dillingham
Editorial Production: nSight, Inc.
Technical Reviewer: Todd Meister; Technical Review services provided by Content Master, a member of CM Group, Ltd.
Copyeditor: Richard Carey
Indexer: Lucie Haskins
Cover: Twist Creative • Seattle and Joel Panchot

To my parents, for all the love and unconditional support you gave that kid who only liked computers.

And to my three girls, Inma, Inmita, and María, for putting up with me daily and yet being able to give me so much love and happiness.

—José M. Aguilar

Contents at a Glance

Contents

What do you think of this book? We want to hear from you!

Microsoft is interested in hearing your feedback so we can continually improve our books and learning resources for you. To participate in a brief online survey, please visit:

microsoft.com/learning/booksurvey

What do you think of this book? We want to hear from you!

Microsoft is interested in hearing your feedback so we can continually improve our
books and learning resources for you. To participate in a brief online survey, please visit:

microsoft.com/learning/booksurvey

Introduction

SignalR, Microsoft's latest addition to the web development technology stack, is a framework that facilitates the creation of amazing real-time applications, such as online collaboration tools, multiuser games, and live information services, whose development has traditionally been quite complex.

This book provides a complete walkthrough of SignalR development from scratch, but it will also deal with more advanced topics. The idea is that after reading it you will be familiar with the possibilities of this framework and able to apply it successfully in practice in the creation of real time systems of any size. It can also be used as a reference manual because, although not exhaustively, it includes most features of practical application in the development of SignalR systems, and it provides the bases for fully mastering them.

Who should read this book

The aim of this book is to help developers understand, know, and program SignalR-based components or applications. It can be of special interest to developers who need to make use of real-time immediacy in existing applications or who want to create new systems based on this paradigm.

Developers specializing in the back end will learn to implement real-time services that can be consumed from any client and to address scenarios such as those requiring scalability or quality improvement via unit tests. Those who are more oriented to the front end will see how they can consume real-time services and add spectacular features to their creations on the client side. Web developers, especially, will find a really simple way to break the limitations characteristic of the HTTP-based world, thanks to the use of push and the asynchrony of these solutions.

Assumptions

In this book, we will assume that the reader has a good knowledge of C# and programming within the .NET environment in general. Also, because SignalR itself and many of the examples and contents are focused on the web world, it is necessary to know the protocols on which it rests, as well as having a certain knowledge of the basic languages of these environments, such as HTML and, in particular, JavaScript.

Although not strictly necessary, the reader might benefit from some prior knowledge about development with jQuery, Windows Phone 8, or WinRT for the chapters that develop examples and contents related to them. Familiarity with techniques such as unit testing, mocking, and dependency injection to get the most out of the final chapters could also prove helpful.

Who should not read this book

Readers who do not know the .NET platform and C# will not be able to benefit from this book. If you do not have prior knowledge of JavaScript, it will be difficult to follow the book's explanations.

Organization of this book

This book is structured into nine chapters, throughout which we will go over different aspects of the development of real-time multiuser systems with SignalR, starting from scratch and all the way up to the implementation of advanced features of this framework.

Chapter 1, "Internet, asynchrony, multiuser...wow!" and Chapter 2, "HTTP: You are the client, and you are the boss," are purely introductory, and they will help you understand the technological context and the foundations on which this new framework rests.

In Chapter 3, "Introducing SignalR," we will present SignalR at a high level, showing its position in the Microsoft web development technology stack and other related concepts such as OWIN and Katana.

From this point, we will begin to look in detail at how to develop applications by using SignalR. We will dedicate Chapter 4, "Persistent connections," and Chapter 5, "Hubs," to study development from different levels of abstraction, using persistent connections and hubs. In Chapter 6, "Persistent connections and hubs from other threads," we will study how to integrate these components with other technologies within the same application, and in Chapter 7, "Real-time multiplatform applications," we will see how to implement multiplatform clients.

Chapter 8, "Deploying and scaling SignalR," will show different deployment scenarios and the scaling solutions offered by SignalR. In Chapter 9, "Advanced topics," we will find miscellanea where we will deal with more advanced aspects, such as security, extensibility, testing, and others.

Finding your best starting point in this book

Although this book is organized in such a way that it can be read from beginning to end following a path of increasing depth in the contents addressed, it can also be used as a reference by directly looking up specific chapters, depending on the level of knowledge the reader starts with and their individual needs.

Thus, for developers who are approaching SignalR for the first time, the recommendation would be to read the book from beginning to end, in the order that the chapters have been written. However, for those who are acquainted with SignalR and have already developed with it in any of its versions, it will suffice to take a quick look at the first three chapters and then to pay closer attention to the ones dedicated to development with persistent connections or hubs to find out aspects they did not know about or changes from previous versions. From there, it would be possible to go directly to resolving doubts in specific areas, such as the scalability features of the framework, implementing authorization mechanisms, or the procedure for performing unit tests on hubs.

In any case, regardless of the chapter or section, it is a good idea to download and install the related example projects, which will allow practicing and consolidating the concepts addressed.

Conventions and features in this book

This book presents information using the following conventions designed to make the information readable and easy to follow:

- Boxed elements with labels such as "Note" provide additional information or alternative methods for successfully completing a task.

- Text that you type (apart from code blocks) appears in bold.

- A plus sign (+) between two key names means that you must press those keys at the same time. For example, "Press Alt+Tab" means that you have to hold down the Alt key while you press the Tab key.

- A vertical bar between two or more menu items (for example, "File | Close") means that you should select the first menu or menu item, then the next one, and so on.

System requirements

To be able to adequately follow the examples shown in this book and practice with them, it is necessary to have, at least, the following hardware and software items:

- A computer equipped with a processor whose speed is at least 1.6 GHz (2 GHz recommended).

- 2 GB RAM (4 GB is advisable).

- A video card compatible with DirectX 9, capable of resolutions above 1024x768.

- The operating systems Windows 7 SP1, Windows 8, Windows 8.1, or Windows Server editions above 2008 R2 SP1.

- Internet Explorer 10.

- Visual Studio 2012 or above, in any of its editions. It is possible to use Express versions in most cases.

- An Internet connection.

Some examples might require that you have a system account with administrator permissions or that you install complements such as the Windows Phone SDK. In some chapters, external resources are also used, such as Windows Azure services.

Code samples

Throughout this book you can find examples, and even complete projects, to illustrate the concepts dealt with. The majority of these, as well as other additional examples, can be downloaded from the following address:

http://aka.ms/SignalRProg/files

Follow the instructions to download the SignalRProgramming_codesamples.zip file.

> **Note** In addition to the code samples, your system should have Visual Studio 2012 or 2013 installed.

Notes on the version

This book has been written using version 2.0.0 of SignalR, so throughout it you will find various references to that specific version.

However, the SignalR team at Microsoft is constantly striving to improve its product, so it frequently issues software updates. The numbering of these versions is usually of the 2.0.x or 2.x.0 type. Besides corrections, these updates might include some new or improved features, but not breaking changes or significant modifications of the development APIs.

In any case, the contents of the book will still be valid after updating components to these new versions, although it will obviously be necessary to modify the existing references in the source code of the examples, especially in the case of references to script libraries.

Thus, if we have a code such as the following:

```
<script src="/scripts/jquery.signalR-2.0.0.min.js"></script>
```

after installing version 2.0.1 of SignalR, it should be changed to this:

```
<script src="/scripts/jquery.signalR-2.0.1.min.js"></script>
```

Installing the code samples

To install the code samples, just download the file indicated and decompress it into a folder in your system.

Using the code samples

After decompressing the file, a folder structure will have been created. The folders are organized in the same order as the chapters in the book, starting with Chapter 4, which is where we will begin to look at examples of code:

...

Chapter 04 – Persistent connections

Chapter 05 – Hubs

Chapter 06 – External access

...

Inside each of these folders you can find a subfolder for each sample project included. These subfolders are numbered in the order that the concepts are dealt with in the book:

...

Chapter 08 – Scaling

1-AzureServiceBus

2-SqlServer

...

Inside these folders you can find the specific solution file (*.sln) for each example. The solutions are completely independent of each other and include a fully functional example that is ready to be run (F5 from Visual Studio), although in some cases it will be necessary to make some prior adjustments in configurations. In such cases, detailed instructions are always given for this on the main page of the project or in a readme.txt file.

Acknowledgments

As trite as it might sound, a book such as this would not be possible without the collaboration of many people who have helped with their time and effort for it to become a reality, and it is only fair to dedicate them a special word of thanks.

In particular, I would like to thank my editor at campusMVP.net, Jose M. Alarcón (on Twitter at @jm_alarcon) for his involvement, his ability in the project management, coordination, and revision, as well as for his sound advice, all of which have led us here.

Javier Suárez Ruíz's (@jsuarezruiz) collaboration has also been essential, for his contributions and SignalR client implementation examples in non-web environments such as Windows Phone or WinRT.

I would like to thank Victor Vallejo, of campusMVP.net, for his invaluable help with the text.

On the part of Microsoft, I want to give thanks to the acquisitions editor, Devon Musgrave, for his interest in this project from the start, without which this book would have never been made. I also want to thank project editor Carol Dillingham for her expert work. Thanks go out to technical reviewer Todd Meister, copy editor Richard Carey, project manager Sarah Vostok of nSight, and indexer Lucie Haskins. And thanks to Sarah Hake and Jenna Boyd of O'Reilly Media for their support.

Lastly, I would like to thank Damian Edwards and David Fowler for their invaluable input. It is a privilege to have been able to benefit from the suggestions and contributions of the creators of SignalR to make this book as useful as possible.

Errata & book support

We have made every effort to ensure the accuracy of this book and its companion content. Any errors that have been reported since this book was published are listed at:

http://aka.ms/SignalRProg/errata

If you find an error that is not already listed, you can report it to us through the same page.

If you need additional support, email Microsoft Press Book Support at *mspinput@ microsoft.com*.

Please note that product support for Microsoft software is not offered through the addresses above.

We want to hear from you

At Microsoft Press, your satisfaction is our top priority, and your feedback our most valuable asset. Please tell us what you think of this book at:

http://aka.ms/tellpress

The survey is short, and we read every one of your comments and ideas. Thanks in advance for your input!

Stay in touch

Let's keep the conversation going! We're on Twitter: *http://twitter.com/MicrosoftPress*.

CHAPTER 1

Internet, asynchrony, multiuser... wow!

An application that combines Internet, asynchrony, and multiple users cooperating and interacting at the same time always deserves a "wow!". At some point, we have all doubtlessly been amazed by the interactivity that some modern web systems can offer, such as Facebook, Twitter, Gmail, Google Docs, Office Web Apps, or many others, where we receive updates almost in real time without having to reload the page.

For example, when we are editing a document online using Office Web Apps and another user also accesses it, we can see that they have entered the document and follow the changes that they are making. Even in a more everyday scenario such as a simple web chat, the messages being typed by our friend just appear, as if by magic. Both systems use the same type of solution: asynchronous data transfer between the server and the clients in real time.

We developers who have had some experience in the world of the web are accustomed to the traditional approach proposed by the protocols that govern this environment—that is, the client is the active agent who makes requests asking for information, and the server merely answers. This is a probable reason for why we are so excited at the prospect of applications where the client side is directly updated by the server—for example, due to a new user having entered to edit the document or because our chat room buddy has written a new message in the chat. Pure magic.

The world is undoubtedly demanding this immediacy: users need to know right away what is happening in their environment, the documents they are working on, their social networks, their online games, and an increasing number of areas of their daily life. Instead of having to seek information as they used to do just a few years ago, now they want the information to come to them as soon as it is generated.

These needs have been evident at web protocol level for some time, because the long-standing HTTP, as defined in its day, cannot meet them efficiently. In fact, the organizations that define web standards and protocols, and also browser developers, are aware of this and have been working for years on new mechanisms for communication between the client and the server in opposite direction to the conventional one—that is, allowing the server to take the initiative in communications.

This has materialized into new protocols that can be used with a degree of reliability, although they are still rather far from universal solutions. The great diversity of client and server platforms, and even of network infrastructures, makes the adoption of these new mechanisms difficult and slow. Later on, we will delve in detail into these aspects.

However, these are not the only issues that have to be addressed when developing real-time multiuser applications. Communications, as we know, constitute unstable and unpredictable variables, which make management and distribution of messages to users quite complicated. For example, in a chat room application, we could have users with very different bandwidths connected to the same room, and those bandwidths might even fluctuate throughout the chat session. To prevent the loss of messages in this scenario, the server should be capable of storing them temporarily, sending them to their recipients, and monitoring which users have received them already, always taking into account the conditions of communication with each user and the potential breakdowns that might occur during delivery, sending data again if necessary. In a sense, this is very similar to the features that we can find in traditional SMTP servers, but with the added requirement of the immediacy needed by real-time systems. It is easy to picture the complexity and difficulty associated with the implementation of a system such as the one described.

Until recently, there was no component or framework in the area of .NET technologies provided by Microsoft that was capable of providing a complete solution to the problems of implementing this type of application. Certainly, there are many technologies capable of offering connected and disconnected services, such as the familiar Web Services, WCF, or the more recent Web API. However, none of them was specifically designed for asynchronous environments with real-time collaboration between multiple users. In fact, although it was possible to create this type of system with such platforms, it was not a trivial task even for the most experienced developers, and it frequently produced very inefficient systems with many performance problems and limited scalability.

Throughout these pages, we will learn how to implement impressive features of this kind using SignalR, a remarkable framework—powerful, flexible, and scalable—which will facilitate our task to the point of making it trivial.

For this purpose, we will first present a brief review of the problems that we find when developing real-time multiuser applications, some of which we have already mentioned. We will quickly look at HTTP operation and its limitations for supporting these types of systems, and we will introduce the *push* concept. We will also describe the standards that are currently in the process of being defined by W3C and IETF, as well as techniques that we can currently use for implementing push on HTTP. This will allow us to achieve a deep understanding of the scenario in which we are working and the challenges surrounding the development of applications boasting the immediacy and interactivity that we have described. In turn, this will help us gain a better understanding of how SignalR works and the basis on which it rests.

Next, we will formally introduce SignalR, describing its main features, its position within the stack of Microsoft technologies for web development, and the different levels of abstraction that it allows over the underlying protocols and which will help us remain separated from lower-level details so that we can just focus on creating spectacular features for our users. We will also take this chance to speak about OWIN and Katana, two new agents which are becoming increasingly prominent in various technologies, SignalR included.

We will study in depth the various techniques and abstractions provided by this framework to create interactive multiuser real-time applications, both on the client and server sides, and we will learn to make use of their power and flexibility. Naturally, for this we will provide different code examples that will help us understand its basis in a practical way and thus illustrate how we can use this framework in real-life projects.

We will also describe how SignalR is independent of web environments: although they might seem to constitute its natural environment, this framework goes far beyond them, allowing the provision of real-time services from any type of application and, likewise, their consumption from practically any type of system. We will see several examples of this.

Another aspect of great importance, to which we will devote several pages, is reviewing the deployment and scalability of SignalR applications. We will study the "out-of-the-box" tools that come with this platform and point to other possible solutions when addressing scenarios where such tools are not powerful enough. Additionally, we will look at different techniques designed to monitor the status of our servers and improve their performance in high-concurrency environments.

Finally, we will go into advanced aspects of programming with SignalR, which will give us deeper insight as to how the framework works, including security, creating decoupled components using dependency injection, SignalR extensibility, unit testing, and other aspects of interest.

Welcome to multiuser real-time asynchronous applications. Welcome to SignalR!

CHAPTER 2

HTTP: You are the client, and you are the boss

HTTP (HyperText Transfer Protocol) is the "language" in which the client and the server of a web application speak to each other. It was initially defined in 1996[1], and the simplicity and versatility of its design are, to an extent, responsible for the success and expansion of the web and the Internet as a whole.

Although it is still valid in traditional web scenarios, there are others, such as real-time applications or services, for which it is quite limited.

HTTP operations

An HTTP operation is based on a request-response schema, which is always started by the client. This procedure is often referred to as the pull model: When a client needs to access a resource hosted by a server, it purposely initiates a connection to it and requests the desired information using the "language" defined by the HTTP protocol. The server processes this request, returns the resource that was asked for (which can be the contents of an existing file or the result of running a process), and the connection is instantly closed.

If the client needs to obtain a new resource, the process starts again from the beginning: a connection to the server is opened, the request for the resource is sent, the server processes it, it returns the result, and then the connection is closed. This happens every time we access a webpage, images, or other resources that are downloaded by the browser, to name a few examples.

As you can guess by looking at Figure 2-1, it is a synchronous process: after sending the request to the server, the client is left to wait, doing nothing until the response is available.

---

[1] Specification of HTTP 1.0: *http://www.w3.org/Protocols/HTTP/1.0/spec.html*

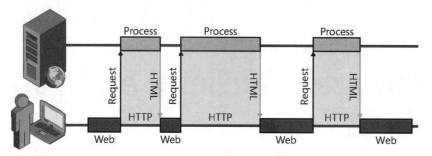

FIGURE 2-1 HTTP communication between a browser and a web server.

Although this operation is a classic in web systems, the HTTP protocol itself can support the needs for asynchrony of modern applications, owing to the techniques generally known as AJAX (Asynchronous JavaScript And XML).

Using AJAX techniques, the exchange of information between the client and the server can be done without leaving the current page. At any given moment, as shown in Figure 2-2, the client can initiate a connection to the server by using JavaScript, request a resource, and process it (for example, updating part of the page).

What is truly advantageous and has contributed to the emergence of very dynamic and interactive services, such as Facebook or Gmail, is that these operations are carried out asynchronously—that is, the user can keep using the system while the latter communicates with the server in the background to send or receive information.

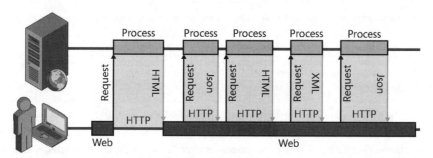

FIGURE 2-2 AJAX in a webpage.

This operating schema continues to use and abide by the HTTP protocol and the client-driven request-response model. The client is always the one to take the initiative, deciding when to connect to the server.

However, there are scenarios in which HTTP is not very efficient. With this protocol, it is not easy to implement instant-messaging applications or chat rooms, collaboration tools, multiuser online games, or real-time information services, even when using asynchrony.

The reason is simple: HTTP is not oriented to real time. There are other protocols, such as the popular IRC[2], which are indeed focused on achieving swifter communication to offer more dynamic and interactive services than the ones we can obtain using pull. In those, the server can take the initiative and send information to the client at any time, without waiting for the client to request it expressly.

Polling: The answer?

As web developers, when we face a scenario in which we need the server to be the one sending information to the client on its own initiative, the first solution that intuitively comes to our minds is to use the technique known as *polling*. Polling basically consists in making periodic connections from the client to check whether there is any relevant update at the server, as shown in Figure 2-3.

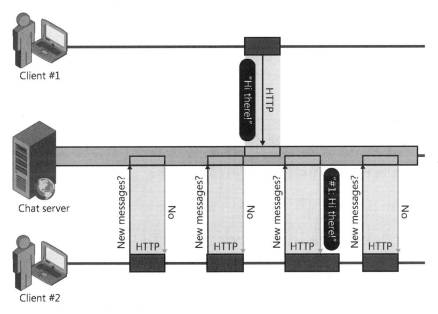

FIGURE 2-3 Polling in a chat room service.

The main advantages of this solution are, first, its easy implementation and, second, its universal application: it works in every case, with all browsers and with all servers, because it does nothing more than use the standard features of HTTP. And, of course, we still use the pull model.

However, sometimes the price of polling is too high. Constant connections and disconnections have a high cost in terms of bandwidth and processing at both ends of communication. The worst part is that this cost increases proportionally to our need for faster updates and the number of clients making use of the service at a given time. In an application providing real-time updates, it is easy to imagine the load that a server has to bear when it has thousands of users connected, requesting several updates per second.

---

[2] Internet Relay Chat (IRC) protocol: *http://www.ietf.org/rfc/rfc1459.txt*

There are techniques to mitigate these problems insofar as possible. One of them is to use adaptive intervals so that the interval between queries regularly adapts to the current system load or to the probability of new updates. This solution is quite easy to implement and can significantly improve resource consumption in some scenarios.

There is a more conservative variant of polling, but it degrades user experience. It is the technique called *piggy backing*, which consists in not making deliberate queries from the client and, instead, taking advantage of any interaction between the user and the system to update any necessary information. To illustrate this, consider a web mail service: instead of making periodic queries to check for the arrival of new messages, those checks would be performed each time the user accessed a page, an email, or any other feature. This can be useful in scenarios that do not require great immediacy and in which the features of the system itself mean that we can be sure that the user will interact with the application frequently.

Of course, these variants can be combined with each other to achieve more efficient usage of resources, offering at the same time a reasonable user experience. For example, to obtain the updates, it would be possible to update the status of a client via piggy backing when the client interacts with the server, using polling with or without adaptive periodicity when there is no such interaction.

In conclusion, polling is a reasonable option despite its disadvantages when we want a solution that is easy to implement and that can be used universally and in scenarios in which a very high update frequency is not required. In fact, it is used a lot in current systems. A real-life example of its application is found in the web version of Twitter, where polling is used to update the timeline every 30 seconds.

Push: The server takes the initiative

We have already said that there are applications where the use of pull is not very efficient. Among them, we can name instant-messaging systems, real-time collaboration toolsets, multiuser online games, information broadcasting services, and any kind of system where it is necessary to send information to the client right when it is generated.

For such applications, we need the server to take the initiative and be capable of sending information to the client exactly when a relevant event occurs, instead of waiting for the client to request it.

This is precisely the idea behind the push, or server push, concept. This name does not make reference to a component, a technology, or a protocol: it is a concept, a communication model between the client and the server where the latter is the one taking the initiative in communications.

This concept is not new. There are indeed protocols that are push in concept, such as IRC, the protocol that rules the operation of classic chat room services, or SMTP, the protocol in charge of coordinating email sending. These were created before the term that identifies this type of communication was coined.

For the server to be able to notify events in real time to a set of clients interested in receiving them, the ideal situation would be to have the ability to initiate a direct point-to-point connection with them. For example, a chat room server would keep a list with the IP addresses of the connected clients and open a socket type connection to each of them to inform them of the arrival of a new message.

However, that is technically impossible. For security reasons, it is not normally possible to make a direct connection to a client computer due to the existence of multiple intermediate levels that would reject it, such as firewalls, routes, or proxies. For this reason, the customary practice is for clients to be the ones to initiate connections and not vice versa.

To circumvent this issue and manage to obtain a similar effect, certain techniques emerged that were based on active elements embedded in webpages (Java applets, Flash, Silverlight apps, and so on). These components normally used sockets to open a persistent connection to the server—that is, a connection that would stay open for as long as the client was connected to the service, listening for anything that the server had to notify. When events occurred that were relevant to the client connected, the server would use this open channel to send the updates in real time.

Although this approach has been used in many push solutions, it is tending to disappear. Active components embedded in pages are being eliminated from the web at a dramatic speed and are being substituted for more modern, reliable, and universal alternatives such as HTML5. Furthermore, long-term persistent connections based on pure sockets are problematic when there are intermediary elements (firewalls, proxies, and so on) that can block these communications or close the connections after a period of inactivity. They can also pose security risks to servers.

Given the need for reliable solutions to cover these types of scenarios, both W3C and IETF—the main organizations promoting and defining protocols, languages, and standards for the Internet— began to work on two standards that would allow a more direct and fluent communication from the server to the client. They are known as WebSockets and Server-Sent Events, and they both come under the umbrella of the HTML5 "commercial name."

WebSockets

The WebSockets standard consists of a development API, which is being defined by the W3C (World Wide Web Consortium, *http://www.w3.org*), and a communication protocol, on which the IETF (Internet Engineering Task Force, *http://www.ietf.org*) has been working.

Basically, it allows the establishment of a persistent connection that the client will initiate whenever necessary and which will remain open. A two-way channel between the client and the server is thus created, where either can send information to the other end at any time, as shown in Figure 2-4.

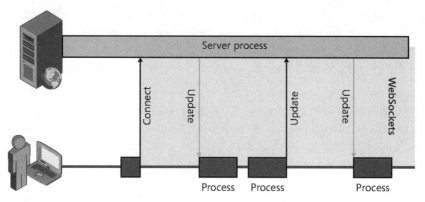

FIGURE 2-4 Operation of the WebSockets standard.

Although at the moment the specifications of both the API and the protocol are quite far advanced, we cannot yet consider this technology to be universally applicable.

We can find implementations of WebSockets in many current browsers, such as Internet Explorer 10, Internet Explorer 11, Chrome, and Firefox. Some feature only partial implementations (Opera mini, Android browser), and in others, WebSockets is simply not available[3].

Aside from the problem of the different implementation levels at the client side, the fact that the standard includes an independent protocol for communication (although initially negotiated on HTTP) means that changes also have to be made on some infrastructural elements, and even on servers, so that connections using WebSockets are accepted.

For example, it has not been possible to use WebSockets easily on Microsoft technologies up until the very latest wave of developments (Internet Explorer 10, ASP.NET 4.5, WCF, IIS 8, and so on), in which it has begun to be supported natively.

From the perspective of a developer, WebSockets offers a JavaScript API that is really simple and intuitive to initiate connections, send messages, and close the connections when they are not needed anymore, as well as events to capture the messages received:

```
var ws = new WebSocket("ws://localhost:9998/echo");
ws.onopen = function() {
    // Web Socket is connected, send data using send()
    ws.send("Message to send");
    alert("Message is sent...");
};
ws.onmessage = function(evt) {
    var received_msg = evt.data;
    alert("Message is received...");
};
ws.onclose = function () {
    // WebSocket is closed.
    alert("Connection is closed...");
};
```

---

[3] Source: *http://caniuse.com/WebSockets*

As you can see, the connection is opened simply by instantiating a WebSockets object pointing to the URL of the service endpoint. The URL uses the ws:// protocol to indicate that it is a WebSockets connection.

You can also see how easily we can capture the events produced when we succeed in opening the connection, data are received, or the connection is closed.

Without a doubt, WebSockets is the technology of the future for implementing push services in real time.

Server-Sent Events (API Event Source)

Server-Sent Events, also known as *API Event Source*, is the second standard on which the W3 consortium has been working. Currently, this standard is in candidate recommendation state. But this time, because it is a relatively straightforward JavaScript API and no changes are required on underlying protocols, its implementation and adoption are simpler than in the case of the WebSockets standard.

In contrast with the latter, Server-Sent Events proposes the creation of a one-directional channel from the server to the client, but opened by the client. That is, the client "subscribes" to an event source available at the server and receives notifications when data are sent through the channel, as illustrated in Figure 2-5.

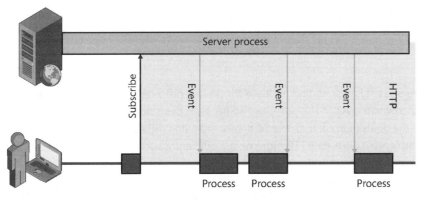

FIGURE 2-5 Operation of the Server-Sent Events standard.

All communication is performed on HTTP. The only difference with respect to a more traditional connection is the use of the content-type text/event-stream in the response, which indicates that the connection is to be kept open because it will be used to send a continuous stream of events—or messages—from the server.

Implementation at the client is even simpler than the one we saw earlier for WebSockets:

```
var source = new EventSource('/getevents');
source.onmessage = function(event) {
    alert(event.data);
};
```

As you can guess, instantiating the EventSource object initiates the subscription of the client to the service whose URL is provided in the constructor, and the messages will be processed in the callback function specified to that effect.

Currently, almost all browsers support this standard except for Internet Explorer and some mobile-specific browsers, and this limits its use in real applications. Also, if we look at it from an infrastructural point of view, we find that although being based on HTTP greatly simplifies its generalization, it requires the aid of proxies or other types of intermediaries, which must be capable of interpreting the content-type used and not processing the connections in the same way as the traditional ones—for example, avoiding buffering responses or disconnections due to time-out.

It is also important to highlight the limitations imposed by the fact that the channel established for this protocol is one-directional from the server to the client: if the client needs to send data to the server, it must do so via a different connection, usually another HTTP request, which involves, for example, having greater resource consumption than if WebSockets were used in this same scenario.

Push today

As we have seen, standards and browsers are both getting prepared to solve the classic push scenarios, although we currently do not have enough security to use them universally.

Nevertheless, push is something that we need right now. Users demand ever more interactive, agile, and collaborative applications. To develop them, we must make use of techniques allowing us to achieve the immediacy of push but taking into account current limitations in browsers and infrastructure. At the moment, we can obtain that only by making use of the advantages of HTTP and its prevalence.

Given these premises, it is easy to find multiple conceptual proposals on the Internet, such as Comet, HTTP push, reverse AJAX, AJAX push, and so on, each describing solutions (sometimes coinciding) to achieve the goals desired. In the same way, we can find different specific techniques that describe how to implement push on HTTP more or less efficiently, such as long polling, XHR streaming, or forever frame.

We will now study two of them, long polling and forever frame, for two main reasons. First, because they are the most universal ones (they work in all types of client and server systems), and second, because they are used natively by SignalR, as we shall see later on. Thus we will move toward the objectives of this book.

Long polling

This push technique is quite similar to polling, which we already described, but it introduces certain modifications to improve communication efficiency and immediacy.

In this case, the client also polls for updates, but, unlike in polling, if there is no data pending to be received, the connection will not be closed automatically and initiated again later. In long polling, the connection remains open until the server has something to notify, as shown in Figure 2-6.

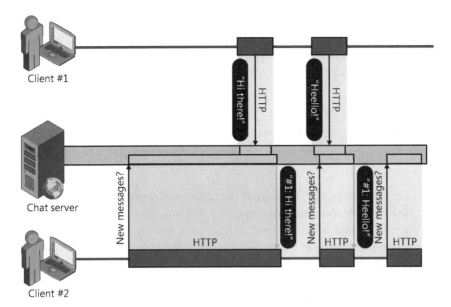

FIGURE 2-6 Long polling.

The connection, which is always initiated by the client, can be closed because of only two things:

- The server sends data to the client through the connection.

- A time-out error occurs due to lack of activity on the connection.

In both cases, a new connection would be immediately established, which would again remain waiting for updates.

This connection is used exclusively to receive data from the server, so if the client needs to send information upward, it will open an HTTP connection in parallel to be used exclusively for that purpose.

The main advantage of long polling is the low delay in updating the client, because as soon as the server has data to update the state of the client, it will be sent through the channel that is already open, so the other end will receive it in real time.

Also, because the number of connection openings and closures is reduced, resource optimization at both ends is much higher than with polling.

Currently, this is a widely used solution due to its relatively simple implementation and the fact that it is completely universal. No browser-specific feature is used—just capabilities offered by HTTP.

Resource consumption with long polling is somewhat higher than with other techniques where a connection is kept open. The reason is that there are still many connection openings and closures if the rate of updates is high, not forgetting the additional connection that has to be used when the client wants to send data to the server. Also, the time it takes to establish connections means that there might be some delay between notifications. These delays could become more evident if the server had to send a series of successive notifications to the client. Unless we implemented some kind of optimization, such as packaging several messages into one same HTTP response, each message would have to wait to be sent while the client received the previous message in the sequence, processed it, and reopened the channel to request a new update.

Forever frame

The other technique that we are going to look at is called *forever frame* and uses the HTML <IFRAME> tag cleverly to obtain a permanently open connection. In a way, this is very similar to Server-Sent Events.

Broadly, it consists in entering an <IFRAME> tag in the page markup of the client. In the source of <IFRAME>, the URL where the server is listening is specified. The server will maintain this connection permanently open (hence the "forever" in its name) and will use it to send updates in the form of calls to script functions defined at the client. In a way, we might say that this technique consists in streaming scripts that are executed at the client as they are received.

Because the connection is kept open permanently, resources are employed more efficiently because they are not wasted in connection and disconnection processes. Thus we can practically achieve our coveted real time in the server-client direction.

Just like in the previous technique, the use of HTML, JavaScript, and HTTP makes the scope of its application virtually universal, although it is obviously very much oriented towards clients that support those technologies, such as web browsers. That is, the implementation of other types of clients, such as desktop applications, or other processes acting as consumers of those services would be quite complex, as shown in Figure 2-7.

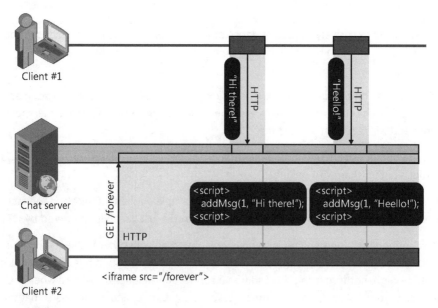

FIGURE 2-7 Forever frame.

This technique is not exempt from disadvantages either. In its implementation, it is necessary to take into account that there might be time-outs caused by the client, the server, or an intermediary element (such as proxies and firewalls). Also, to obtain the best real-time experience, responses must be sent to the client immediately and not withheld in buffers or caches. And, because the responses would accumulate inside the *iframe*, in client memory, we might end up taking up too much RAM, so we have to "recycle" or eliminate contents periodically.

Finally, the fact that the connection is used only to send data from the server to the client makes it necessary to use an additional connection when we want to send it in the opposite direction—that is, from the client to the server.

The world needs more than just push

Until now, we have seen techniques that allow us to achieve push; that is, they allow the server to be able to send information to the client asynchronously as it is generated. We have given the initiative to an element that would normally assume a passive role in communications with the client.

However, in the context of asynchronous, multiuser, and real-time applications, push is but one of the aspects that are indispensable. To create these always surprising systems, we need many more capabilities. Here we list a few of them:

- **Managing connected users**   The server must always know which users are connected to the services, which ones disconnect, and, basically, it must control all the aspects associated with monitoring an indeterminate number of clients.

- **Managing subscriptions**   The server must be capable of managing "subscriptions," or grouping clients seeking to receive specific types of messages. For example, in a chat room service, only the users connected to a specific room should receive the messages sent to that room. This way, the delivery of information is optimized and clients do not receive information that is not relevant to them, minimizing resource waste.

- **Receiving and processing actions**   The server be capable not only of sending information to clients in real time but also of receiving it and processing it on the fly.

- **Monitoring submissions**   Because we cannot guarantee that all clients connect under the same conditions, there might be connections at different speeds, line instability, or occasional breakdowns, and this means that it is necessary to provide for mechanisms capable of queuing messages and managing information submissions individually to ensure that all clients are updated.

- **Offering a flexible API, capable of being consumed easily by multiple clients**   This is even truer nowadays, when there are a wide variety of devices from which we can access online services.

We could surely enumerate many more, but these examples are more than enough to give you an idea of the complexity inherent in developing these types of applications.

Enter SignalR....

CHAPTER 3

Introducing SignalR

SignalR is a framework that facilitates building interactive, multiuser, and real-time web applications (although not only web applications, as we shall see later on), making extensive use of asynchrony techniques to achieve immediacy and maximum performance.

Originally, it was a personal project of David Fowler and Damian Edwards, members of the ASP.NET team at Microsoft, but it is now an officially integrated product in the stack of web technologies. Figure 3-1 gives a simplified idea of its position within the ASP.NET stack, where we can see Web Forms, MVC, and Web Pages as frameworks for building web applications and pages, and Web API and SignalR for building services.

FIGURE 3-1 Conceptual position of SignalR within the ASP.NET technology stack.

As is the case of many of these technologies, the product is completely open source (Apache 2.0 license), but with the advantages of having the full backing and support of the Redmond-based giant. Its development can be tracked, and even contributed to, at GitHub[1], where one can find the source code of the framework and related projects.

After several previews, alphas, and release candidates, version 1.0 of the product was released in February 2013, and its first important update came three months later with version 1.1.0, which included some interesting new features. After that, there were a few more maintenance updates released, mainly to solve bugs and introduce some small improvements.

The 2.0 beta 1 version was released in June 2013, and a few months later, after some other preliminary editions, the final version came out in October 2013, with important new internal features, some breaking changes, and multiple improvements with respect to its predecessor.

Despite the relatively young age of SignalR, it is currently being used successfully in a large number of real projects. For example, SignalR is behind the real-time collaboration features of Office Web Apps, used by SkyDrive, Office365, and SharePoint. Also, in completely different environments,

---

[1] SignalR code repository: *http://www.github.com/signalr*

SignalR brings to life the Browser Link feature introduced with Visual Studio 2013, as well as JabbR (*http://jabbr.net*), a web-based chat room service that is mainly frequented by developers, among whom you might frequently encounter the creators of this framework.

 Note The contents of this book are based on version 2.0 of SignalR. Although most concepts and techniques described here are also valid for previous versions, there might be differences in implementation due to the evolution of the development APIs.

What does SignalR offer?

Basically, SignalR isolates us from low-level details, giving us the *impression* of working on a permanently open persistent connection between the client and the server. To achieve this, SignalR includes components specific to both ends of communication, which will facilitate message delivery and reception in real time between the two.

In a way that is transparent to the developer, SignalR is in charge of determining which is the best technique available both at the client and at the server (long polling, forever frame, WebSockets, and so on) and uses it to create an underlying connection and keep it continuously open, also automatically managing disconnections and reconnections when necessary. As shown in Figure 3-2, we will see and use only one permanently open connection, and SignalR will take care of the dirty work under the hood, making everything function. Thus, with this framework, we frequently say that we work on a virtual persistent connection.

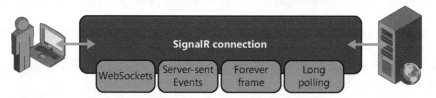

FIGURE 3-2 SignalR virtual connection.

SignalR includes an "out-of-the-box" set of transports—or techniques to keep the underlying connection to the server open—and it determines which one it should use based on certain factors, such as the availability of the technology at both ends. SignalR will always try to use the most efficient transport and will keep falling back until selecting the best one that is compatible with the context.

This decision is made automatically during an initial stage in the communication between the client and the server, known as *negotiation*. It is also possible to force the use of a specific transport by using the client libraries of the framework.

Through the proposed abstraction, SignalR offers a unified programming model that is independent of the technique used in the underlying connection. As developers, we will implement our services on the virtual connection established by the framework. Thus we will have a unified programming model. That is, it is irrelevant to us whether long polling or WebSockets are being used underneath to maintain the connection: we will always use the same API, very powerful, flexible, and optimized for creating real-time applications.

Besides its ease, there is a subsequent advantage: we can also isolate ourselves from the particular aspects of the technologies and their evolution. As developers, we will focus on programming our services, and SignalR will be in charge of managing the connections and the specifics of client and server software throughout. We will not have to worry about when WebSockets will be made universally available: our services will keep adapting and will begin to use WebSockets when that happens.

But there is more. In fact, the features mentioned so far would just help us for a limited period—until WebSockets, the most powerful technology of those proposed, became available.

SignalR also includes a messaging bus capable of managing data transmission and reception between the server and the clients connected to the service. That is, the server can keep track of its clients and detect their connections and disconnections, and it will also have mechanisms to easily send messages to all clients connected or part of them, automatically managing all issues concerning communications (different speeds, latency, errors, and so on) and ensuring the delivery of messages. All this is built on a scalable architecture that will allow our applications' ability to serve their purpose to grow as the number of users using them increases.

Moreover, SignalR includes powerful libraries on the client side that allow the consumption of services from virtually any kind of application, allowing us to manage our end of the virtual connection and send or receive data asynchronously.

In short, in SignalR, we find everything we might need to create multiuser real-time applications.

Two levels of abstraction

We have already spoken about the ability of SignalR to separate us from the particulars of the connection, offering us a homogeneous development surface which is independent of them. However, this is not completely true: in reality, there are two of them.

As shown in Figure 3-3, SignalR offers us two different levels of abstraction over the transports used to maintain the connection with the server. In fact, they make up two APIs or formulas to work on the virtual connection established.

The first one of them, called *persistent connections*, is the lower-level one and is therefore closer to the reality of the connections. In fact, it offers a development surface which is very similar to programming with sockets, although still on the virtual connection established by SignalR.

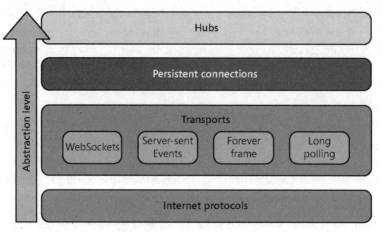

FIGURE 3-3 Levels of abstraction in SignalR.

The second level of abstraction, based on components called *hubs*, is much further away from the underlying connections and protocols, offering a very imperative programming model similar to RPC[2], where the traditional boundaries separating the client and the server melt away as if by magic.

Both levels have their spheres of application and will be studied in depth in subsequent chapters of this book.

Supported platforms

On the server side, SignalR can be executed on any operating system capable of running ASP.NET 4.5[3], such as Windows Server 2008 R2 or above, Windows 7 and Windows 8, and Windows Azure. However, if we want to make use of the most efficient transport, it is necessary to have at least Windows Server 2012 or Windows 8. These two options are obviously the most recommended.

The ideal web server to execute SignalR applications is IIS 8 or above, both in its full and Express editions, because this is the first version of the service that can accept connections via WebSockets. SignalR will also work in previous versions such as 7 and 7.5, but without being able to use WebSockets. In any case, the server must support extensionless URLs and operate in integrated pipe-line mode.

In development time, it is possible to use Visual Studio 2012 or 2013, in both cases it being rec-ommended that we use IIS Express for testing. Cassini is not supported. If, as is the usual case, we are working on a client edition of the operating system (such as Windows 8 or 8.1), it is not a good idea to use the full edition of IIS for testing during development due to limitations in the number

---

[2] Remote Procedure Call.

[3] For ASP.NET 4 projects, SignalR 1.*x* could be used, although WebSockets will not be available even when it is executed on an operating system that does support this standard.

of simultaneous connections allowed. Obviously, this problem will not exist when running IIS on Windows Server.

From the point of view of the client, as we shall see later on, SignalR supports a wide variety of platforms, ranging from the web to rich desktop clients and mobile devices, although the transports available will vary depending on the technology. For example, web-specific clients provide support for virtually all browsers currently available, although in some versions, WebSocket transports or Server-Sent Events will not be available.

On the official site of the product (*http://www.asp.net/signalr*), you can find the complete list of client platforms officially supported.

OWIN and Katana: The new kids on the block

However, as we shall see in more depth later on, the server components of SignalR are not only capable of being executed on the popular duo ASP.NET/IIS; they can work on various types of host thanks to OWIN-based architecture. OWIN is a concept that we will come across frequently throughout this book, and it is worth pausing here to explain it.

Open Web Interface for .NET[4] (OWIN) is an open specification led by the community and published under the Creative Commons license, which defines a standard interface to communicate servers with web applications, using abstractions that allow these two components, historically so tied to each other, to be decoupled. As in other occasions, this is not something radically new or out of the blue. It is derived from similar ideas already tested on platforms such as Node, Ruby, and Python.

The main goal of these indirections is twofold. First, separating applications and web servers allows more independence for both, so they can be evolved separately. For example, if SignalR had been built directly on ASP.NET, the product cycles of both frameworks would have been permanently tied, as it currently happens with Web Forms: its update depends on the arrival of a new version of the complete platform. Because this is not the case with SignalR, it will be able to evolve independently and adapt faster to the changes that this flexible and volatile world requires.

Second, this abstraction will allow our applications to be more portable, usable in various execution environments (hosters) and even on different technological platforms.

In practice, OWIN defines, among other things, a context consisting of a dictionary of values with standardized keys that the server, whichever it is, will send to the applications to provide them with information about the request, the client, parameters, and so on, as well as the way in which the applications will return the result to the host process. We might say that OWIN imposes a barrier beyond which there is to be no reference to the specific implementations of the server, isolating the application from the particulars of the latter.

---

[4] Official site of the OWIN specification: *http://owin.org/*

The OWIN standard distinguishes five main agents that make up the chain of responsibilities needed to process requests coming from a client. Each suggests the possibilities for modularization proposed by this specification:

■ **Host**   The process on which the server and the application are executed.

■ **Server**   When executed on a host, opens a port and remains listening to communicate with the clients, processing the requests using the "protocol" defined by OWIN. Sometimes the server needs to have adaptors available that are capable of translating data into OWIN semantics. It is also possible to find software components that act at the same time as server and host of an application.

■ **Middleware**   Transverse components installed between the server and the application, capable of examining, directing, or modifying requests and responses to obtain a result. Normally, here we find very specialized modules that perform specific tasks such as routing requests to the appropriate component, managing security, and so on.

■ **Web framework**   A special type of middleware that is much more complex and reaches further than modules, because its mission is to provide an API, tools, and functionalities that simplify the process of building applications, which can be used to process requests with a higher level of abstraction. Sometimes these frameworks need adaptors to understand the information received from the server using the OWIN specification.

■ **Web application**   Usually built on a framework and in charge of the final processing of requests.

Figure 3-4 shows these roles in the context of the architecture of OWIN-based solutions.

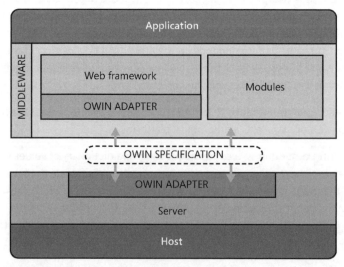

FIGURE 3-4 Architecture of OWIN-based solutions.

This architecture can materialize in diverse scenarios where these roles can be played by different software components, allowing the flexibility and independence that OWIN aims for. For example, the same SignalR application could work on the technology stacks shown in Figure 3-5.

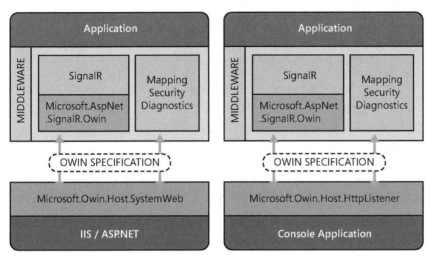

FIGURE 3-5 Two possible deployment scenarios of the same SignalR application.

Another key feature of OWIN is the *application delegate* or *AppFunc*, which is the delegate that will be in charge of processing each request. This delegate is defined as follows, receiving as a parameter the dictionary containing the data on the context of the request and returning a Task object representing the task to be processed:

```
using AppFunc = Func<
    IDictionary<string, object>, // Environment
    Task>; // Done
```

These asynchronous tasks are implemented on different middleware modules or frameworks, which can be chained to each other to create complex pipelines for the processing of requests.

Figure 3-6 shows the location of middleware components in the processing flow of requests, where they are established as middlemen through which both requests and responses pass, all within the dictionary that contains the context. This vantage position gives them the option of either capturing a request and processing it completely or simply acting as a gateway to other middleware modules of the pipeline with the possibility of altering the data of the request or its response.

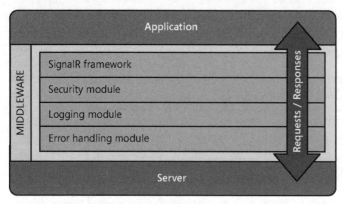

FIGURE 3-6 Processing of requests through the OWIN pipeline.

But undoubtedly the most interesting feature, which represents a great improvement compared to the traditional way of developing applications on ASP.NET, is that in OWIN-based applications we will include only the modules that we need to use, thus creating lighter and more efficient applications.

OWIN is just that: a specification. It does not include any reference implementation, and it is here where Katana comes into play.

Katana[5] is an open source project created by Microsoft and distributed under the Apache 2.0 license, which contains a set of components that facilitate creating and executing web applications based on the OWIN specification.

In this project, we can find components to perform hosting of applications that are compatible with OWIN (for example, SignalR or WebAPI applications) on ASP.NET (`Microsoft.Owin.Host. SystemWeb`) or in self-hosting environments such as console applications or Windows services, using the `Microsoft.Owin.Host.HttpListener` package to receive requests directly.

It also includes many middleware modules that provide generic functionalities to the frameworks or OWIN applications using them, including compression (via the `Microsoft.Owin.Compression` package), CORS[6] (`Microsoft.Owin.Cors`), security (`Microsoft.Owin.Security.*`), and access to static files (`Microsoft.Owin.StaticFiles`).

It is good to see that functions traditionally implemented by frameworks or applications, often duplicated, have been relocated as OWIN modules that are reusable and shared by all of them. For example, not long ago, support for CORS had to be implemented in WebAPI, SignalR, or MVC independently. However, after OWIN, there is a specific middleware that can give coverage to this technique to allow cross-origin requests in a unified way.

The components of the Katana project are those on which the hosting independence of SignalR is based, so in the following chapters, we will see several examples of their use.

---

[5] Website of the Katana project: *http://katanaproject.codeplex.com/*

[6] Cross Origin Resource Sharing.

Installing SignalR

The easiest way to include SignalR in a project is by using the NuGet package manager. This great tool makes it easy to carry out the formerly lengthy process of downloading the components, copying the binaries to the project, and adding the references.

SignalR is distributed in diverse packages, where we can find server-side components, satellite assemblies with resources localized to different cultures, and various client implementations of these types of services.

It is possible to get the official packages available by using the graphic interface or entering the following command into the package management console[7]:

```
PM> Get-Package microsoft.aspnet.signalr -ListAvailable
```

Thus, in a web application, we will normally install the `Microsoft.AspNet.SignalR` package, which includes both server components and client libraries based on JavaScript. If we want to consume the services from any type of .NET application (including WinRT, Windows Phone 8, and Silverlight 5), we must install only the `Microsoft.AspNet.SignalR.Client` package on it.

```
PM> Install-package Microsoft.aspnet.signalr
```

It is also possible to create SignalR components directly from the development environment. In Visual Studio 2012, as long as we have installed the "ASP.NET and Web Frameworks 2012.2" update or a later one, it is possible to add components of this framework, as shown in Figure 3-7.

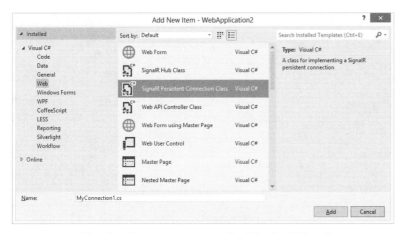

FIGURE 3-7 Adding SignalR components to a Visual Studio 2012 project.

Visual Studio 2013 includes out-of-the-box SignalR templates, so we can also add components of the main available versions directly, as shown in Figure 3-8.

---

[7] You can access the Package Manager Console in Visual Studio via "Tools > Library Package Manager > Package Manager Console".

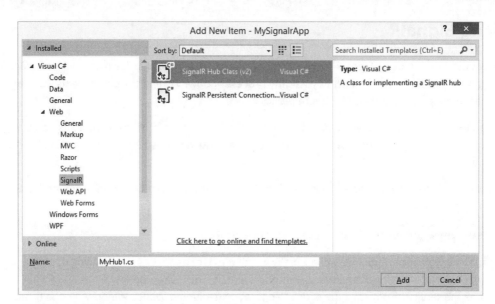

FIGURE 3-8 Adding SignalR components to a Visual Studio 2013 project.

In both cases, when we add these elements to our project, the necessary libraries will be downloaded and installed, and also some basic code with which to work will be included.

CHAPTER 4

Persistent connections

The lower-level API with which we can approach the persistent connection that SignalR offers is illustrated in Figure 4-1. This API provides us with a layer of abstraction that isolates us from the complexities inherent to keeping a permanent connection open between the client and the server and from the transports used to send information between both ends.

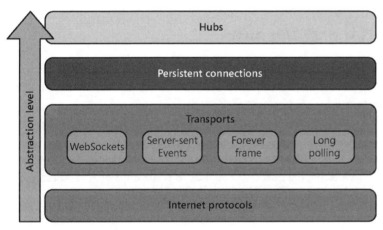

FIGURE 4-1 Abstraction levels used by SignalR.

In practice, this API gives us access to the communication channel that is quite similar to the one used traditionally when working at a low abstraction level with sockets: On the server side, we can be notified when connections are opened and closed and when data are received, as well as sending information to clients. On the client side, we can open and close connections, as well as sending and receiving arbitrary data. Also, just like with sockets, messages have no format; that is, they are *raw* data—normally text strings—that we will have to know how to interpret correctly at both ends.

From the point of view of the client, its operation is very easy. We just have to initiate a connection to the server, and we will be able to use it to send data right away. We will perform the reception of information using a callback function that is invoked by the framework after its reception.

The server side is not very complex either. Take a look at Figure 4-2. Persistent connections are classes that inherit from `PersistentConnection` and override some of the methods that allow taking control when a relevant event occurs, such as the connection or disconnection of new clients or the reception of data. From any of them, we will be able to send information to the client that has caused the event, to all clients connected to the service, or to a group of them.

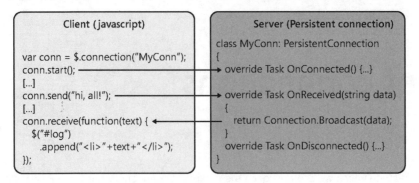

FIGURE 4-2 Conceptual implementation of persistent connections.

Now we will delve into all these aspects.

Implementation on the server side

For the clients to be able to connect to a SignalR service, first it is necessary to include this framework in our web project. For example, we can quickly do it by entering the following command in the NuGet package manager console:

```
PM> Install-package Microsoft.AspNet.Signalr
```

Each persistent connection is externally reachable via a URL, so, in a similar way to using other frameworks such as MVC or Web API, the next step could be to configure SignalR and associate each persistent connection to the path through which it will be available.

Mapping and configuring persistent connections

As usual, this is a process that must take place during application startup. In previous versions of SignalR, this registration was carried out in the global.asax, using extensions directly on the route collection of the application. However, since version 2.0, there is greater integration with OWIN[1], and this has changed the way it is implemented. In fact, from said version onwards, we need to register and configure SignalR in the middleware collection of the system in the startup process of the application.

We will come back to this, but for now it will suffice to know that the host process on which our application runs, based on OWIN, will search for a class called `Startup` in the root namespace of the application, and when it finds it, it will execute its `Configuration()` method. We will see that this convention can also be modified.

When the `Configuration()` method is executed, the execution environment will provide it with an argument in the form of an object implementing the `IAppBuilder` interface, which basically represents the application being initialized and contains a dictionary with configuration parameters

---

[1] OWIN (Open Web Interface for .NET): *http://owin.org/*

and methods that allow us to configure the different OWIN middleware that will process the requests, such as SignalR, Web API, authentication, tracing, and so on.

Configuration is normally performed by using extension methods on `IAppBuilder`. These methods are provided by the frameworks themselves or by middleware to facilitate their implementation. In our case, we will use the `MapSignalR()` method, defined by SignalR as an extension method for `IAppBuilder` in the Owin namespace, to link the used persistent connections to the paths through which we access them, as shown in the following OWIN startup class:

```
public class Startup
{
    public void Configuration(IAppBuilder app)
    {
        app.MapSignalR<EchoConnection>("/echo");

        // Configuration of other OWIN modules
    }
}
```

In any case, what we will achieve by calling `MapSignalR()` is "mapping" the paths of the type "/echo/something" to the class where we will implement the persistent connection, which in this case we have called `EchoConnection`. This path identifies the endpoint where the clients must be connected to consume the services. Obviously, at this point, there must be as many calls to the `MapSignalR<TConnection>()` method as the number of connections that are offered to the clients.

When this first step is completed, we are in position to implement the SignalR service, which will consist only in writing a class inheriting from `PersistentConnection` (defined in the `Microsoft.AspNet.SignalR` namespace):

```
public class EchoConnection: PersistentConnection
{
    // ...
}
```

This class will be instantiated by SignalR each time an HTTP connection is opened from a client to the server to process the request, which might depend on the transport selected each time. For example, if *WebSockets* is used as a transport, after the connection is established, the instance of `PersistentConnection` will remain active until the client disconnects, because it will be used both to send and receive data from the server. Contrariwise, if we use forever frame, an object will also be instantiated each time the client sends data, because those data are transmitted using a different request from the one used to obtain "push."

Therefore, it is generally not a good idea to use instance members on this class to maintain system state because the instances are created and destroyed depending on the transport used to keep the connection open. For this, static members are normally used, although always appropriately protected from concurrent accesses that could corrupt their content or cause problems inherent to multithreaded systems. We also have to take into account that using the memory for storing shared data limits the scale-out capabilities of SignalR, because it will not be possible to distribute the load among several servers.

Events of a persistent connection

The `PersistentConnection` class offers virtual methods that are invoked when certain events occur that are related to the service and the connections associated with the class, such as the arrival of a new connection, the disconnection of a client, or the reception of data. To take control and enter logic where we want, it will suffice to override the relevant methods.

The most frequently used methods, which correspond to the events mentioned, are the following:

```
protected Task OnConnected(IRequest request, string connectionId)
protected Task OnDisconnected(IRequest request, string connectionId)
protected Task OnReceived(IRequest request, string connectionId,
                         string data)
```

First, note that all of them return a `Task` type object. This already gives us a clear idea of the extensive use of asynchrony capabilities present in the latest versions of the .NET platform and languages, inside which the goal is to always implement code that can be quickly and synchronously executed, or to return a background task represented by a `Task` object that performs it asynchronously.

We can also observe that there are always at least two parameters sent to the methods: an `IRequest` object and a text string called `connectionId`.

The first one, `IRequest`, allows accessing specific information on the request received, such as cookies, information about the authenticated user, parameters, server variables, and so on, as shown in Figure 4-3. The `IRequest` interface is a specific SignalR abstraction that allows separating the implementation of services from ASP.NET. As we pointed out when we mentioned OWIN, this will allow them to be hosted in any .NET application. We will look at this in more depth later on.

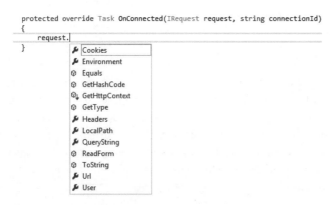

FIGURE 4-3 IntelliSense showing the members of IRequest.

The second parameter, `connectionId`, is a unique identifier associated with the connection that is generated by SignalR automatically during the initial negotiation process. The framework will use a GUID[2] by default, as shown in Figure 4-4.

---

[2] Globally Unique Identifier: *http://en.wikipedia.org/wiki/Globally_unique_identifier*

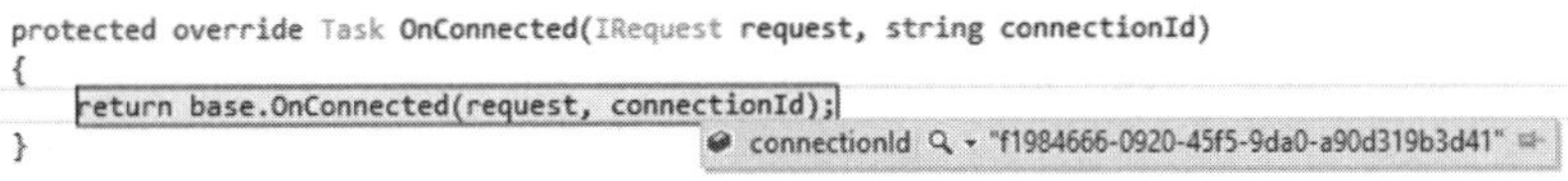

```
protected override Task OnConnected(IRequest request, string connectionId)
{
    return base.OnConnected(request, connectionId);
}
```
connectionId 🔍 ▾ "f1984666-0920-45f5-9da0-a90d319b3d41" ▥

FIGURE 4-4 Value of a `connectionID`.

We can use the connection identifier to send direct messages to specific clients or to perform any type of personalized monitoring on them.

The following code shows the implementation of a simple service, which just counts the number of users connected to it and internally displays said number on the debug console. Note the use of *thread-safe* constructions to avoid problems associated with concurrent access from different execution threads to the static variable where the value is stored. These are precautions that we must take mandatorily when implementing this kind of service:

```
public class VisitorsCountConnection: PersistentConnection
{
    private static int connections = 0;
    protected override Task OnConnected(IRequest request,
                                        string connectionId)
    {
        Interlocked.Increment(ref connections);
        Debug.WriteLine("Visitors: " + connections);
        return base.OnConnected(request, connectionId);
    }
    protected override Task OnDisconnected(IRequest request,
                                           string connectionId)
    {
        Interlocked.Decrement(ref connections);
        Debug.WriteLine("Visitors: " + connections);
        return base.OnDisconnected(request, connectionId);
    }
}
```

Other less utilized methods also exist in the `PersistentConnection` class, such as `OnReconnected()` and `OnRejoiningGroups()`. The former can be useful to take control when there is a reconnection—that is, when the client has connected to the server again after the physical connection of the transport has closed due to a time-out, a communication problem between the two ends, an application crash, a server reboot, or any other such incident. From the point of view of the SignalR connection, it is still the same client and has the same identifier, thus the invocation of `OnReconnected()` instead of treating it as a new connection. The `OnRejoiningGroups()` method allows taking control when a connection is reopened after a time-out and determining to which groups the connection should be reassigned.

The `OnReceived()` method of the persistent connection allows processing the data sent by the clients. In this method, the information submitted will be received as a text string:

```
protected override Task OnReceived(IRequest request,
                                   string connectionId,
                                   string data)
{
```

```
        // Do something interesting here
}
```

Of course, if an object serialized in any format came in this `string`, we should deserialize it manually before processing it. If it was JSON serialized, which will likely be the usual case, we could use the Json.NET library, which will be available in our project because it is required by SignalR:

```
using Newtonsoft.Json;
// ...
protected override Task OnReceived(IRequest request,
                                   string connectionId,
                                   string data)
{
    var message = JsonConvert.DeserializeObject<ChatMessage>(data);
    if (message.MessageType == MessageType.Private)
    {
        var text = message.Text;
        // ...
    }
    // ...
}
```

Sending messages to clients

There are tools available to the classes that inherit from `PersistentConnection`, which allow sending information to all connected clients, to specific clients identified by their `connectionId`, or to groups of clients.

To send a message asynchronously to all clients connected to the service, we will use the `Connection` property to invoke the `Broadcast()` method as follows:

```
protected override Task OnConnected(IRequest request,
                                    string connectionId)
{
    // Notify all connected clients
    return this.Connection.Broadcast(
                "New connection: " + connectionId);
}

protected override Task OnDisconnect(IRequest request,
                                     string connectionId)
{
    // Notify all connected clients
    return this.Connection.Broadcast("Bye bye, " + connectionId);
}
```

In this example, each time a new client connects to the service, the notification text is sent to all connected clients (including the newcomer) through the SignalR connection. And, in the same way, we make use of the `OnDisconnected()` method, by which we are informed of the disconnection of a client, to notify the rest of the users.

The parameter that we pass to `Broadcast()` is an object type (as shown in Figure 4-5), which means that we can send any type of object, which SignalR will serialize to JSON automatically.

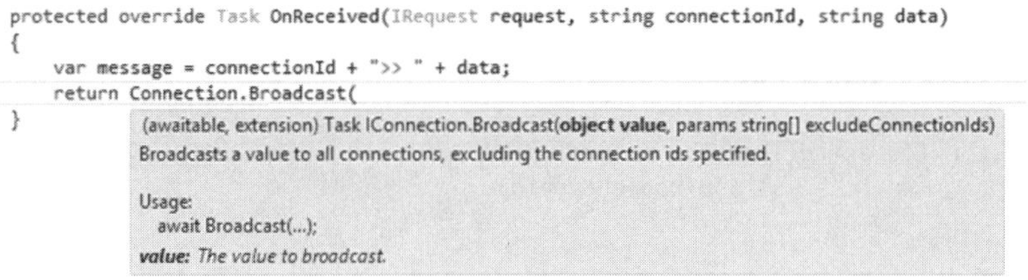

```
protected override Task OnReceived(IRequest request, string connectionId, string data)
{
    var message = connectionId + ">> " + data;
    return Connection.Broadcast(
```
```
    (awaitable, extension) Task IConnection.Broadcast(object value, params string[] excludeConnectionIds)
    Broadcasts a value to all connections, excluding the connection ids specified.

    Usage:
        await Broadcast(...);
    value: The value to broadcast.
```

FIGURE 4-5 BroadCast() receives an object type parameter.

The `Broadcast()` method also accepts an optional parameter where we can specify a collection of `connectionIds` to which the message will not be sent. The following example shows how to use this feature to send a notification to all users of the service except the one who has just connected:

```
protected override Task OnConnected(IRequest request,
                                    string connectionId)
{
    return this.Connection.Broadcast(
            "A new user is online! Let's give them a warm welcome!",
            connectionId  // Do not notify the current user

    );
}
```

The list of identifiers excluded from the return is given in a parameter of the `params string[]` type, so they can be specified directly as parameters separated by commas or as an array of text strings:

```
protected override Task OnConnected(IRequest request,
                                    string connectionId)
{
    return this.Connection.Broadcast(
            "A new user is online! Let's give them a warm welcome!",
            new[] { connectionId }

    );
}
```

To send messages to a specific client, we need to know its `connectionId`. Normally, this is not a problem, because this information will be available in the methods from which we will use these calls. The following example displays a welcome message to the client initiating a connection only:

```
protected override Task OnConnected(IRequest request,
                                    string connectionId)
{
    return this.Connection.Send(connectionId,
                                "Welcome, " + connectionId);
}
```

A very interesting aspect that we already anticipated is the fact that, both in the Send() method and in Broadcast(), the message to be sent to the clients is an object type. This means that messages are not limited to text; it is entirely possible to send any type of object, which will be automatically serialized in JSON format before being returned to the client. This allows sending messages with a structure beyond the mere character string:

```
protected override Task OnConnected(IRequest request,
                                    string connectionId)
{
    var message = new {
                        type = MessageType.NewUser,
                        id = connectionId
                      };
    return this.Connection.Broadcast(message);
}
```

 Note If the object supplied to Send() or Broadcast() is of the ArraySegment<byte> type, it will not be serialized. This could be useful if we already have the JSON representation of the object to be sent, because it would prevent double serialization of the object.

Although the most frequent procedure for making deliveries will be using the methods just described, the Send() method has some additional overloads. One of them receives as arguments a list of strings representing the connection identifiers to which we want to send the message. Another, actually used internally by Broadcast() to make the delivery, simply receives a ConnectionMessage type object that defines the recipients, the message, and, optionally, the connection identifiers that we want to exclude:

```
var connMessage = new ConnectionMessage(
                            Connection.DefaultSignal, textMessage);
return Connection.Send(connMessage);
```

The preceding code would be equivalent to making a broadcast with the value of textMessage. In fact, the Broadcast() method uses Send() internally in a way that is quite similar to the one shown. Connection.DefaultSignal is a unique code made up by the full name of the persistent connection class preceded by a constant prefix, which in this case indicates that the message must be sent to all the users "subscribed" to this signal, which are all those connected to the persistent connection.

Asynchronous event processing

As you can imagine, calls to the Send() or Broadcast() methods that we have already used in some of our examples could take too long to execute if communications between both ends are very slow, or if the number of connections is very large. If they were executed synchronously, the threads in charge of performing these tasks would be blocked until said tasks ended. In high load environments, this is truly a waste of resources; we want these threads to be released as soon as possible so that they can keep managing requests and providing their services.

For this reason, those commands are executed asynchronously, returning a `Task` object representing the task that will take care of them in the background. Consequently, we can return the result of the call from the body of the method, as we have been doing with the code shown up until now:

```
return this.Connection.Broadcast(message);
```

Following this same example, we must use asynchrony inside the methods of the persistent connection whenever we are to perform long tasks, and especially those requiring the use of external elements such as the access to web services or external APIs, or heavy queries to databases.

The following example shows how to use the async/await construct of C# 5 to invoke asynchronous methods in a very clean way:

```
protected override async Task OnConnected(IRequest request,
                                          string connectionId)
{
    // Store the new connection in the database
    await _services.SaveNewConnectionAsync(connectionId);

    // And then, send the notifications
    await this.Connection.Broadcast("A new user is online!");
    await this.Connection.Send(connectionId,
                               "Welcome, " + connectionId);
}
```

Connection groups

We have seen how SignalR allows sending messages to individual clients, identified by their `connectionId`, or to all clients connected to a service. Although these capabilities cover multiple scenarios, it would still be difficult to undertake certain tasks that require selective communication with a specific group of connections.

Imagine a chat service with different rooms. When a user enters a specific room and writes a text, ideally it would be sent only to the users present in said room. However, with the functionalities studied up to this point, implementing this very simple feature would not be easy.

For this reason, SignalR offers the possibility of grouping connections based on whatever criteria we deem relevant. For example, in a chat, we might create a group for each room; in an online game, we could group the users competing in the same match; in a multiuser document editor similar to Google Docs, we could create a group for every document being edited.

To manage those groups, we use the `Groups` property, available in the `PersistentConnection` class and thus in all its descendants. This property is of the `IConnectionGroupManager` type, and, among other things, it provides methods to add a connection identified by its `connectionId` to a group and, likewise, remove it.

The following example shows how we might interpret the commands `join <groupname>` and `leave <groupname>` coming from a client, to respectively add the connection to the group specified and remove it from it:

```
protected override Task OnReceived(IRequest request,
                                    string connectionId,
                                    string data)
{
    var args = data.Split(new[] {" "},
                            StringSplitOptions.RemoveEmptyEntries);

    if(args.Length == 2 && args[0].ToLower()=="join")
    {
        return this.Groups.Add(connectionId, args[1]);
    }
    if (args.Length == 2 && args[0].ToLower() == "leave")
    {
        return this.Groups.Remove(connectionId, args[1]);
    }
    // ...
}
```

The groups do not need to exist previously nor do they require any kind of additional managing. They are simply created when the first connection is added to them and are automatically eliminated when they become empty. And, of course, one connection can be included in as many groups as necessary.

To send information through the connections included in a group, we can use the Send() method as follows:

```
protected override Task OnReceived(IRequest request,
                                    string connectionId,
                                    string data)
{
    int i;
    if ((i = data.IndexOf(":")) > -1)
    {
        var groupName = data.Substring(0, i);
        var message = data.Substring(i + 1);
        return this.Groups.Send(groupName, message);
    }
    // ...
}
```

As you can see, the preceding code would interpret a message such as "signalr:hello!" by sending the text "hello!" to all clients connected to the "signalr" group.

Also, there is an overload of the Send() method that allows specifying a list of group names as the recipient:

```
var groupNames = new[] { "firstgroup", "secondgroup"};
this.Groups.Send(groupNames, message);
```

Unfortunately, for reasons related to the structural scalability of SignalR, we cannot obtain information about the groups, such as the list of connections included in them, not even how many there are. Neither can we know, a priori, what groups are active at a given moment. If we want to include these aspects in our applications, we must implement them ourselves, outside SignalR.

The OWIN startup class

We have previously seen where to enter the mapping and configuration code of our persistent connections and, in general, of any middleware based on OWIN. We will now go back to that briefly, to go over some details that were left pending.

When an OWIN-based system starts up, the host process on which it is executed will try to execute configuration code that must be implemented in a member predefined by convention. By default, it will try to execute the `Configuration()` method of the `Startup` class, which must be located in the root namespace of the application. However, to adapt it to our preferences, it is possible to modify this convention in one of the following ways:

- Specifying the class and the method that we want to employ by using the assembly attribute `OwinStartup`:

```
[assembly:OwinStartup(typeof(MyApp.MyStartupClass),
                      methodName: "MyConfigMethod")]
```

- Including the entry "`owin:AppStartup`" in the `<AppSettings>` section of the .config file of the application and setting as a value the fully qualified name of the class and the method to be used:

```
<configuration>
    <appSettings>
        ...
        <add key="owin:AppStartup"
             value="MyApp.MyStartupClass.MyConfigMethod"/>
    </appSettings>
    ...
</configuration>
```

In either case, the configuration method can be static or an instance method (although in the latter case the class must have a public constructor without parameters), and it must necessarily be defined with an `IAppBuilder` parameter:

```
namespace MyApp
{
    public class MyStartupClass
    {
        public void MyConfigMethod(IAppBuilder app)
        {
            // Configure OWIN app here
        }
    }
}
```

Because all the OWIN middleware of the application will be initialized in this method, it might be advisable to take the specific configuration of SignalR to an independent class. Obviously, if we are using the conventions of ASP.NET MVC or Web API on file location, it will probably be a much better idea to enter it into the /App_Start directory and, if the configuration code is too long, we should even separate it into an independent class and file. The following example shows a possible way to organize these files:

```
//
// File: /App_Start/Startup.cs
//
public class Startup
{
    public void Configuration(IAppBuilder app)
    {
        SignalRConfig.Setup(app);
    }
}


//
// File: /App_Start/SignalRConfig.cs
//
public class SignalRConfig
{
    public static void Setup(IAppBuilder app)
    {
        app.MapSignalR<EchoConnection>("/echo");
    }
}
```

In any case, this does not constitute a norm to be used mandatorily. The point is to stick to the conventions defined and well-known by the development team so that things are located where it is expected they should be.

Implementation on the client side

SignalR offers many client libraries with the purpose that practically any kind of application can use the connection provided by the framework. Although later on we will see examples of implementations of other types of clients, for the moment we will deal with creating clients from the web using JavaScript, mainly because it is easy and widely done.

In any case, the concepts and operating philosophy that we are going to see are common to all clients and project types.

Initiating the connection by using the JavaScript client

An important aspect to underline is that this client is completely and solely based on JavaScript, so it can be used in any kind of Web project: Web Forms, ASP.NET MVC, Web Pages, PHP, or even from pure HTML pages.

In fact, to access services in real time from an HTML page, it is enough to reference jQuery (version 1.6.4 or above)—because the client is implemented as a plug-in of this renowned framework—and then the jquery.signalR library (version 2.0.0 or above). We can find both of them in the /Scripts folder when we install the `Microsoft.AspNet.SignalR.JS` package from NuGet, or the complete `Microsoft.AspNet.SignalR` package, which includes both the client and server components for web systems.

```
<script src="Scripts/jquery-1.6.4.min.js"></script>
<script src="Scripts/jquery.signalR-2.0.0.min.js"></script>
```

After they are referenced, we can begin to work with SignalR from the client side. The first thing we have to do is open a connection to the server. For this, it is necessary for the client to know the URL by which the persistent connection is accessible. As we said before, it is assigned during application startup. Here you can see an example:

```
public class Startup
{
    public void Configuration(IAppBuilder app)
    {
        app.MapSignalR<EchoConnection>("/realtime/echo");
    }
}
```

Given the previous configuration, which maps the path /realtime/echo to the persistent connection implemented in the EchoConnection class, the following code shows how to create and open a connection to it using JavaScript:

```
<script type="text/javascript">
    $(function() {
        var connection = $.connection("/realtime/echo");
        connection.start();
        // ...
    });
</script>
```

As you can see, this call is being entered in the page initialization, following the customary pattern used to develop with jQuery. Although it does not necessarily have to be this way, this technique ensures that the code will be executed when the page has loaded completely and the DOM is ready to be operated on.

The call to the `start()` method is asynchronous, so the execution of the script will continue on the next line even if the connection has not been opened yet. This particular detail is very important, because we will not be able to use the connection until it has been established. If this does not happen, an exception will be thrown with a very clear message:

```
var connection = $.connection("/realtime/chat");
connection.start();
connection.send("Hi there!");
```

"SignalR: Connection must be started before data can be sent. Call .start() before .send()"

Fortunately, this method has overloads that allow us to specify a callback function that will be executed when the connection is open and the process of transport negotiation with the server has been completed:

```
var connection = $.connection("/realtime/echo");
connection.start(function() {
    // Connection established!
    connection.send("Hi there!");
});
```

It is important to know that the specified callback function will be executed whenever the connection is initiated. That is, if the start() method is invoked from another point in the client code, the previously registered callback function will also be executed when the connection process completes successfully.

It is also possible to use the well-known promise[3] pattern and the implementation of jQuery based on Deferred[4] objects to take control when the connection has been successful, as well as in the event that an error has occurred. This is the recommended option:

```
var connection = $.connection("/realtime/echo");
connection.start()
    .done(function() {
        connection.send("Hi there!"); // Notify other clients
    })
    .fail(function() {
        alert("Error connecting to realtime service");
    });
```

After the connection is established, we can begin to send and receive information by using the mechanisms that are described later in this chapter.

From this point onwards, we can also close the connection explicitly, by invoking the connection.stop() method, or obtain the identifier of the current connection, generated by the server during the negotiation phase, through the connection.id property.

---

[3] The promise pattern: *http://wiki.commonjs.org/wiki/Promises*

[4] The Deferred object in jQuery: http://api.jquery.com/category/deferred-object/

Support for older browsers

A problem that might arise when we open the connection using the `start()` method is that the user's browser might be too old and not have the JSON parser built in—for example, as it happens with Internet Explorer 7. In this case, execution will stop, indicating the problem and even its solution:

```
var connection = $.connection("/realtime/chat");
connection.start();
connection.send("Hi there!");
```
"SignalR: Connection must be started before data can be sent. Call .start() before .send()"

The json2.js file that we are told must be referenced can be easily obtained from NuGet with the following command in the console:

```
PM> Install-package json2
```

When this is done, we would have to include only the reference to the script before doing so with SignalR:

```
<script src="Scripts/jquery-1.6.4.min.js"></script>
<script src="Scripts/json2.min.js"></script>
<script src="Scripts/jquery.signalR-2.0.0.min.js"></script>
```

Support for cross-domain connections

SignalR includes "out-of-the-box" support for connections with a different server from the one that has served the script currently being executed, something that is normally not allowed for security reasons. This type of request, called *cross-domain*, requires the use of some kind of special technique to avoid this restriction that is usual in browsers. Examples of those techniques are JSONP[5] or, only in some browsers, the use of the CORS[6] specification.

JSONP is not particularly recommended for security reasons, but if our service must provide support to clients using older browsers such as Internet Explorer 7, it might be the only option available to obtain connections from external domains. This feature is disabled by default at server level, but it can be activated by supplying a `ConnectionConfiguration` object during initial mapping, setting its `EnableJSONP` property to `true`:

```
public class Startup
{
    public void Configuration(IAppBuilder app)
    {
        var config = new ConnectionConfiguration()
                {
```

---

[5] JSONP (JSON with Padding): *http://en.wikipedia.org/wiki/JSONP*

[6] CORS (Cross-Origin Resource Sharing): *http://en.wikipedia.org/wiki/Cross-origin_resource_sharing*

```
                        EnableJSONP = true
                };
        app.MapSignalR<EchoConnection>("/realtime/echo", config);
    }
}
```

This way, the server will be ready to accept connections using long polling transport with JSONP.

Because CORS is quite a cross-cutting technique and independent of frameworks and applications, it is implemented as OWIN middleware; therefore, to allow this type of connection, it will be necessary to first download the module using NuGet:

```
PM> Install-Package microsoft.owin.cors
```

After this, we can specify that we want to use CORS in our initialization method, entering the module into the OWIN pipeline with the extension method UseCors() so that it is executed before the SignalR middleware:

```
public class Startup
{
    public void Configuration(IAppBuilder app)
    {
        app.Map("/realtime/echo",
            map => {
                    map.UseCors(CorsOptions.AllowAll);
                    map.RunSignalR<EchoConnection>();
                }

        );
    }
}
```

Note that in this case we have used a different construct to map and configure the service available in the path /realtime/echo. First, we have used the Map() extension to specify the path just once, followed by a lambda that receives as a parameter the mapping that we are defining (in turn, an IAppBuilder object). On this parameter, we have used the extensions provided by the different modules to enter them into the pipeline associated to the URL provided:

- UseCors() enables the use of CORS at the server, according to the options sent as an argument in the form of a CorsOptions object. CorsOptions.AllowAll is an object preconfigured in a very permissive mode; it allows all origins, verbs, and headers. However, it is possible to supply it a customized CorsOptions object to fine-tune its configuration and usage policies.

- RunSignalR() is the equivalent of the MapSignalR() method that we had been using up until now, but as opposed to it, we do not need to supply it the path because it has already been defined.

At the client side, SignalR will automatically detect that we are making a cross-domain connection if when the connection is made it notices that an endpoint has been specified that is hosted in a domain different than the one of the current page. In this case, it will try to use CORS to make the connection. Only if it is not possible will it automatically fall back to JSONP, using long polling as the transport.

In scenarios where we need to force this last option, we can specifically indicate that we want to use JSONP when initiating the connection from the client. At this moment, it is possible to send an object with settings that allow fine-tuning said process:

```
var connection = $.connection("http://localhost:3701/realtime/echo");
connection.start({ jsonp: true })
        .done(function() {
            alert(connection.transport.name);
        });
```

The `connection.transport` property contains the transport used by the current connection.

Sending messages

As you can probably guess, to send information to the server from the JavaScript client, we will use the `send()` method available in the `connection` object, which represents the connection created before.

This method accepts the object to be sent as a parameter. It will be received in the data parameter of the `OnReceived()` method of the server in the form of a text string, as we saw previously:

```
// =================================================================
// Client code (Javascript)
connection.send("Hi there!");  ──┤ Persistent Connection ├──┐

// =================================================================
// Server code
public class ChatConnection : PersistentConnection
{

    protected override Task OnReceived(
                IRequest request, string connectionID, string data)  ◄──┘
    {
        // Broadcasts the message to all connected clients
        return this.Connection.Broadcast(data);
    }
}
```

Of course, we can send any object type. SignalR will serialize it automatically before sending it:

```
$("#buttonSend").click(function () {
    var obj = {
        messageType: 1, // Broadcast message, type = 1
        text:        $("#text").val(),
        from:        $("#currentUser").val(),
    };
    connection.send(obj);
});
```

Because what would arrive at the server would be a text string with the JSON representation of the object, to manipulate the data comfortably it would be necessary to deserialize the *string* and turn it into a CLR object, as we have already seen:

```
// Server code
protected override Task OnReceived(IRequest request,
                                   string connectionId,
                                   string data)
{
    var message = JsonConvert.DeserializeObject<ChatMessage>(data);
    if (message.MessageType == MessageType.Broadcast)
    {
        return this.Connection.Broadcast(
                   "Message from "+message.From +
                   ": " + message.Text);
    }
    // ...
}
```

Although the send() method is expected to adhere to the promise pattern in the future, this is currently not so, and there is no direct way of knowing when the transfer process has ended or whether there has been an error in its execution.

Nevertheless, it is possible to detect errors on the connection by using the error() method of the connection to set the callback function to be executed when there is any problem on it:

```
var connection = $.connection("/chat");
connection.error(function (err) {
    alert("Oops! It seems there is a problem. \n" +
              "Error: " + err.message);
});
connection.start();
```

The callback function receives a JavaScript object from which we can obtain information describing the problem that has occurred, as shown in Figure 4-6.

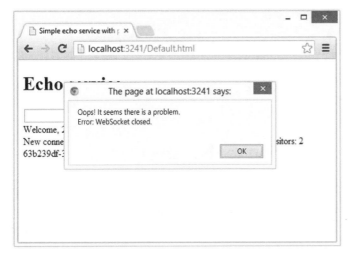

FIGURE 4-6 Connection interrupted captured by the callback.

Receiving messages

The reception of data sent from the server is performed at the JavaScript client by registering the callback that will be executed each time information is received. This registration is performed by calling the `received()` method of the object that represents the connection with the server and supplying it the function for data handling:

```
connection.received(function (msg) {
    $("#contents").append("<li>" + msg + "</li>");
});
```

As you can see, as a parameter, this function receives the data sent from the server in the form of a directly usable object. SignalR will be responsible for serializing and deserializing the data on both ends.

Thus, if a character string has been sent from the server, we can obtain it and process it directly at the client, as in the preceding example. Conversely, if structured data are sent from the server, they are automatically serialized to JSON, and in the input parameter of our callback function we will directly receive the JavaScript object ready for use:

```
// =====================================================
// Server code
protected override Task OnConnected(IRequest request,
                                    string connectionId)
{
    var message = new
    {
        type = MessageType.NewUser,
        id = connectionId,
        text = "New user!"
    };
```

```
    return this.Connection.Broadcast(message);
}

// ====================================================
// Client code (Javascript)
connection.received(function (msg) {
    $("#contents").append(msg.text + ". Id: " + msg.id);
});
```

Sending additional information to the server

We have seen that the events available at the server receive an IRequest type parameter through which it is possible to access the environment of the request that is behind the persistent connection. Thus, using this object, it would be possible to retrieve, among other things, the identity of the user authenticated into the system, information sent in cookies, or even the parameters of the query string or server headers.

For example, if you are using cookie-based authentication, when a user is authenticated in a website, the browser will automatically include the authentication cookie in all requests to SignalR, which offers the possibility of implementing code such as the following at the server:

```
protected override Task OnConnected(IRequest request,
                                    string connectionId)
{
    string message = request.User.Identity.IsAuthenticated
                        ? "Welcome, " + request.User.Identity.Name
                        : "You must be logged in!";

    return Connection.Send(connectionId, message);
}
```

In the same vein, when it is necessary to send additional information from the client to the server, we can make use of cookies. They are easy to manage, and they allow entering arbitrary information into requests that are going to be made *a posteriori*, as illustrated in the following example:

```
// Client side:
var username = prompt("Your username");
document.cookie = "username=" + username;
var connection = $.connection("/realtime/chat");
...
connection.start();


// Server side:
protected override Task OnConnected(IRequest request,
                                    string connectionId)
{
    Cookie cookie;
    var username =
        request.Cookies.TryGetValue("Username", out cookie)
        ? cookie.Value
        : connectionId;
```

```
      var message = "Welcome, " + username + "!";
      return Connection.Send(connectionId, message);
}
```

Another possibility would be to use the query string to send information. For this, the SignalR client allows us to specify an additional parameter at the point at which the connection is defined. In this parameter, we can add key-value mappings, either in the form of a string or an object, which will be annexed to all the requests made to the SignalR server:

```
// Client side:
var name = prompt("Your username");
var conn = $.connection(
               "/realtime/chat",
               "username="+name // or { username: name  }
);
...
conn.start();


// Server side:
protected override Task OnConnected(IRequest request,
                                    string connectionId)
{
    var userName = request.QueryString["username"] ?? connectionId;
    var message = "Welcome, " + userName + "!";
    return Connection.Send(connectionId, message);
}
```

Other events available at the client

The connection object has a large number of events that allow us to take control at certain moments in the life cycle of the connection if we register the callback methods that we want to be invoked when the time comes. The most interesting ones are the following:

- received() and error(), which we already saw and which allow us to specify the function to be executed when data are received or when an error occurs in the connection.

- connectionSlow(), which allows entering logic when the connection is detected to be slow or unstable.

- stateChanged(), invoked when the state of the connection changes.

- reconnected(), when there is a reconnection of the client after its connection has been closed due to time-out or any other cause.

In the SignalR repository in GitHub[7], you can find the documentation about methods, events, and properties offered by the JavaScript client connections.

---

[7] Javascript client documentation: *https://github.com/SignalR/SignalR/wiki/SignalR-JS-Client*

Transport negotiation

We have seen that, after the reference to the connection is obtained, the `start()` method really initiates communication with the server, thus beginning the negotiation phase in which the technologies or techniques to be used to maintain the persistent connection will be selected.

First, there will be an attempt to establish the connection using WebSockets, which is the only transport that really supports full-duplex on the same channel and is therefore the most efficient one. If this is not possible, to determine which is the most efficient solution available at both ends, a fallback procedure will begin:

- In the browsers that support it (basically all with the exception of Internet Explorer), contact will be attempted using Server-Sent Events, which at least provides a standard mechanism to obtain *push*.

- In Internet Explorer, the possibility of using forever frame will be examined.

If neither of the previous steps has succeeded, to maintain the persistent connection, long polling will be tried.

It is easy to trace this process, because the SignalR web client allows us to activate the tracing of events with the JavaScript console available in major browsers. (See Figure 4-7.) This option is enabled at the moment the connection is created, setting the third parameter of the `$.connection()` method to `true`:

```
var connection = $.connection("/realtime/chat", null, true);
```

Or, in an equivalent and much more legible way, directly on the `logging` property of the connection:

```
var connection = $.connection("/myconn");
connection.logging = true;
```

FIGURE 4-7 Trace of the SignalR client in Internet Explorer 11.

We can also trace requests using Fiddler[8] or the development tools available in our browsers to trace requests, and thus we can view the main terms of the "agreement" reached by the client and the server.

Figure 4-8 shows the tracing of connections using the development tools of Chrome, where you can see the process of content negotiation between this browser and IIS 8. Both support WebSockets.

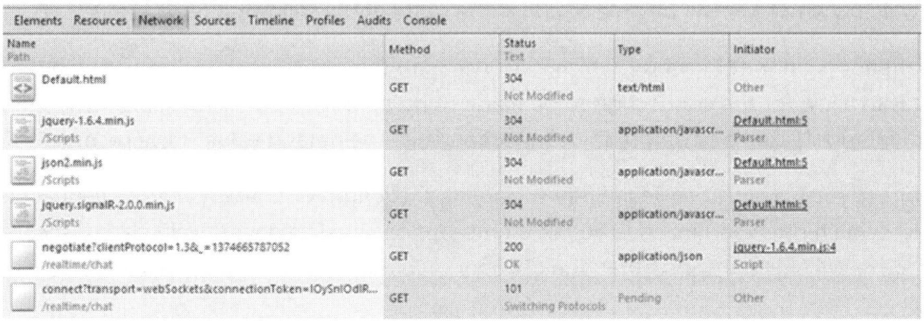

Name Path	Method	Status Text	Type	Initiator
Default.html	GET	304 Not Modified	text/html	Other
jquery-1.6.4.min.js /Scripts	GET	304 Not Modified	application/javascr...	Default.html:5 Parser
json2.min.js /Scripts	GET	304 Not Modified	application/javascr...	Default.html:5 Parser
jquery.signalR-2.0.0.min.js /Scripts	GET	304 Not Modified	application/javascr...	Default.html:5 Parser
negotiate?clientProtocol=1.3&_=1374665787052 /realtime/chat	GET	200 OK	application/json	jquery-1.6.4.min.js:4 Script
connect?transport=webSockets&connectionToken=IOySnIOdIR... /realtime/chat	GET	101 Switching Protocols	Pending	Other

Elements Resources **Network** Sources Timeline Profiles Audits Console

FIGURE 4-8 Process of transport negotiation with Chrome.

However, Fiddler[9] is used in Figure 4-9 to show the negotiation procedure of Internet Explorer 7 and how the fallback mechanism works to select the best transport supported by it—forever frame:

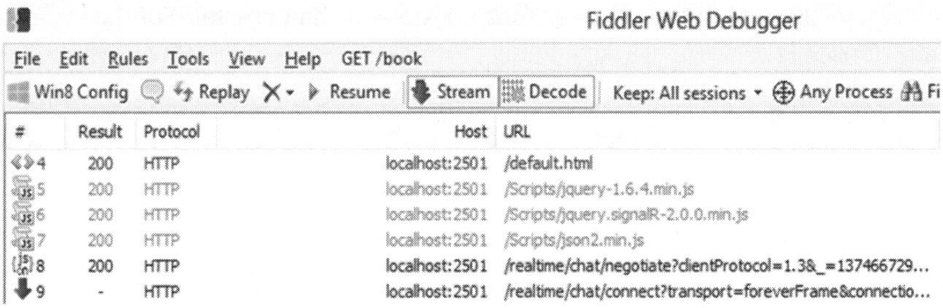

Fiddler Web Debugger

File Edit Rules Tools View Help GET /book

Win8 Config Replay X ▾ ▶ Resume ⬇ Stream Decode Keep: All sessions ▾ Any Process Fi

#	Result	Protocol	Host	URL
4	200	HTTP	localhost:2501	/default.html
5	200	HTTP	localhost:2501	/Scripts/jquery-1.6.4.min.js
6	200	HTTP	localhost:2501	/Scripts/jquery-2.0.0.min.js
7	200	HTTP	localhost:2501	/Scripts/json2.min.js
8	200	HTTP	localhost:2501	/realtime/chat/negotiate?clientProtocol=1.3&_=137466729...
9	-	HTTP	localhost:2501	/realtime/chat/connect?transport=foreverFrame&connectio...

FIGURE 4-9 Transport negotiation procedure with Internet Explorer 7.

Finally, Figure 4-10 shows the trace by the Firefox console (Firebug) of the negotiation of a cross-domain connection, which is resolved employing the WebSocket transport using CORS.

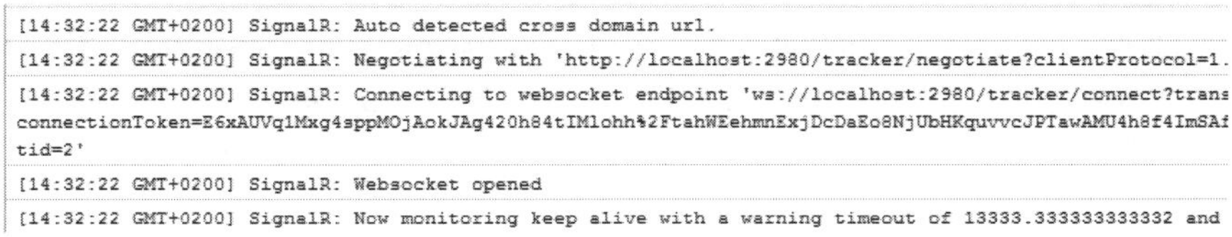

```
[14:32:22 GMT+0200] SignalR: Auto detected cross domain url.
[14:32:22 GMT+0200] SignalR: Negotiating with 'http://localhost:2980/tracker/negotiate?clientProtocol=1.
[14:32:22 GMT+0200] SignalR: Connecting to websocket endpoint 'ws://localhost:2980/tracker/connect?trans
connectionToken=E6xAUVq1Mxg4sppMOjAokJAg420h84tIMlohh%2FtahWEehmnExjDcDaEo8NjUbHKquvvcJPTawAMU4h8f4ImSAf
tid=2'
[14:32:22 GMT+0200] SignalR: Websocket opened
[14:32:22 GMT+0200] SignalR: Now monitoring keep alive with a warning timeout of 13333.333333333332 and
```

FIGURE 4-10 Cross-domain connection negotiation with Firefox.

---

[8] Fiddler: *http://www.fiddler2.com*

[9] Notes on the use of Fiddler with SignalR: *https://github.com/SignalR/SignalR/wiki/Using-fiddler-with-signalr*

Adjusting SignalR configuration parameters

SignalR allows us to adjust certain parameters that affect the way in which connections are made, as well as other aspects related to their management. This is done through a configuration object available in the global object `GlobalHost`. As we shall see throughout this book, this object allows static access to some interesting functions of SignalR, but for now, we will focus on its `Configuration` property, which is where we will be able to adjust the value of the following parameters:

- `TransportConnectTimeout`, which is a `TimeSpan` that specifies the length of time that a client is to allow for the connection to be made using a transport, before falling back to another with inferior features or before the connection fails. The default value is five seconds.

- `ConnectionTimeout` is a `TimeSpan` specifying the length of time for which a connection must remain open and inactive before a time-out occurs. The default value is 110 seconds. It is effective only for transports that don't support keep alive, or if keep alive is disabled.

- `DisconnectTimeout` specifies the length of time from when a connection is closed until the disconnect event is fired. The default value is 30 seconds.

- `KeepAlive` is a nullable `TimeSpan` that allows us to specify the length of time between messages sent to the server indicating that the client remains active. The default value is 10 seconds, but we can disable it by setting a null value; see Figure 4-11. In any case, we cannot enter a value smaller than two seconds nor greater than one third of the value of `DisconnectTimeout`.

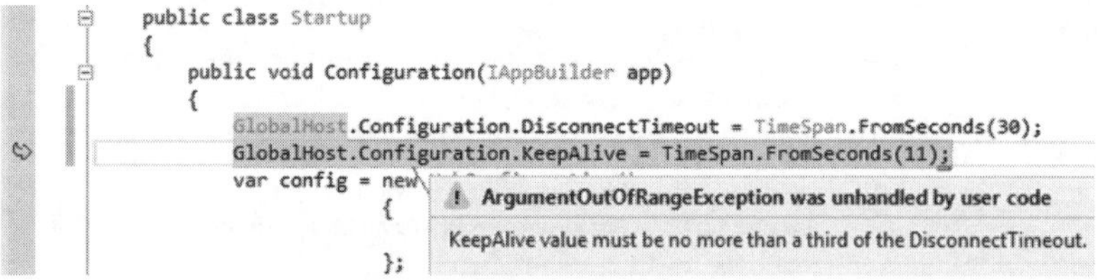

FIGURE 4-11 Exception during application startup.

- `DefaultMessageBufferSize` is an integer indicating the size of the message buffer for a specific signal (connection, group, users, and so on). The default value is 1,000.

- `LongPollDelay` is a `TimeSpan` that allows us to specify the length of time that a client must wait before opening a new long polling connection after having sent data to the server. The default value is 0.

Some of these parameters, such as `TransportConnectTimeout` or `KeepAliveTimeout`, are sent to the client in the negotiation phase of the connection so that it can apply them during said connection.

Naturally, for them to take effect, the changes on the configuration properties should be made during application startup—for example, like this:

```
public class Startup
{
    public void Configuration(IAppBuilder app)
    {
        GlobalHost.Configuration
                .DisconnectTimeout = TimeSpan.FromSeconds(30);

        app.MapSignalR<EchoConnection>("/echo");
    }
}
```

Note These settings are also valid when we use hubs, because they are global configurations of the server.

Complete example: Tracking visitors

We will now look at the code of a complete example, both on the client and server sides, with the purpose of consolidating some of the concepts addressed throughout this chapter.

Specifically, we will track the mouse of the visitors of a page and send this information to the rest of the users in real time. Thus, every visitor will be able to see the position of other users' cursors on their own screen and follow their movement across it.

Figure 4-12 shows the system being executed on a busy page.

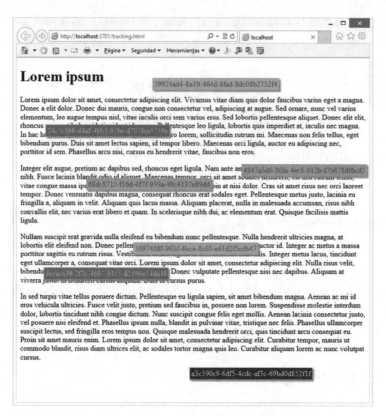

FIGURE 4-12 System for tracking users in real time in operation.

Project creation and setup

For the purpose of creating the application that we will develop over the following pages, it is necessary to first create a project of the "ASP.NET Web Application" type from Visual Studio 2013 and then select the "Empty" template to create a completely empty project[10]. The version of the .NET framework used must be at least 4.5.

After we have created it, we must install the following package using NuGet:

```
PM> install-package Microsoft.AspNet.SignalR
```

---

10   In Visual Studio 2012, we can achieve the same goal by creating a project from the template "ASP.NET Empty Web Application."

Implementation on the client side

HTML markup (tracking.html)

```html
<!DOCTYPE html>
<html xmlns="http://www.w3.org/1999/xhtml">
<head>
    <title></title>
    <script src="Scripts/jquery-1.6.4.min.js"></script>
    <script src="Scripts/jquery.signalR-2.0.0.min.js"></script>
    <script src="Scripts/tracking.js"></script>
    <style>
        .client {
            position: absolute;
            background-color: white;
            -moz-box-shadow: 10px 10px 5px #888;
            -webkit-box-shadow: 10px 10px 5px #888;
            box-shadow: 3px 3px 3px #888;
            border: 1px solid #a0a0a0;
            padding: 3px;
        }
    </style>
</head>
<body>
    <h1>Lorem ipsum</h1>
    <p>Lorem ipsum dolor sit amet, [...]</p>
    <p>Integer elit augue, [...] </p>
</body>
</html>
```

Scripts (Scripts/Tracking.js)

```javascript
$(function() {

  /* SignalR client */
  var connection = $.connection("/tracker");
  connection.start(function () {
      startTracking();
  });

  connection.received(function (data) {
      data = JSON.parse(data);

      var domElementId = "id" + data.id;
      var elem = createElementIfNotExists(domElementId);
      $(elem).css({ left: data.x, top: data.y }).text(data.id);
  });

  function startTracking() {
      $("body").mousemove(function (e) {
          var data = { x: e.pageX, y: e.pageY, id: connection.id };
          connection.send(data);
      });
  }
```

```javascript
/* Helper functions */
function createElementIfNotExists(id) {
    var element = $("#" + id);
    if (element.length == 0) {
        element = $("<span class='client' " +
                    "id='" + id +"'></span>");
        var color = getRandomColor();
        element.css({ backgroundColor: getRgb(color),
                      color: getInverseRgb(color) });
        $("body").append(element).show();
    }
    return element;
}

function getRgb(rgb) {
    return "rgb(" + rgb.r + "," + rgb.g + "," + rgb.b + ")";
}

function getInverseRgb(rgb) {
    return "rgb(" + (255 - rgb.r) + "," +
                    (255 - rgb.g) + "," + (255 - rgb.b) + ")";
}

function getRandomColor() {
    return {
        r: Math.round(Math.random() * 256),
        g: Math.round(Math.random() * 256),
        b: Math.round(Math.random() * 256),
    };
}
});
```

Implementation on the server side

Persistent connection (TrackerConnection.cs)

```csharp
using System.Threading.Tasks;
using Microsoft.AspNet.SignalR;

public class TrackerConnection : PersistentConnection
{
    protected override Task OnReceived(IRequest request,
                                       string connectionId,
                                       string data)
    {
        return Connection.Broadcast(data);
    }
}
```

Startup code (Startup.cs)

```
using Owin;

public class Startup
{
    public void Configuration(IAppBuilder app)
    {
        app.MapSignalR<TrackerConnection>("/tracker");
    }
}
```

CHAPTER 5

Hubs

Indubitably, persistent connections provide all that we might need to create real-time multiuser applications through a really simple and intuitive API. Nevertheless, the creators of SignalR have taken it one step further, offering a much higher level of abstraction above Internet protocols, transports, and persistent connections: hubs. (See Figure 5-1.) Hubs use an imperative development model based on the flexibility of JavaScript and the dynamic features of C#, which creates an illusion of continuity between the client and the server, two physically separated environments.

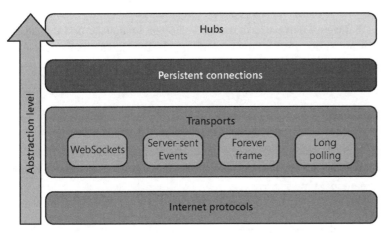

FIGURE 5-1 Abstraction levels used by SignalR.

Hubs are thus the higher-level API that we can use to access the persistent connection created by SignalR. We can create the same applications using persistent connections, but if we choose hubs, it will be simpler.

Although there are two different approaches to working with hubs in SignalR, the most common model used in web environments allows us to make direct calls between client-side and server-side methods transparently. This is two-way RPC; that is, from the client, we will directly invoke methods available at the server, and vice versa. See Figure 5-2.

Obviously, there is nothing magical about this. To make it possible, on the client side, SignalR automatically creates proxy objects with the façade of server Hub classes, and in their methods, it enters remote calls to their real methods. Conversely, when the server invokes a method of the client, it is resolved by using dynamic types and a special protocol that "packages" these calls at the server and sends them to the other end through push by using the underlying transport. They then arrive at the client, where they are interpreted and executed. Later in this chapter, in the section "Sending messages to clients," we'll look at this process in greater detail.

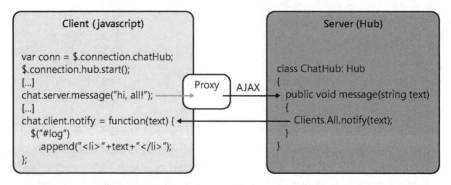

FIGURE 5-2 Conceptual implementation of services using hubs.

The use of hubs is recommended when we need to send different types of messages with various structures between the client and the server. As you know, persistent connections operate mainly on text strings, which means that we have to perform the parsing of data manually, and this can sometimes be laborious. But if we use hubs, most of the work is done by the SignalR framework itself, in exchange for a very small additional load.

Server implementation

Creating a hub-based application usually involves the deployment of components both on the server and client sides. In this section, we will focus on the server side, and we will study how to configure, create, and use hubs to create real-time services.

Hub registration and configuration

Unlike persistent connections, services based on hubs do not require specific mapping for each one during startup to associate them with the URLs that access them, because they are all accessible through a single base URL that the framework sets by default with the value "/SignalR".

For this reason, it will be necessary to perform only one mapping during startup, something that we can do in the OWIN startup class. As we have seen, by convention, this class in most cases will be called `Startup`, will be found in the root namespace of the project, and will contain a method called `Configuration()` where the configuration code will be found:

```
public class Startup
{
    public void Configuration(IAppBuilder app)
    {
        app.MapSignalR();
    }
}
```

`MapSignalR()` is an extension method of `IAppBuilder` provided by SignalR to facilitate mapping and configuration of the hub service. Notice, as opposed to its generic overload `MapSignalR<TConnection>`, which we use to map persistent connections, that we do not have to specify the classes that implement the services: this call suffices to map all the hubs of the system. Of course, if both hubs and persistent connections are used in the same applications, their mappings should appear separately in the configuration:

```
public void Configuration(IAppBuilder app)
{
    // Map persistent connections
    app.MapSignalR<MyPersistentConnection>("/myconnection");
    app.MapSignalR<OtherPersistentConnection>("/other");

    // Map hubs to "/signalr" by default
    app.MapSignalR();
}
```

We can modify the default path to access the services and adapt the path to our needs or preferences:

```
app.MapSignalR("/realtime", new HubConfiguration());
```

In this case, the base URL for accessing the hubs will be /realtime. Also, in the second parameter, we can modify some configuration options of our hubs, such as the dependency resolution component to be used or whether the generation of dynamic proxies and JSONP are enabled. We'll look at all these aspects as we delve deeper into the use of hubs in SignalR in this chapter.

Creating hubs

Services are implemented in classes that inherit from the Hub class, available in the `Microsoft.AspNet.SignalR` namespace:

```
public class EchoHub: Hub
{
    // ...
}
```

Hubs are instantiated through calls. Each time a client sends a message to the server, an object of this type will be created to process it. Hubs will also be instantiated when new connections or disconnections are detected, so we can enter customized logic in these cases, as we shall see. It is important to bear this in mind so as not to use instance members on the hub to maintain the state: after the current request is processed, the object will be eliminated, so this information would be lost.

This short life cycle is similar to the one found in Web API or ASP.NET MVC controllers, but it is different from the one found in `PersistentConnection` objects, which could remain active for as long as the connection lasts, depending on the transport used.

The name selected for the hub class is an important detail because later, on the client side, it will be used to reference the service. Nevertheless, it's possible to specify a different name for that by using the [HubName] attribute:

```
// This service will be referenced as "EchoService"
// instead of "EchoHub"
[HubName("EchoService")]
public class EchoHub: Hub
{
    // ...
}
```

Inside the class, we will implement the methods that will be exposed to the clients and that will allow us to take control upon the arrival of messages.

Receiving messages

When a client needs to send data to a hub, it invokes one of its methods and supplies it the required parameters, in the same vein as RPC. That is, in this case, we do not have a single point for receiving information on the server side like the OnReceived() method of persistent connections; here we can implement as many methods as we need in the class, and each of them will act as a possible point of entry and implementation of processing logic.

The following code shows a hub with the signature of methods that could be useful for a simple chat service:

```
public class ChatHub: Hub
{
    public void Broadcast(string text) { ... }
    public void Message(string to, string text) { ... }
    public void SendToGroup(string group, string text) { ... }
    public void ChangeNick(string newNickname) { ... }
    public void Join(string group) { ... }
    public void Leave(string group) { ... }
    // ...
}
```

 Note Any public method within a hub can be invoked from outside, which could potentially become a security hole. Be careful with this.

In the following examples, you can see how one of these methods could be invoked from a JavaScript client using the automatically generated proxy (we will look at this in depth later on):

```
var newNick = prompt("Enter your new nickname");
hubProxy.server.changeNick(newNick); // Calls method ChangeNick()
                                     // on the server
```

Or from a generic .NET client:

```
hubProxy.Invoke("ChangeNick", "Joe"); // Calls method ChangeNick()
                                      // on the server
```

As you can see, the name of the method is used from the client to make the call, although it is possible to specify an alternative one using the [HubMethodName] attribute:

```
// This method will be referenced as "SendPrivate"
// instead of "Message"
[HubName("SendPrivate")]
public void Message(string to, string text) { ... }
```

SignalR allows us to overload the methods exposed to the client; but internally, when determining which method is to be executed, only the number of parameters supplied will be considered and not their type. Therefore, the following methods defined in a hub are valid and could be invoked from the client side without any problems:

```
public class ChatHub: Hub
{
    public Task Send(string message) {...}
    public Task Send(string message, string target) {...}
    ...
}
```

However, a definition like the following would generate ambiguity problems, and trying to execute either of these two actions would return an error:

```
public class ChatHub: Hub
{
    public Task Send(string message, string target) {...}
    public Task Send(string message, MessageType type) {...}
    ...
}
```

After the framework determines what method to execute, depending on the name of the method and the number of arguments supplied in the call from the client side, they are directly mapped to the parameters expected by the method on the server side, type conversion being automatically managed on both ends. Internally, a mechanism similar to the one we find in the binder of ASP.NET MVC or Web API is used; not only will it be capable of transforming values into native types used by the parameters, but it will also do the same thing with complex types like the one shown in the following example:

```
public class ChatHub: Hub
{
    // ...
    public void SendPrivate(PrivateMessage msg)
    {
        // ...
    }

}
```

```
public class PrivateMessage
{
    public string From { get; set; }
    public string To { get; set; }
    public string Message { get; set; }
    public int MsgId { get; set; }
}
```

Thus, from a JavaScript client, the call to the method might be like this:

```
hubProxy.server.sendPrivate({ from: "john",
                              to: "peter",
                              message: "Hi!",
                              msgId: "18"
});
```

In complex objects, binding will be performed without regard to uppercase or lowercase. That is, the preceding code would work exactly the same way if it was written like this:

```
hubProxy.server.sendPrivate({ From: "john",
                              TO: "peter",
                              MeSsAgE: "Hi!",
                              msgid: "18"
});
```

It is also possible to receive complete graphs, such as the following:

```
// Hub:
public class PeopleHub: Hub
{
    public bool SavePerson(Person person)
    {
        // TODO: Persist this person in db
    }
}

// Data structures
public class Person
{
    public string Name { get; set; }
    public int Age { get; set; }
    public Address Address { get; set; }
}

public class Address
{
    public string Street { get; set; }
    public string Zip { get; set; }
}
```

From a JavaScript client, it could be invoked as follows:

```
peopleHub.server.savePerson({
    name: "John",
    age: 32,
    address: {
```

```
        street: "Madison Avenue",
        zip: "1234"
    }
});
```

Another interesting feature of these methods is that they allow the direct return of any type of value; SignalR will be the one in charge of serializing them to make them available to the client that made the call. In the following example, we can see the implementation of a method with a return and its retrieval by a JavaScript client, where we can again observe the use of the promise pattern to obtain the result of this operation:

```
// =========================================================
// Server code
public class Calc: Hub
{
    // ...
    public int Sum(int a, int b)
    {
        return a + b;
    }
}

// =========================================================
// Client code (JavaScript)
hubProxy.server.sum(3, 4)
        .done(function(result) {
            alert(result);
        });
```

Asynchrony is also present in the implementation of the methods of the hub. If, inside a method, the process to be performed is too costly and it depends on external factors—for example, the connection to a web service or a complex query to a database—we can return a Task<T> object representing the process in the background that will return a T type object:

```
public Task<int> Sum(int a, int b)
{
    return Task.Factory.StartNew(() =>
            {
                Thread.Sleep(5000); // Simulate an external call
                return a + b;
            });
}
```

And, of course, we can also use the recommended async/await construct of C# in the implementation of asynchronous features:

```
public async Task<int> Sum(int a, int b, int c)
{
    var partialResult = await DoSum(a, b);
    var result = await DoSum(partialResult, c);
    return result;
}
```

```
// Private methods

private async Task<int> DoSum(int a, int b)
{
  await Task.Delay(1000);
  return a + b;
}
```

Sending messages to clients

The same concept applied to sending messages from the client to the server is also employed in the opposite direction. Through its `Clients` property, the Hub class offers a wide variety of tools to determine the recipients of the message and "invoke their methods" in a simple way thanks to the flexibility provided by .NET dynamic types.

The following code shows an invocation of the `showAlert()` method in all the clients connected when one of them calls the `Alert()` method of the hub:

```
public class AlertService: Hub
{
    public void Alert(string msg)
    {
        this.Clients.All.showAlert(msg);

    }
}
```

· `Clients.All` returns a reference to all connected clients in the form of a dynamic object that we can subsequently use to directly code the call to the method that we want to execute in all of them. Notice that the use of dynamic types is what makes the preceding code not fail in compilation despite the fact that there is no `showAlert()` method in the object on which we are making the call.

Internally, still at the server, all invocations to methods that are made on this dynamic object are captured and, following the command[1] pattern, their specifications are entered into a data packet, which is what is really sent to the clients. When the information reaches the other end, the data will be interpreted to execute whatever logic has been implemented.

The structure sent from the server to the clients looks more or less like this:

```
{
    "C": "d-B,2|F,2|G,3|H,0",
    "M": [
            {
                "H":"AlertService",
                "M":"showAlert",
                "A":["I felt a great disturbance in the force"]
            }
        ]
}
```

---

[1] Command pattern: *http://en.wikipedia.org/wiki/Command_pattern*

Although this data packet has a lot of control information, we can intuitively understand that when a client receives this information it will know that the message has been sent from the "AlertService" hub and that it must execute the "showAlert" local method, supplying it the text "I felt a great disturbance in the force" as an argument. Depending on the type of client (JavaScript, .NET, WP, and so on), it will be executed in one way or another. For example, with a JavaScript client, the packet will be translated into a call to the `client.showAlert()` method of the proxy created for the hub and its parameter will be supplied the specified text, as shown in Figure 5-3:

```
hubProxy.client.showAlert = function (msg) {
    alert(msg);
};
```

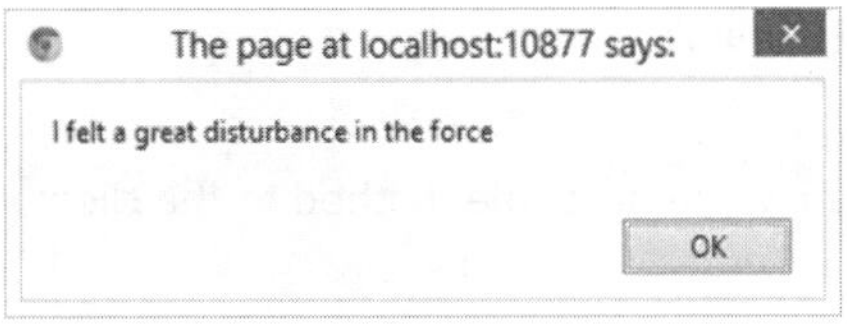

FIGURE 5-3 Alert shown after receiving the message from the server.

It is important to take into account that no checks are performed at the server on the name of the method or the coincidence of its signature, parameters, or types—there would be no way to do so, because they are physically separated. Therefore, the call specification will simply be "packaged"; if we make any mistake, no error will be generated: the packet will be sent to the recipients, but they will not know how to interpret it, and thus the effects will not be as expected.

If we go back to the server side, we find that besides `Clients.All`, we can use various constructions to select the recipients of the calls. All of them are used in the same way, because they return a dynamic object on which we must make the invocations of the functions on the client side. The delivery tools offered by SignalR hubs are as follows:

- **`Clients.All`**   Allows us to "invoke" a method in all the clients connected to the hub, with no exceptions.

```
public class ChatHub: Hub
{
    public Task Broadcast(string text)
    {
        // Invokes the function "Message" in all connected clients
        return Clients.All.Message(text);
    }
}
```

- **`Clients.AllExcept(connections)`**   Indicates that the call must be sent to all the clients, except those whose `connectionIds` are passed as an argument in the form of an array or strings, or simply separated by commas, because the parameter received by this method is a `params string[]`:

```
Clients.AllExcept(darkSideUser1, darkSideUser2)
        .Message("May the force be with you");
```

```
// Or
string[] darkSidePeople = _getDarkSidePeople();
Clients.AllExcept(darkSidePeople)
      .Message("May the force be with you");
```

■ **Clients.Caller**   Identifies that the recipient of the invocation is the client that has made the call to the hub method currently being executed.

```
public Task Broadcast(string message)
{
    Task broadcast =  Clients.All.Message("Broadcast: " + message);
    Task notification = Clients.Caller.Message(
                            ">> Your message was sent!");
    return broadcast.ContinueWith(_ => notification);
}
```

■ **Clients.Client(connectionId)**   Sends the invocation of the method to the client with the specified connection identifier only.

```
Clients.Client(lukeConnectionId).Message("Use the force");
```

■ **Clients.Clients(connectionIds)**   Sends the invocation of the method to the clients whose connection identifier is specified in the form of an **IList<string>**:

```
var jedis = _rebelServices.GetJedisConnectionIds();
Clients.Clients(jedis).Message("Use the force");
```

■ **Clients.Others**   Represents all the clients connected except the one who has invoked the method being executed. It is equivalent to using **AllExcept()** and supplying it the identifier of the current connection.

```
public Task Broadcast(string message)

{
    return Clients.Others.Message("Broadcast: " + message);
}
```

■ **Clients.Group(groupName, excludeConnectionIds)**   Allows invoking functions only in clients belonging to the group specified as an argument. Although we will go into deeper details later in this chapter in the section "Managing groups," it should be remarked here that hubs, like persistent connections, allow creating arbitrary groups and linking clients to them.

```
public Task MessageToGroup(string group, string text)

{
    return Clients.Group(group).Message(text);
}
```

The second parameter is useful to enter the identifiers of the clients that, despite belonging to the specified group, must not receive the message.

- **Clients.Groups(groupNames, excludeConnectionIds)**   Similar to the preceding method, sends the invocation of the method to the clients belonging to the groups specified in the form of string lists.

```
public Task MessageToAdmins(string text)
{
    var groups = new[] { "admins", "superadmins", "ninjas" };
    return Clients.Groups(groups).Message(text);
}
```

- **Clients.OthersInGroup(groupName)**   Allows us to select all the clients belonging to a group, except the one making the current call to the hub.

```
public Task BroadcastToGroup(string group, string text)
{
    return Clients.OthersInGroup(group).Message(text);
}
```

- **Clients.OthersInGroups(groupNames)**   Allows us to specify all the clients belonging to the groups entered as recipients of the message, except the client making the current call to the hub.

```
public Task BroadcastToGroups(IList<string> groups, string text)
{
    return Clients.OthersInGroups(groups).Message(text);
}
```

- **Clients.User(userName)**   Enables us to state the specific user on which the method will be invoked but, in contrast to Clients.Client(), in this case we will use their name as the search criterion. In the next section, "Sending messages to specific users," we will come back to this, but for now it will suffice to know that this name will initially be the name of the user authenticated in the system:

```
public Task ObiWanMessage()
{
    return Clients.User("luke").Message("Use the force");
}
```

An important detail to keep in mind, which we have anticipated in some of the previous examples, is that the invocation of any method from the client side on a selection of recipients returns a Task type object, which allows employing it as a return of asynchronous methods or using the capabilities offered by this type to coordinate processes executed in parallel, as well as easy use of the async/await constructs of the language:

```
public async Task Alert(string msg)
{
    await Clients.All.showAlert(msg);
    await Clients.Caller.showAlert("Your alert has been sent");
}
```

Sending messages to specific users

We previously saw that we can invoke a method on a specific client by using its connection identifier via a construct similar to `Clients.Client(id).MethodToInvoke(params)`.

We also briefly commented on another option: using the `User(userName)` selector, thus adding an additional way of selecting the recipient or recipients of the message by their user names.

```
public Task ObiWanMessage()
{
    return Clients.User("luke").Message("Use the force");
}
```

In the preceding example, the message will be sent to all the SignalR clients that are authenticated in the system as "luke". Note that, as opposed to `Clients.Client()`, which locates the recipient uniquely, in this case it would be possible to send the message via several connections, as many as are associated to the authenticated user.

The small distinguishing nuance is the distinction between the terms "client" and "user." A client is equivalent to a connection and has a unique identifier, whereas a user can have several active connections (for example, by having several tabs open in their browser), each one with a different identifier.

Nevertheless, the best thing about this feature is its flexibility. When SignalR needs to know the name of the user, it employs a class that implements the `IUserIdProvider` interface, whose single method will be in charge of returning the user name, using information from the current request, if necessary.

The default implementation is found in the `PrincipalUserIdProvider` class, defined in the `Microsoft.AspNet.SignalR.Infrastructure` namespace, and it returns the name of the authenticated user:

```
public class PrincipalUserIdProvider : IUserIdProvider
{
    public string GetUserId(IRequest request)
    {
        if (request == null)
            throw new ArgumentNullException("request");
        if (request.User != null && request.User.Identity != null)
            return request.User.Identity.Name;
        else
            return (string) null;
    }
}
```

Obviously, we can implement our own logic to obtain the name of the user associated to a connection. For example, the following code shows how we could use the content of a cookie for this:

```
public class CookiesUserIdProvider : IUserIdProvider
{
    public string GetUserId(IRequest request)
    {
        if (request == null)
            throw new ArgumentNullException("request");
        Cookie cookie;
        if (request.Cookies.TryGetValue("username", out cookie))
        {
            return cookie.Value;
        }
        else
        {
            return null;
        }
    }
}
```

SignalR will know that it must use this class instead of the one included out of the box because we are going to specifically indicate so by registering this class in a component called the dependency resolver. In Chapter 9, "Advanced topics," we will delve into the dependency resolver. For now, it will suffice to understand that the following code, entered in the application startup, tells SignalR that when it needs an object of the IUserIdProvider type it must use the delegate that we are providing it to obtain the instance. In this case, we will always provide it an instance of the CookiesUserIdProvider type:

```
GlobalHost.DependencyResolver.Register(
    typeof(IUserIdProvider),
        ()=> new CookiesUserIdProvider()
);
```

State maintenance

Clients automatically include state information in the calls they make to the methods of a hub. This information consists of a key-value dictionary that contains data that might be of use to either end. From the point of view of the server, this gives us the possibility of accessing these data from the body of the methods, again thanks to .NET dynamic types.

Thus, on the client side, we can create and use arbitrary properties that could be directly accessed from the server method invoked. In the case of a JavaScript client, these properties are created inside the state property of the proxy, as you can see in the following code:

```
// ==========================================================
// Client code (Javascript)
hubProxy.state.UserName = "Obi Wan";      // Accessible from server ───────────
hubProxy.state.MsgId = 1;                 // Accessible from server ─────────┐
                                                                              │
hubProxy.server.alert ("I felt a great disturbance in the force");           │
                                                                              │
                                                                              │
// ==========================================================                │
// Server code                                                               │
public Task Alert(string msg)                                                │
{                                                                            │
    var alert = string.Format("#{0} alert from {1}: {2}",                    │
                            Clients.Caller.MsgId, ◄────────────────────────┘
                            Clients.Caller.UserName, ◄──────────────────────
                            msg);
    return Clients.All.ShowAlert(alert);
}
```

Obviously, we can access data relative only to the client that invoked the current method; for this reason, we use the familiar `Clients.Caller` property to access such data.

It is also possible to modify the values at the server. The new state will be transferred to the client in the response to the invocation. Notice that in this case we are directly applying an autoincrement operator on the `MsgId` property:

```
public Task Alert(string msg)
{
    var alert = string.Format("#{0} alert from {1}: {2}",
                            Clients.Caller.MsgId++,
                            Clients.Caller.UserName,
                            msg);
    return Clients.All.ShowAlert(alert);
}
```

The new value of the `MsgId` property will be returned to the client as part of the response to the call to the method. Upon arrival, the local value of the property will be updated.

This capability can be useful for the purpose of simplifying the signature of the methods of the hub, although we should bear in mind that the state information that we include at the client will travel in all requests, to maintain synchronization between both ends, so we must use it carefully.

Later, in "State maintenance" in the "Client implementation" section, we will look at the mechanisms behind this interesting feature.

Accessing information about the request context

When using hubs, in method signatures we include only the parameters that the methods need to receive from the client to perform the task assigned to them. Consequently, obtaining information from the context of the request or even the identifier of the connection that makes the call is not as direct as when we used persistent connections, where we received these data as parameters of the methods provided by the `PersistentConnection` base class.

Nevertheless, it is just as easy. To access the context data, the `Hub` class offers the `Context` property—of the `HubCallerContext` type—through which it exposes properties, including `ConnectionId`, `Headers`, `QueryString`, or `User`. See Figure 5-4.

FIGURE 5-4 Members of the `Context` property of the `Hub` class.

As its name implies, in `Context.ConnectionId` we will always have the identifier of the connection that the hub is currently instantiating and executing.

```
public Task NewUser()
{
    var message = "New user: " + Context.ConnectionId;
    return Clients.Others.ShowAlert(message);
}
```

Other properties of `Context`, such as `Headers`, `QueryString`, `RequestCookies`, and `User`, are just shortcuts to members of the `Request` property, which is the one that really contains the information about the request.

Although one might expect the type of this `Request` property to be the traditional `System.Web.HttpRequest`, this is not so. The property uses the `IRequest` type, which is a SignalR-specific abstraction and which allows accessing information on the context of the request in a decoupled way, without needing to know exactly what its implementation is. If we keep poring over the code of the framework, we will see that this interface is implemented in a class that, in turn, obtains all the data it needs using the OWIN standard. This constitutes a complete isolation from the host in which the application is executed.

Notification of connections and disconnections

Hubs also detect when new clients connect, as well as disconnections and reconnections, allowing us to enter logic at these points. In a similar way to persistent connections, we will achieve this by overriding three methods defined in the Hub class:

```
public abstract class Hub : IHub, IDisposable
{
    public virtual Task OnDisconnected() { ... }
    public virtual Task OnConnected()    { ... }
    public virtual Task OnReconnected()  { ... }
    ... // Other members of Hub
}
```

Because, as we have seen, the context information is available through the Context property of the Hub, none of these methods defines input parameters. Also, as with the PersistentConnection class, they all return a Task type object.

```
public class AlertService : Hub
{
    public override Task OnConnected()
    {
        return Clients.All.ShowAlert(
                "There is a new user ready to send alerts to!"
        );
    }
    ... // Other members of AlertsService

}
```

If inside one of these methods we perform an operation that is quick and direct and does not require using asynchrony or creating a Task, we can simply return the result of invoking the corresponding method of the base class:

```
public override Task OnConnected()
{
    // Do something sync here

    return base.OnConnected();
}
```

Managing groups

We have already seen how to send messages to clients belonging to a group by using the Clients.Group() and Clients.OthersInGroup() methods, but first, we must obviously find some way both to associate clients to SignalR groups and to disassociate them.

Both operations can be performed very easily through the `Groups` property of the hubs, which gives us the `Add()` and `Remove()` properties for asynchronously adding a connection and removing it from a group:

```
public class Chat: Hub
{
    public Task Join(string groupName)
    {
        return Groups.Add(Context.ConnectionId, groupName);
    }
    public Task Leave(string groupName)
    {
        return Groups.Remove(Context.ConnectionId, groupName);
    }

    ... // Other members of the Chat
}
```

As with persistent connections, to avoid limiting the scale-out possibilities of SignalR applications, we are unable to ask what groups are available or what connections are included in each of them. If we were to need these functionalities for our applications, we would have to implement them outside the SignalR framework.

Maintaining state at the server

During the development of an application on SignalR, the need can frequently arise to save any type of state maintenance on the server side. We have already seen how to do it at the client side, but because the client is inherently fragile and because the information travels continually between both ends, this is not always a viable option and we have to search for other solutions. For example, if we are implementing an online game, the reasonable thing to do is store the state of the different players at the server, and not at the client, for the duration of the match. Or suppose that we need a list with the users connected to a chat service. SignalR does not offer any way to get it, so our only option would be to keep a list at the server with information about these users.

As a first approach that is valid in many scenarios, we could consider using data structures stored in the server memory. Depending on our needs, we could use variables, lists, dictionaries, or any other structure, but it is important to remember that they must be defined statically, because hubs have a very short life cycle, being created and destroyed in each call or event of the connection. Thus we might be tempted to write code like the following:

```
// Note: UserData is a custom class to store
// our user's current status.

public class ChatHub : Hub
{
    private static Dictionary<string, UserData> _users =
                        new Dictionary<string, UserData>();
    private static int _usersCount = 0;
```

```
public override Task OnConnected()
{
    _usersCount++;
    var user = new UserData()
                    {
                        Active = true,
                        Name = "user" + _usersCount,
                        Color = "blue",
                        ConnectedAt = DateTime.Now
                    };
    _users[Context.ConnectionId] = user;
    return base.OnConnected();
}

// ...More code
}
```

Although conceptually this would solve our problem—allowing us to have state information available to use in our application—if we were to test it, we would notice after a few minutes that it does not work properly in multiuser environments. Concurrent access of several users would cause the information kept in the dictionary and even the counter itself to begin to display corruption issues, generating inconsistencies and problems during execution.

This aspect is of vital importance in all SignalR applications because, by definition, we are building multiuser systems where we will likely have a high degree of concurrency, so it is necessary to take precautions to prevent simultaneous access of these members. In Chapter 4, "Persistent connections," we saw that we can perform increment atomic operations on integers by using the features offered by the static class System.Threading.Interlocked:

```
Interlocked.Increment(ref _usersCount);
```

And, with the dictionary, the problem is solved in an equally easy way. Data corruption happens because, by design, the Dictionary class of the .NET Framework is not thread safe for writing; that is, it does not guarantee its consistency in scenarios with multiple concurrencies where there might be execution threads adding elements and other execution threads eliminating them.

Fortunately, since version 4 of the .NET Framework, we have an option especially designed for this: ConcurrentDictionary. This class is available in the System.Collections.Concurrent[2] namespace, together with other concurrent versions of familiar structures such as lists, stacks, or queues, and it provides a key-value dictionary that can be used safely in multiprocess scenarios. Therefore, the only change that we would need to make to the previous code would be in the definition of the store used:

```
private static ConcurrentDictionary<string, UserData> _users =
    new ConcurrentDictionary<string, UserData>();
```

---

[2] Documentation of the System.Collections.Concurrent namespace: *http://msdn.microsoft.com/en-us//library/system.collections.concurrent.aspx*

This way, we would now be storing the system state in the server memory safely while having concurrent accesses. We can use this state information from the actions or events of the hub, as in the following example:

```
public class ChatHub: Hub
{
    private static int _usersCount = 0;
    private static ConcurrentDictionary<string, UserData>
            _users = new ConcurrentDictionary<string, UserData>();

    public override Task OnConnected()
    {
        Interlocked.Increment(ref _usersCount);
        var user = new UserData()
                    {
                        Active = true,
                        Name = "user" + _usersCount,
                        Color = "blue",
                        ConnectedAt = DateTime.Now
                    };
        _users[Context.ConnectionId] = user;
        return base.OnConnected();
    }

    public Task ChangeNickname(string newName)
    {
        UserData user;
        if (_users.TryGetValue(Context.ConnectionId, out user))
        {
            var oldName = user.Name;
            user.Name = newName;
            return Clients.All.Message(
                    oldName + " now is " + newName, "system");
        }
        return null;
    }

    public Task Send(string message)
    {
        UserData user;
        if (_users.TryGetValue(Context.ConnectionId, out user))
        {
            var m = string.Format("[{0}]: {1}", user.Name, message);
            return Clients.All.Message(m);
        }
        return null;
    }
    ... // Other methods
}
```

The technique shown is absolutely valid, and it yields great performance because it is based on the store that is most efficient and closest to the server: its memory. However, it is not exempt from drawbacks.

The first obvious problem is that memory is a volatile resource. If the server is restarted, the application breaks down, or an update is installed, all the information stored would be lost immediately. In some services, this might not be a great issue, but in other systems, we will not be able to allow this behavior and we will therefore have to discard this solution.

Another serious problem would emerge if we had to scale out the system horizontally—that is, adding new servers to balance the load, as shown in Figure 5-5. (Later, we'll see that SignalR provides tools to do this.) In this scenario, each connection could be dealt with by a different server, so the state of the application would be distributed among all of them without any synchronization of the information stored. Thus, relying on server memory to store state information can prove unreliable in these situations.

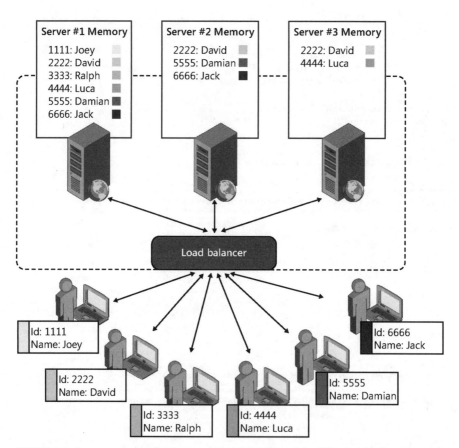

FIGURE 5-5 Server memory after horizontal scale-out. The state of the application is inconsistent.

This is neither a peculiar limitation nor exclusive to SignalR; it is quite logical and common to all application servers whose load we want to share among several nodes. For example, in standard ASP.NET applications, the use of in-memory session variables causes the same scalability problems, and this is why there are alternative options such as session state servers or providers in charge of storing the state in distributed stores, such as the cache system in Windows Azure.

SignalR does not offer any out-of-the-box solution for these situations, and it is the responsibility of the developer to have a centralized and non-volatile persistence system capable of storing this information and retrieving it quickly. The approach would therefore be to migrate to a structure such as the one shown in Figure 5-6, where a component or additional system is introduced whose responsibility will be exclusively focused on storing and managing the application state information and making it available to all its nodes.

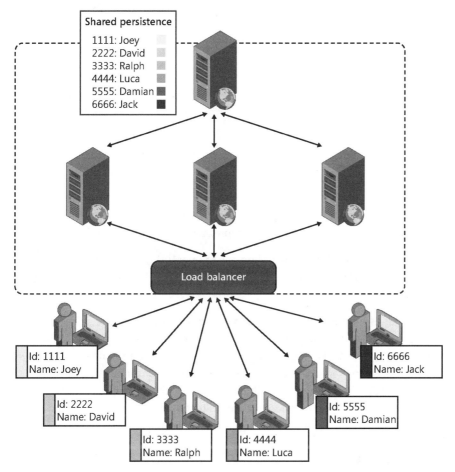

FIGURE 5-6 Shared storage component.

We could implement this system on virtually any technology or platform, from a relational database such as SQL Server, solutions for structured storing in the cloud such as those provided by Azure, or systems specialized in offering high-efficiency distributed storage, such as Redis, Memcached, MongoDB, and many more. Among others, the following criteria can help us select the solution that matches our needs:

- **Efficiency** For real-time multiuser applications, remember that immediate response is a basic requirement. However, it is also important to bear in mind that the immediacy needs can be different depending on the type of application: a multiuser shooter does not have the same requirements as a chat room service.

- **Persistence and non-volatility**   Normally, it is important for our software to ensure these aspects of the information.

- **Scalability**   For state storage solution, if the number of users grows exponentially, it might be necessary to distribute this very component among several physical nodes. If we cannot scale out the persistence mechanism, the scalability of our system will be irredeemably limited to it.

- **Security**   This component must offer features to protect the information proportional to the importance of the state data to be stored.

- **Operation environment**   The solution selected must be technically compatible with this environment. Also, the availability of interfaces allowing its use with .NET applications must be considered.

- **Knowledge and experience**   This is especially important for the development and maintenance team, who will have to use it to implement state persistence and keep it operating throughout the system's life.

Along with the preceding criteria, of course, we must include other aspects of the product, such as its reliability, integrity, maintainability, community, support, licensing model, and so on.

Now that we have taken a first look at operation environments distributed across several nodes, this is a good time to anticipate a very important point that we delve into in Chapter 8, "Deploying and scaling SignalR."

In distributed scenarios such as the one described previously, SignalR creates a challenge with no precedent in more traditional web applications: how to get the messages to reach their recipients. Something so relatively simple as sending a broadcast message to all users connected to one same point stops being trivial when there are several nodes to which a balancer has been assigning the users. For now, we will just reflect upon this; in Chapter 8, we will describe the problem in depth and we will go over the solution that SignalR offers for these situations.

Client implementation

The SignalR framework offers specific client libraries for the different types of systems that can consume services in real time: JavaScript, generic .NET applications, Windows Phone, and so on. They are all similar, yet obviously adapted to the peculiarities of their respective execution environments.

In Chapter 7, "Real-time multiplatform applications," we will see other examples of use, but for now, we will continue to focus on the JavaScript client because it is easy to implement and very useful for a natural environment for this type of system: the web.

JavaScript clients

There are two different ways of working with SignalR using JavaScript: with or without an automatic proxy. We have already anticipated many aspects of the first way in earlier sections, and it is really the most spectacular and easy to use because SignalR, on its own, takes care of a large portion of the work needed to achieve bidirectional communication with the server. Contrariwise, if we choose not to use an automatic proxy, we will have to make a little more effort to reach the same goals, because we will use a syntax that is more generic and aseptic, quite similar to the one used in other types of clients, as shown in the following example:

```
// With automatic/dynamic proxy:
proxy.server.alert("Here I am");

// Without automatic proxy:
proxy.invoke("alert", "Here I am");
```

We will continue studying the JavaScript client using the dynamic proxy, although later on we will also see some examples of direct use of the API without this aid.

Generating the proxy

To initiate the connection to the hub by using the JavaScript client with a dynamic proxy, we must reference the following script libraries from the page[3]:

```
<script src="/scripts/jquery-1.6.4.min.js"></script>
<script src="/scripts/jquery.signalR-2.0.0.min.js"></script>
<script src="/signalr/js"></script>
```

> **Note** It is important to take into account the root path where the application is published when passed during production. For this reason, unless we are implementing the client on a pure HTML page, it is a good idea to use the methods provided by the different technologies to generate the URL based on virtual addresses of the resources, relative to the root of the site:
>
> ```
> // In ASP.NET MVC 4 or above
> <script src="~/signalr/js"></script>
>
> // In ASP.NET MVC 3
> <script src="@Url.Content("~/signalr/js")"></script>
>
> // WebForms
> <script src="<%: ResolveClientUrl("~/signalr/hubs")%>"></script>
> ```

The first two scripts included, already used in the implementation of clients using persistent connections, are basic. SignalR's client library for JavaScript (jquery.signalR) is a plug-in for JQuery, and

---

[3] Remember that the version numbers of the script files referenced from the code can vary depending on the updates that you have installed in your project.

for this reason, both must be included in the page and in this order. Otherwise, a runtime script error will be generated, as shown in Figure 5-7, indicating the measures to be taken to solve it.

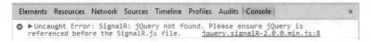

FIGURE 5-7 Error loading the main SignalR script in incorrect order.

Next we find a new reference to a script located at /Signalr/js. The first part of this path ("/Signalr") is the address where the framework is expecting connections from the clients wanting to consume the services provided by the hubs. This path is common to all hubs in the application, and as we have seen, it can be easily modified in the call to the MapSignalR() method that the server executes during application startup, although normally the one provided by default will be valid and we will not need to change it.

The second part ("/js") indicates the resource to be downloaded, in this case the proxy components that will allow easy access to the methods exposed by the different hubs present at the server.

> **Note** In previous versions of SignalR, only the URL "/Signalr/Hubs" was used to download the proxies, but since version 2.0, "/Signalr/Js" is also allowed because this path is more appropriate for the type of resource that we want to obtain.

When the first request to this URL is received, SignalR will analyze the classes of the application inheriting from Hub and will create a script dynamically. Inside it, we will find a JavaScript object for every hub implemented at the server, which will act as a proxy of it on the client side. This process will take place only once, remaining stored in the memory for the following connections. The result generated—the JavaScript file that will be included in the page by the web client, as shown in Figure 5-8—is sent to the client as it is.

```
http://localhost:48037/signalr/js
 1  /*!
 2   * ASP.NET SignalR JavaScript Library v2.0.0
 3   * http://signalr.net/
 4   *
 5   * Copyright Microsoft Open Technologies, Inc. All rights reserved.
 6   * Licensed under the Apache 2.0
 7   * https://github.com/SignalR/SignalR/blob/master/LICENSE.md
 8   *
 9   */
10
11  /// <reference path="..\..\SignalR.Client.JS\Scripts\jquery-1.6.4.js" />
12  /// <reference path="jquery.signalR.js" />
13  (function ($, window) {
14      /// <param name="$" type="jQuery" />
15      "use strict";
16
17      if (typeof ($.signalR) !== "function") {
18          throw new Error("SignalR: SignalR is not loaded. Please ensure jquery.
19      }
20
21      var signalR = $.signalR;
```

FIGURE 5-8 Appearance of the JavaScript file generated.

SignalR does not feature "out-of-the-box" implementation of the minimization of the JavaScript code—that is, the removal of all unnecessary characters from the file with the aim of optimizing its download. However, it has been taken into account internally, so we can use the marvelous extensibility features of the product to insert a minimization component in the middle of the process and achieve this goal. We will see how in due time.

Manual generation of JavaScript proxies

Sometimes it can be useful to have the JavaScript proxies in the form of a static file included in the site instead of having to generate it on the fly. This could make things easier for us at design time, because we would be able to benefit from IntelliSense or optimize downloads sending it to a CDN, making a more efficient use of the cache, or compacting and packaging the resulting script in the bundles used by the application.

For this, SignalR comes with a command-line application downloadable via NuGet that we can execute either manually or as part of the build process of the solution. We can obtain the tool, called SignalR.exe, by installing the following package:

```
PM> Install-Package Microsoft.AspNet.SignalR.Utils
```

This command will download and install the executable file in our solution, leaving it ready to be used from the package manager console itself; see Figure 5-9.

FIGURE 5-9 Execution of SignalR.exe from the package manager console.

To generate the JavaScript file of a project, we just enter the following command:

```
PM> signalr ghp /path:[your-hubs-dll-folder] /o:[output-file]
```

The path parameter indicates the path to the folder that contains the assembly in which the hubs for which we want to obtain the proxy are found. Normally, this will be the path to the /bin folder of the project. The o parameter indicates the full path and the name of the file to be generated.

In both cases, the path is relative to the current directory; the default NuGet console will be found in the root folder of the solution (we can query it with the command pwd), so we will be able to use relative paths to simplify the command, like this for example:

```
PM> signalr ghp /path:MyWebApp/bin /o:MyWebApp/scripts/hubs.js
```

We must take into account that the first time we execute this command, the file will be generated but it will not be included in the project, as shown in Figure 5-10. This is something that we have to do manually afterwards from the Visual Studio solution explorer, adding the existing file.

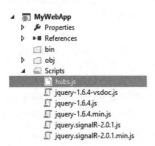

FIGURE 5-10 Proxy generated in the folder but not included in the project.

For better convenience, we can include this procedure as part of the building process of the application very easily. As shown in Figure 5-11, we just have to access the properties of the project and include the following command in the post-compilation command line:

```
$(SolutionDir)\packages\Microsoft.AspNet.SignalR.Utils.2.0.0\tools\signalr.exe ghp /
path:$(TargetDir) /o:$(ProjectDir)/scripts/hubs.js
```

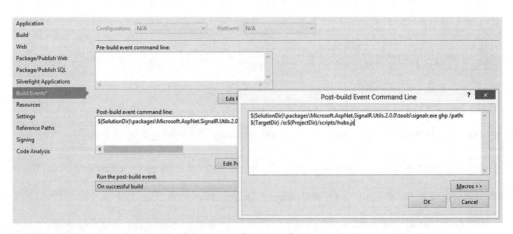

FIGURE 5-11 Automatic generation of the proxy after compiling.

Regardless of which way we generate the .js file, from now on it will obviously be the one that we reference from the pages where we use our hubs:

```
<script src="/scripts/hubs.js"></script>
```

Also, in this case, it would be a good idea to deactivate the automatic proxy generation capability, specifying it in the hub configuration that we can provide during system startup, in the `Startup` class or wherever we have decided to enter the SignalR startup code:

```
public void Configuration(IAppBuilder app)
{
    ...
    app.MapSignalR(new HubConfiguration()
        {
            EnableJavaScriptProxies = false
        });
}
```

When this is done, any attempt to access the automatic proxy generation path, such as /Signalr /Hubs or /Signalr/Js, will generate an error at the client; see Figure 5-12.

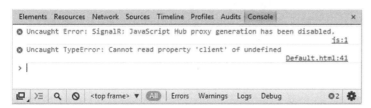

FIGURE 5-12 Error referencing the proxy generation URLs.

Expressly disabling automatic proxy generation can also be useful when the clients of our system are not JavaScript clients but applications of any other type (.NET, Windows Phone, Windows Store, and so on), because these will not need the proxy. We must take into account that the code of the proxies contains a lot of information about the hubs and their actions, and for security, it is a good idea to hide it if their use is not necessary.

Establishing the connection

After the script is at the client, we can initiate the connection to the server by using the following instruction:

```
$.connection.hub.start();
```

The `start()` method implements the promise pattern, so we can enter logic when the connection has been successfully completed or when an error has occurred:

```
$.connection.hub.start()
    .done(function () {
        alert("Connected");
    })
    .fail(function() {
        alert("Connection failed!");
    });
```

Note that the call to the `start()` method is independent of the hubs that we want to use from the client. Initiating the connection simply indicates that we are going to use hubs, but we do not necessarily have to specify which one or ones yet. This is important, because it means that communication with them will be carried out on a single persistent connection and performance will not be affected if we decide to divide up our hubs into several, to organize our code better and to avoid excessively long classes.

The client initiates the negotiation process when the `start()` method is executed. We can trace this process by using the development tools of any browser or external tools such as Fiddler (as shown in Figure 5-13).

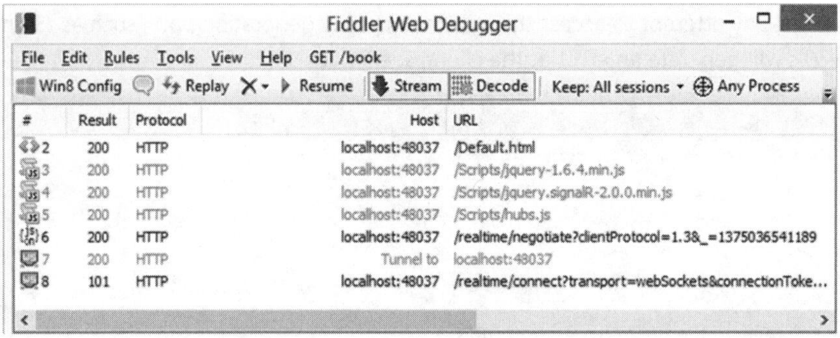

FIGURE 5-13 Negotiation process traced with Fiddler.

Note that one of the parameters that are sent to the server is the version of the SignalR protocol that the client expects to use, 1.3 in this case. This is important, because from version 2.0 of SignalR the server will be able to respond to different client protocols, which will allow client and server to understand each other even if they do not share the exact same version of the framework. Thus a SignalR 2.0 server can give service to connections made using version 1.0 of the client libraries. However, it will not work in the opposite way: a 1.0 server would not be able to give service to clients of a later version.

By default, the JavaScript client will try to communicate with the hub system available at the URL "/Signalr", although if the URL has been modified at the server, we will also have to modify it here before initiating the connection:

```
// Server initialization code
public void Configuration(IAppBuilder app)
{
    var config = new HubConfiguration();
    app.MapSignalR("/realtime", config);
}

// Client code
$.connection.hub.url = "/realtime";
... // Other client initialization
$.connection.hub.start();
```

This feature also opens the possibility of connecting to services published in different servers to the one that has served the current page.

```
$.connection.hub.url = "http://myserver.com/myurl";
```

The SignalR client will detect cross-domain scenarios automatically and will use the appropriate technique for the connection to be successfully established. However, to serve this type of request, the hub will have to have been previously configured at the server. The configuration mechanism is identical to the one already described when we studied persistent connections:

- If we want the server to respond to requests from external domains using CORS, we have to activate the appropriate OWIN middleware. For this, we first install the package from NuGet:

  ```
  PM> Install-Package microsoft.owin.cors
  ```

  Next, we enter it into the OWIN pipeline before SignalR. Note that, as we did with persistent connections, we use the Map() extension to create a configuration section associated to a URL, to which we add the modules that we want. In practice, it is as if we created a bifurcation in the pipeline starting off from the specified path:

  ```
  // Server initialization code
  public void Configuration(IAppBuilder app)
  {
      app.Map("/chat", map =>
      {
          map.UseCors(CorsOptions.AllowAll);
          map.RunSignalR();
      });
  }
  ```

- If we also need to activate JSONP to allow older browsers to access the services, we could indicate it in the hub configuration object that we can supply to RunSignalR() or MapSignalR():

  ```
  app.Map("/chat", map =>
  {
      map.UseCors(CorsOptions.AllowAll);
      var config = new HubConfiguration()
                      {
                          EnableJSONP = true
                      };
      map.RunSignalR(config);

  });
  ```

Sending messages to the server

As you know, in the dynamically generated script, there will be a proxy object for every hub in the server. Each hub will have a representative on the client side, which we can access via the `$.connection.[hubName]` property. The following code shows how we can reference the proxy of a hub called "AlertService" at the server:

```
// Client code
var proxy = $.connection.alertService;
```

Note that to ensure coherence with the syntax and naming standards of JavaScript, during the generation of the proxy, the name of the class has been converted to camel casing style with the first character automatically in lowercase. This detail is very important, because if this naming convention is not respected, access to the hub will not be possible:

```
var proxy = $.connection.AlertService; // Error: "AlertService"
                                       // doesn't exist
```

This conversion is performed whenever we have not used the [HubName] attribute to explicitly specify a name for the hub. In this case, the name will be used exactly as stated in this annotation.

Now we shall pause for a moment to look at what has happened behind the scenes that enables us to access the proxy like this. Here is the code of a simple hub, followed by a portion of the code generated dynamically for it by SignalR:

```
// ========================================================
// Server code
public class AlertService : Hub
{
    public Task Alert(string msg)
    {
        // Code
    }
}


// ========================================================
// Portion of client code (generated script)
...

proxies.alertService = this.createHubProxy('alertService');
proxies.alertService.client = { };
proxies.alertService.server = {
    alert: function (msg) {
            return proxies.alertService.invoke.apply(
                proxies.alertService,
                $.merge(["Alert"], $.makeArray(arguments))
            );
        }
};
```

In the `proxies` object that appears in the generated code is where the different objects are stored that will act as proxies of the hubs detected at the server. Later on, we will be able to access them using the expression `$.connection.[hubName]`. On this object, we see that in this case an `alertService` property is declared to store the proxy created. This is the one that we used earlier to obtain a reference to said proxy, when we used the following code:

```
var proxy = $.connection.alertService;
```

As you can see, inside this proxy a `server` property has been created, which is a faithful reproduction of its counterpart at the server; it includes a method for each method found in the hub. Obviously, in their implementation, we will find only the code needed to perform the invocation to the server asynchronously.

By default, the name of each method is also converted to adapt it to the customary naming conventions in JavaScript: the `Alert()` method of the server will be mapped to an `alert()` method at the client. However, the name will not be converted if we use the `[HubMethodName]` attribute to expressly state the name by which the method will be available.

Therefore, to call methods from the client that are available at the server, the only thing we have to do is use the `server` property of the proxy towards the hub and invoke it directly, supplying it the required parameters:

```
var proxy = $.connection.alertService;
... // Open connection
proxy.server.alert("Here I am!");
```

> **Note** In the case of methods overloaded at the server, only the signature of the one with the least number of parameters will appear in the proxy, but we will still be able to invoke them from the client without any problems.

The call to the server methods implements the promise pattern, so to take control when the call has been made successfully or when it has failed for any reason, we can use the constructions that we already know. In the first case, it is also possible to retrieve the value returned by the method executed.

```
// ==========================================================
// Server code
public int Divide(int a, int b)
{
    return a / b;
}

// ==========================================================
// Client code (JavaScript)
var a = prompt("a?");
var b = prompt("b?");
proxy.server.divide(a, b)
    .done(function (result) {
        alert("Result: " + result);
```

```
        })
        .fail(function (err) {
            alert("Error: " + err);
        });
```

In this example, the function defined in the done() method will receive the result of the operation performed by the server as an argument. In case of failure, the function specified in fail() will receive an object where we can find the description of the error that occurred (for example, "divide by zero attempt"), if this option has been expressly enabled at startup. Note the use of the #if DEBUG compilation directive to prevent detailed error messages from reaching production:

```
public class Startup
{
    public void Configuration(IAppBuilder app)
    {
        var config = new HubConfiguration();
        #if DEBUG
            config.EnableDetailedErrors = true;
        #endif
        app.MapSignalR(config);
    }
}
```

By default, when detailed errors are not enabled, a generic message will be sent, indicating that an error has occurred in the call to the method of the hub.

To handle errors in a more precise way, from the hub we can throw exceptions of the HubException type at any moment, supplying it a message describing the error and, if necessary, an arbitrary object with additional information:

```
// Server code
public Task ChangeNickname(string newNickname)
{
    if (!nameIsValid(newNickname))
    {
        throw new HubException(
                "Nickname not valid",
                new { user = Context.User.Identity.Name, attempted = newNickname }
        );
    }
    … // Change the nickname
}
```

The HubException exception thrown will be automatically serialized by SignalR, and we will receive it in the fail() function associated to the call to the server:

```
// Client code
proxy.server.changeNickname(newNickname)
    .fail(function(err) {
        if (err.source === 'HubException') {
            console.log(e.data.user+" -> "+ e.message);
        }
    });
```

> **Note** For these types of exceptions, the value of EnableDetailedErrors will not be taken into account. They will always be serialized and sent to the client as they are.

Sending additional information

Just as it happened in the world of persistent connections, the clients of a hub can send additional information in requests by using the mechanisms provided by web protocols. This information can be retrieved at the server with the `Context` property of the hub.

For example, a JavaScript client can enter information in a cookie, and its value will be available at the server side because it will travel with each request made to the server:

```
// Client (JavaScript) code
document.cookie = "Username=phil";
$.connection.hub.start();
…

// Server code (Hub)
public Task Send(string message)
{
    Cookie cookie;
    var username =
        Context.RequestCookies.TryGetValue("Username", out cookie)
        ? cookie.Value
        : Context.ConnectionId;
    return Clients.All.Message(username + " >> " + message);
}
```

Another option is to enter additional values into the query string of the different requests originated at the client. For this, we can set arbitrary values in the qs ("query string") property of the hub at the client before opening the connection, and these values will be available later at the server:

```
// Client code

$.connection.hub.qs = "username=phil";
// Or, alternatively:
$.connection.hub.qs = { username: "phil" };

$.connection.hub.start();

// Server code (Hub)

public Task Send(string message)
{
    var username = Context.QueryString["Username"] ?? "Unknown";
    return Clients.All.Message(username + " dice " + message);
}
```

It should be again noted that this information will travel when requests are made to the server. In a transport such as WebSockets, there will normally be only one request that will remain open, while other transports such as long polling will open many more connections. Therefore, the value obtained at the server will be the one sent from the client at the time of the most recent request.

Receiving messages sent from the server

We have seen that when we make calls from the server to methods that exist in clients, what actually happens is that the specifications of that call are "packaged" into a data structure and sent to all its recipients using push. See Figure 5-14.

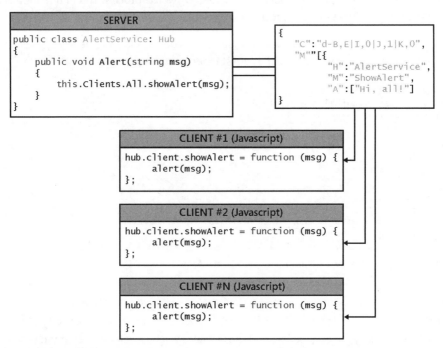

FIGURE 5-14 Calls from the server to client-side methods.

From the point of view of the client, what SignalR does is interpret the data packet received and invoke the relevant methods. That is, it processes the events received.

In the JavaScript client, methods that can be "executed" from the server must be defined in the `client` property of the proxy object:

```
var alertHub = $.connection.alertService;
alertHub.client.showAlert = function (msg) {
    alert(msg);
};
alertHub.client.newUser = function (userId) {
    alert("New user with id: " + userId);
};
```

It is necessary to make these specifications before the connection is opened; otherwise, they will not work. It is also important to highlight that the name of the method used at the server must match the name at the client exactly, except that the match is case-insensitive. The following commands at the server will execute the logic expected at the client:

```
public override Task OnConnected()
{
    return Clients.All.NewUser(Context.ConnectionId);
}

    // Is equivalent to
public override Task OnConnected()
{
    return Clients.All.newuser(Context.ConnectionId);
}
```

However, if a nonexistent method is invoked from the server, there will be no errors on either end. The server will send the clients the data packet with the command specification, and the clients will not execute any action upon its reception, because the name of the method received will not match any existing one.

Logging

The client component of SignalR for JavaScript allows registering a trace with the most relevant events that occur during the lifetime of the connection, which can be very helpful when debugging the applications. To activate this trace, we just have to add the following line to the initialization code:

```
$.connection.hub.logging = true;
```

From that moment on, it will be possible to query the trace in the browser's console, as shown in Figure 5-15 and Figure 5-16. Note that, as well as the negotiation process, we can view the events thrown from the server—that is, the methods invoked on the client side.

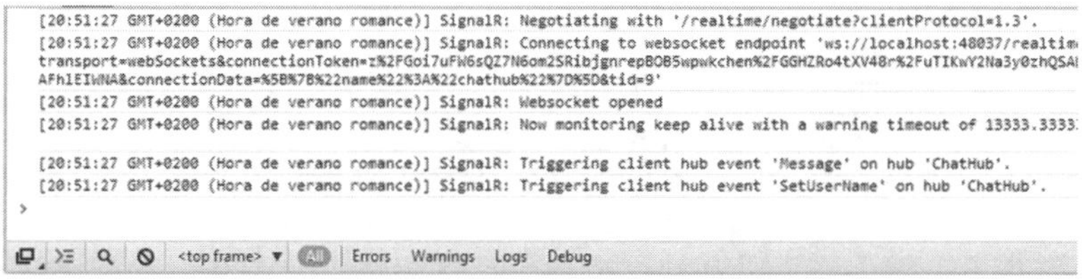

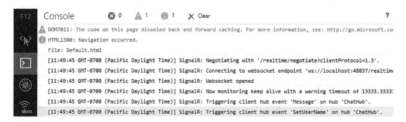

FIGURE 5-15 Log of the JavaScript client in Google Chrome.

FIGURE 5-16 Log of the JavaScript client in Internet Explorer 11 Developer Tools.

Actually, if we need to, we can even include custom information in this log easily (see Figure 5-17):

```
$.connection.hub.start()
    .done(function () {
        $.connection.hub.log("My id: " + $.connection.hub.id);
    });
```

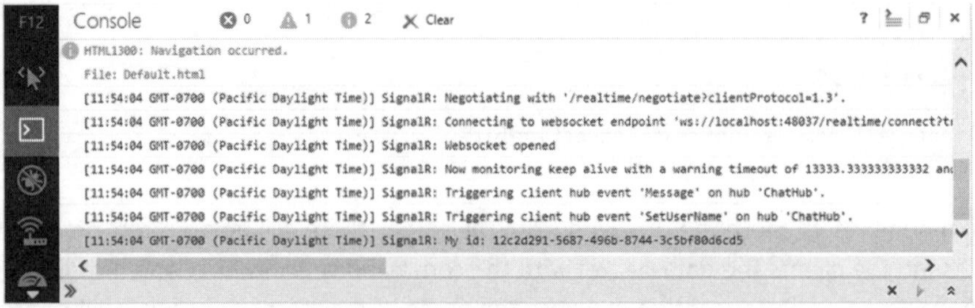

FIGURE 5-17 Custom information in the SignalR trace.

> **Note** The identifier assigned to the current client is available in the `$.connection.hub.id` property.

The information logged in this way will always have the prefix "SignalR:", so it is easy to identify it in the trace.

State maintenance

We have previously seen that it is possible to define variables at the client that can be queried or modified directly from the server:

```
// =========================================================
// Client code (Javascript)
hubProxy.state.UserName = "Obi Wan";      // Accessible from server ———
hubProxy.state.MsgId = 1;                 // Accessible from server ———

hubProxy.server.alert ("I felt a great disturbance in the force");


// =========================================================
// Server code
public Task Alert(string msg)
{
    var alert = string.Format("#{0} alert from {1}: {2}",
                              Clients.Caller.MsgId++,◄
                              Clients.Caller.UserName,◄
                              msg);
    return Clients.All.ShowAlert(alert);
}
```

As we said earlier and as you can infer from the code, these variables must be defined in the hub's proxy, inside the object stored in its state property. In this case, the name of the variable used at the server must match the one defined at the client exactly, including letter case.

The internal operation of this feature is based on the command pattern and is quite simple. Given the above code, where we saw the setting of two state properties and a call to a remote method at the client, the information sent in the client-server direction would be approximately as follows:

```
data = {
    "H":"alertservice",
    "M":"Alert",
    "A":["I felt a great disturbance in the force"],
    "I":6,
    "S":{
        "UserName":"Obi Wan",
        "MsgId":7
        }
}
```

As you can see, the message sent encapsulates both the specification of the invocation to be performed on the server side ("H": hub, "M": method, "A": args) and all the state variables ("S": state) that have been defined. It is therefore important to use them prudently to avoid excessive bandwidth consumption.

After processing the method at the server, the information returned to the client is more or less as follows:

```
{
    "S": {
        "MsgId":8
    },
    "I":"6"
}
```

In this case, we see that the client is returned a structure that contains information about several aspects, including the new value of the state variables modified during server processing (note the increase of the MsgId variable). Thus, when the data packet reaches the client, the latter can extract the property values and modify them on its local copy, maintaining a consistent application state between calls.

Implementing the client without a proxy

There might be scenarios where using a proxy is inconvenient, such as applications with a large number of hubs or applications that expose a large number of operations to their clients. In such— perhaps somewhat extreme—cases, using a proxy might be too costly in terms of the bandwidth and processing capacity needed on both ends. Also, a hacker could very easily obtain information about the hubs and their actions, which constitutes a perfect x-ray of the server's attack surface.

However, we are not required to use proxies. Yes, they simplify development, but SignalR offers an additional alternative to directly communicate with hubs in scenarios where we do not want to use a proxy.

In this case, the API is in fact quite similar to the one we find in other clients such as the generic .NET client, where we do not have this type of syntactical sweetener. We will now very quickly study its main features, because the concepts are identical to those explained until now, this being just a different syntax to achieve the same purposes.

Establishing the connection

To initiate a connection to a hub without using proxies, it will not be necessary to reference the /SignalR/Hubs script or whichever one we have set as we were doing before. Here it will suffice to include jQuery and SignalR in the page:

```
<script src="Scripts/jquery-1.6.4.min.js"></script>
<script src="Scripts/jquery.signalR-2.0.0.min.js"></script>
```

Next we must obtain a reference to the connection to the hub server and open it, similar to what we have done in previous examples:

```
var connection = $.hubConnection();
connection.start()
    .done(function () {
        // Code
    });
```

The URL where it is assumed by default that SignalR will be available at the server is /Signalr, which is the one used in the default mapping. However, we can modify it by supplying it to the $.hubConnection() method as a parameter, as you can see in the following example:

```
// Client side
    var connection = $.hubConnection("/realtime");


// Server side configuration(startup.cs):
app.MapSignalR("/realtime", new HubConfiguration());
```

Finally, if we are not using proxies, the best thing to do is to disable them at the server, something that can be done by specifying it when the hub is configured:

```
public void Configuration(IAppBuilder app)
{
    app.MapSignalR(new HubConfiguration()
                {
                    EnableJavaScriptProxies = false
                });
}
```

Of course, if we have configured the generation of the proxy as a static file, we must not forget to eliminate it too.

Invoking server methods

Even if we are not using the automatically generated proxy, on the client side we will always need an object representing the hub on which we can work, allowing us to invoke the methods and receive the events of the server.

We can create one of these objects, which is but a proxy after all, based on the connection previously referenced, like this:

```
var connection = $.hubConnection();
var proxy = connection.createHubProxy("AlertService");
```

To perform an operation from the server side, we use the `invoke()` method directly on the proxy that we have created:

```
var connection = $.hubConnection();
var proxy = connection.createHubProxy("AlertService");
connection.start().done(function () {
    proxy.invoke("Alert", "I felt a great disturbance in the force");
});
```

As you can guess, the first argument is the name of the method or action to be invoked on the server side. In this case, the name is not case-sensitive: we will get the same result if we invoke the methods "alert" and "ALERT".

The second argument and the following ones are values that are going to be supplied to the action for its execution. They can be any type; the server will be in charge of converting them to those specified in the method signature.

As usual, the `invoke()` method implements the promise pattern, so we can take control when execution has ended, whether in success—at which point we can obtain the return values—or in an error:

```
proxy.invoke("divide", 100, prompt("Divisor?"))
    .done(function(result) {
        alert(result);
    })
    .fail(function(err) {
        alert(err);
    });
```

State maintenance

This programming model also offers the ability to maintain state in client variables that are accessible from the server. In the same way as we saw when using dynamic proxies, we can use the `state` property for this:

```
... // Code
var proxy = connection.createHubProxy("AlertService");
proxy.state.MsgId = 1;                 // Property accessible from server
proxy.state.UserName = "Obi Wan";  // Property accessible from server
```

Receiving messages sent from the server

When methods of the client side are invoked from the server, we can capture these calls using the `On()` method as follows:

```
proxy.on("ShowAlert", function(msg) {
    alert(msg);
});
```

The first parameter supplied to this method is the name of the event or action invoked from the server, specified as a case-insensitive character string. The second one is the code to be executed, in the form of an anonymous function, with the parameters that have been sent to it from the remote end.

Complete example: Shared drawing board

In this example, we will use hubs to implement a simplified version of a shared drawing board system, with the purpose of showing how some of the concepts presented in this chapter work in practice.

Users will be able to draw freely on the canvas, and their actions will be visible to the other connected clients in real time. Furthermore, we will allow selecting the stroke color and erasing the entire drawing board at any moment. Each point drawn is stored at the server in a buffer so that the first thing that new clients receive is a full copy of the content of the drawing board at the time of their connection.

The result we want to obtain is shown in Figure 5-18.

FIGURE 5-18 Shared drawing board.

Project creation and setup

For the purpose of creating the application that we will develop over the following pages, it is necessary first to create a project of the "ASP.NET Web Application" type from Visual Studio 2013 and then
to select the "Empty" template to create a completely empty project[4]. The version of .NET Framework
used must be at least 4.5.

After we have created it, we must install the following package using NuGet:

```
PM> install-package Microsoft.AspNet.SignalR
```

---

[4] In Visual Studio 2012 we can achieve the same goal by creating a project from the template "ASP.NET Empty Web
Application."

Implementation on the client side

HTML markup (drawingboard.html)

```html
<!DOCTYPE html>
<html xmlns="http://www.w3.org/1999/xhtml">
<head>
    <title>Drawing board</title>
    <script src="Scripts/jquery-1.6.4.min.js"></script>
    <script src="Scripts/jquery.signalR-2.0.0.min.js"></script>
    <script src="/signalr/js"></script>
    <script src="Scripts/DrawingBoard.js"></script>
    <style>
        div { margin: 3px; }
        canvas { border: 2px solid #808080; cursor: default; }
    </style>
</head>
<body>
    <div>
        <div>
            <label for="color">Color: </label>
            <select id="color"></select>
        </div>
        <canvas id="canvas" width="300" height="300"></canvas>
        <div>
            <button id="clear">Clear canvas</button>
        </div>
    </div>
</body>
</html>
```

Scripts (Scripts/DrawingBoard.js)

```javascript
$(function () {

    //////////////////////////////////////////////////////////////
    // Standard drawing board functionalities
    //////////////////////////////////////////////////////////////

    var colors = ["black", "red", "green", "blue", "yellow", "magenta", "white"];
    var canvas = $("#canvas");
    var colorElement = $("#color");
    for (var i = 0; i < colors.length; i++) {
        colorElement.append(
            "<option value='" + (i + 1) + "'>" + colors[i] + "</li>"
        );
    }
    var buttonPressed = false;
    canvas
        .mousedown(function () {
            buttonPressed = true;
        })
        .mouseup(function () {
            buttonPressed = false;
        })
```

```
        .mousemove(function (e) {
            if (buttonPressed) {
                setPoint(e.offsetX, e.offsetY, colorElement.val());
            }
        });

var ctx = canvas[0].getContext("2d");
function setPoint(x, y, color) {
    ctx.fillStyle = colors[color-1];
    ctx.beginPath();
    ctx.arc(x, y, 2, 0, Math.PI * 2);
    ctx.fill();
}
function clearPoints() {
    ctx.clearRect(0, 0, canvas.width(), canvas.height());
}

$("#clear").click(function () {
    clearPoints();
});

/////////////////////////////////////////////////////////////
// SignalR specific code
/////////////////////////////////////////////////////////////

var hub = $.connection.drawingBoard;
hub.state.color = colorElement.val(); // Accessible from server
var connected = false;

// UI events
colorElement.change(function () {
    hub.state.color = $(this).val();
});
canvas.mousemove(function (e) {
    if (buttonPressed && connected) {
        hub.server.broadcastPoint(
            Math.round(e.offsetX), Math.round(e.offsetY)
        );
    }
});
$("#clear").click(function () {
    if (connected) {
        hub.server.broadcastClear();
    }
});

// Event handlers
hub.client.clear = function () {
    clearPoints();
};
hub.client.drawPoint = function (x, y, color) {
    setPoint(x, y, color);
};
hub.client.update = function (points) {
    if (!points) return;
    for (var x = 0; x < 300; x++) {
        for (var y = 0; y < 300; y++) {
```

```
                if (points[x][y]) {
                    setPoint(x, y, points[x][y]);
                }
            }
        }
    };

    // Voila!
    $.connection.hub.start()
        .done(function () {
            connected = true;
        });

});
```

Implementation on the server side

Hub (DrawingBoard.cs)

```
public class DrawingBoard : Hub
{
    private const int BoardWidth = 300;
    private const int BoardHeight = 300;
    private static int[,] _buffer = GetEmptyBuffer();
    public Task BroadcastPoint(int x, int y)
    {
        if (x < 0) x = 0;
        if (x >= BoardWidth) x = BoardWidth-1;
        if (y < 0) y = 0;
        if (y >= BoardHeight) y = BoardHeight - 1;

        int color = 0;
        int.TryParse(Clients.Caller.color, out color);
        _buffer[x, y] = color;
        return Clients.Others.DrawPoint(x, y, Clients.Caller.color);
    }
    public Task BroadcastClear()
    {
        _buffer = GetEmptyBuffer();
        return Clients.Others.Clear();
    }

    public override Task OnConnected()
    {
        return Clients.Caller.Update(_buffer);
    }

    private static int[,] GetEmptyBuffer()
    {
        var buffer = new int[BoardWidth, BoardHeight];
        return buffer;
    }
}
```

Startup code (Startup.cs)

```
public class Startup
{
    public void Configuration(IAppBuilder app)
    {
        app.MapSignalR();
    }
}
```

CHAPTER 6

Persistent connections and hubs from other threads

All server implementations seen up to this point in the book have had something in common: they have always been responding to direct messages from a client. Even though they are push systems, a client has always been initiating the procedure:

- In a chat, when a user sends a message to the server, this message is sent to the rest of the connected users.

- In the tracking system that we showed in Chapter 4, "Persistent connections," a user's mouse movement was the action that originated the notification to the other users.

- In the shared drawing board example in Chapter 5, "Hubs," when a user drew a point or pressed the button to erase the canvas, the action was sent to the others so that they could update their whiteboards.

Although this is what we will need in most cases, SignalR takes a step further and *allows us to send messages to clients connected to a hub or a persistent connection from another thread of the same application*—that is, outside the hub and without the need for a SignalR client to initiate the sequence explicitly.

Access from other threads

This approach can be very interesting in scenarios where there are unattended or automatically executed processes in the same application where SignalR services are found, and where these processes need to send information to clients who need to receive it in real time.

For example, there might be a background thread obtaining information from a data source (such as stock quotes, meter readings, and so on) and sending it to clients connected to a hub or a persistent connection. It would also be quite easy to create a system that registered the exceptions thrown in an ASP.NET application and sent an alert at exactly that point to a set of users previously connected to a service in real time. Or we could enter logic in the method treating a Web Forms event or an ASP.NET MVC action to notify clients connected to a hub or persistent connection that something important for them has occurred. Any of these cases would consist in accessing hubs or persistent connections from different threads to those where the hubs or persistent connections are running, but always within the same process or app domain. Certainly, the range of possibilities that unfolds thanks to this capability of SignalR is immense.

Although it is probably unnecessary to remark on this, it would also be possible to access real-time services offered by SignalR from other physically separated systems, but such a scenario would be very different: the external system could simply be another client of the services, and to access them, it would have to use client libraries provided by the framework. An example of an external system could be something as simple as a mobile application or as complex as an ERP system, which would need to exchange information with a SignalR server in real time. The structure would be the one displayed in Figure 6-1.

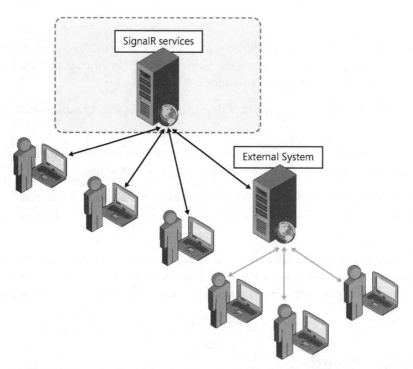

FIGURE 6-1 Accessing SignalR services from physically separate systems.

If we just need the external system to inform the users connected to the services about an event, we could also use more disconnected architectures and create a façade of web services in the application where SignalR resides (using Web API, MVC, WCF, and so on), as shown in Figure 6-2. The external system would notify this façade, and it would transfer the notification to the users, using the techniques that we will look at in this chapter.

Having said this, we are now going to explain how to access SignalR services from other threads of the same application. We will review the other scenarios—connection from external systems both directly and through a façade of services—in Chapter 7, "Real-time multiplatform applications," and Chapter 9, "Advanced topics."

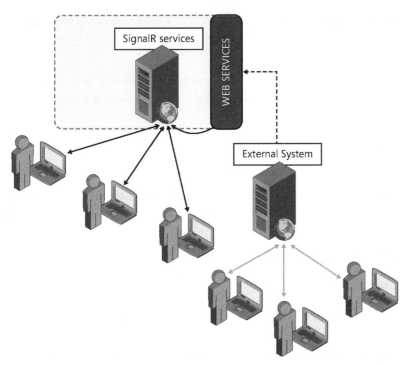

FIGURE 6-2 Accessing SignalR services from external systems via web services.

External access using persistent connections

To submit information to the clients connected to a persistent connection, we simply have to obtain a reference to said connection and use the methods that we normally use inside the PersistentConnection classes.

In the following example, we see how, from a Web Forms application, we could notify connected clients that an event of interest to them has taken place:

```
protected void btnDeleteInvoice_Click(object sender, EventArgs e)
{
    var id = invoiceId.Text;
    _invoiceServices.DeleteInvoice(id);
    var context = GlobalHost.ConnectionManager
                            .GetConnectionContext<ErpNotifications>();

    context.Connection.Broadcast(
            "Invoice #" + id + " deleted by " + User.Identity.Name);
}
```

The GetConnectionContext<T>() method used in the preceding example returns a type T reference to the context of the persistent connection. The call returns an object of the IPersistentConnectionContext type, which gives access to all the functionalities normally available from inside `PersistentConnection`: sending broadcasts directly, sending data to groups, or even actual management of groups of clients. The members available through this interface are the following:

- `Connection`, which provides access to the `IConnection` type object (the same one that we found in the `PersistentConnection` base class) and, at the same time, allows using the following methods:

  - `Send()`, to send messages to specific clients whose `connectionId` is known.

  - `Broadcast()`, to send them to all the clients connected to the persistent connection.

- `Groups`, of the `IConnectionGroupManager` type. Just like the `PersistentConnection` class, it offers services for managing groups and sending messages to them using the following methods:

  - `Add()`, which we can use to add a client, identified by its `clientId`, to a group.

  - `Remove()`, to withdraw a specific client from a group.

  - `Send()`, which allows sending messages to clients that are members of specific groups.

Complete example: Monitoring connections at the server

To illustrate how to implement persistent connections from processes that are external to them, we will now give a complete example consisting of a system with which the server side "spies" the requests made to the website where this component has been installed.

The project consists of a website, implemented in just one page called default.aspx, which will change its content based on a parameter. Free browsing will be allowed, while the requests made by clients of the website will be able to be queried in real time by accessing a monitoring page called "spy.html". We will achieve this by capturing the requests in the `Application_BeginRequest` event of the application global class (Global.asax) and sending a message from here to the clients connected to a persistent connection so that they can display the information. See Figure 6-3.

> **Note** The purpose of this example is simply to show an implementation of persistent connections used from external processes. Using this system can seriously penalize performance at the server, so it is *not recommended at all to use it in production*.

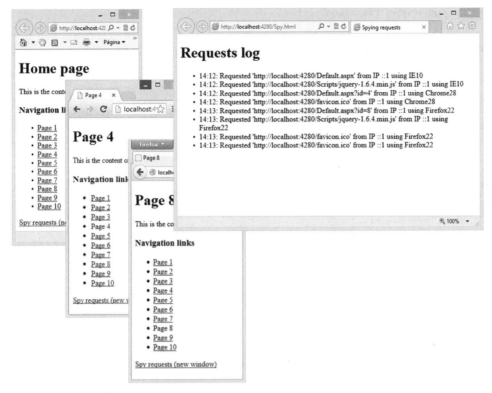

FIGURE 6-3 System for tracing connections in operation.

Project creation and setup

For the purpose of creating the application that we will develop over the following pages, it is necessary to first create a project of the "ASP.NET Web Application" type from Visual Studio 2013 and then select the "Empty" template to create a completely empty project[1]. The version of the .NET Framework used must be at least 4.5.

After we have created it, we must install the following package using NuGet:

```
PM> install-package Microsoft.AspNet.SignalR
```

---

[1] In Visual Studio 2012, we can achieve the same goal by creating a project from the template "ASP.NET Empty Web Application."

Implementing the website

Page markup (default.aspx)

```
<%@ Page Language="C#" AutoEventWireup="true"
        CodeBehind="Default.aspx.cs"
        Inherits="ConnectionSpy.Default" %>

<!DOCTYPE html>
<html xmlns="http://www.w3.org/1999/xhtml">
<head runat="server">
    <title><%: Title %></title>
    <script src="Scripts/jquery-1.6.4.min.js"></script>
</head>
<body>
    <h1><%: Title %></h1>
    <form id="form1" runat="server">
        <div>
            <p>This is the content of the <%: Title %></p>
            <h3>Navigation links</h3>
            <asp:PlaceHolder runat="server" ID="placeHolder">
            </asp:PlaceHolder>
        </div>
        <a href="Spy.html" target="_blank">
            Spy requests (new window)
        </a>
    </form>
</body>
</html>
```

Code-behind (default.aspx.cs)

```
using System;
using System.Text;
using System.Web.UI;
namespace ConnectionSpy
{
    public partial class Default : System.Web.UI.Page
    {
        protected void Page_Load(object sender, EventArgs e)
        {
            int id;
            this.Title = int.TryParse(Request["id"], out id)
                ? "Page " + id
                : "Home page";

            var html = new StringBuilder();
            html.AppendLine("<ul>");
            for (int i = 1; i < 11; i++)
            {
                var text = "Page " + i;
                var link = string.Format(
                    "<li><a href='Default.aspx?id={0}'>{1}</a></li>",
                    i, text
                );
```

```
                html.AppendFormat(link);
            }
            html.AppendLine("</ul>");
            placeHolder.Controls.Add(
                new LiteralControl(html.ToString())
            );
        }
    }
}
```

System for tracing requests (server side)

Persistent connection (ConnectionSpy.cs)

```
using Microsoft.AspNet.SignalR

public class ConnectionSpy: PersistentConnection
{
}
```

Note that the body of the persistent connection is empty. We will not need to take control in it when the SignalR clients connect to it, nor will we need to send messages to clients from here; this will be done from the application global class, as we shall see in the "Application global class (Global.asax.cs)" code.

Startup code (Startup.cs)

```
using Owin;

public class Startup
{
    public void Configuration(IAppBuilder app)
    {
        app.MapSignalR<ConnectionSpy>("/spy");
    }
}
```

Application global class (Global.asax.cs)

```
using System;
using System.Web;
using Microsoft.AspNet.SignalR;

public class Global : HttpApplication
{
  private static IPersistentConnectionContext connSpy =
        GlobalHost.ConnectionManager.GetConnectionContext<ConnectionSpy>();

  protected void Application_BeginRequest(object sender, EventArgs e)
  {
      var context = ((HttpApplication)sender).Context;
      var message = string.Format(
```

```
            "{0}: Requested '{1}' from IP {2} using {3}",
            DateTime.Now.ToShortTimeString(),
            context.Request.Url.ToString(),
            context.Request.UserHostAddress,
            context.Request.Browser.Type
            );
        connSpy.Connection.Broadcast(message);
  }
}
```

We could also have implemented this same process as OWIN middleware, instead of doing it in the application global class. In that case, the module would be the following:

```
using System;
using System.Threading.Tasks;
using Microsoft.AspNet.SignalR;
using Microsoft.Owin;

public class SpyMiddleware : OwinMiddleware
{
    private static IPersistentConnectionContext  connSpy =
            GlobalHost.ConnectionManager.GetConnectionContext<ConnectionSpy>();

    public SpyMiddleware(OwinMiddleware next): base(next) { }

    public override Task Invoke(IOwinContext context)
    {
        var message = string.Format(
            "{0}: Requested '{1}' from IP {2} using {3}",
            DateTime.Now.ToShortTimeString(),
            context.Request.Uri.ToString(),
            context.Request.Host,
            context.Request.Headers["USER-AGENT"]
            );

        return Next.Invoke(context)
                    .ContinueWith(c =>
                        connSpy.Connection.Broadcast(message));
    }
}
```

And to enter this module in the request processing pipeline, we would have to modify the configuration code:

```
public class Startup
{
    public void Configuration(IAppBuilder app)
    {
        app.MapSignalR<ConnectionSpy>("/spy");
        app.Use<SpyMiddleware>();
    }
}
```

Optional changes in configuration (web.config)

For the tracing system to capture all the requests made to the website, whether or not they are processed by ASP.NET, it is a good idea to add the following configuration to the web.config file:

```
<configuration>
    ...
    <system.webServer>
      <modules runAllManagedModulesForAllRequests="true"></modules>
    </system.webServer>
</configuration>
```

Note that this configuration will make the performance at the server even worse.

System for tracing requests (client side)

Spying page (spy.html)

```
<!DOCTYPE html>
<html xmlns="http://www.w3.org/1999/xhtml">
<head>
    <title>Spying requests</title>
    <script src="Scripts/jquery-1.6.4.min.js"></script>
    <script src="Scripts/jquery.signalR-2.0.0.min.js"></script>
</head>
<body>
    <h1>Requests log</h1>
    <ul id="requests"></ul>
    <script>
        $(function () {
            var connection = $.connection("/spy");
            connection.received(function (data) {
                $("#requests").append("<li>" + data + "</li>");
            });
            connection.start();
        });
    </script>
</body>
</html>
```

External access using hubs

If we use hubs, the procedure is similar to what we saw earlier: in the process via which we want to be in contact with clients connected to a hub, we will use the global configuration object GlobalHost. Through its ConnectionManager property, we will obtain a reference to the hub.

The only difference compared to the procedure that we would carry out with persistent connections is that here we will obtain the reference to the hub using the GetHubContext() or GetHubContext<T>() methods.

```
protected void BtnShutdown(object sender, EventArgs e)
{
    var hubcontext = GlobalHost.ConnectionManager
                             .GetHubContext<Chat>();
    hubcontext.Clients.All
    .SendMessage("The system is shutting down!");
    ... // Code
}
```

In the preceding example, we have used the generic method GetHubContext<T>() to obtain the reference using strong typing, although we could have also done it referencing the hub through a character string:

```
var hubcontext = GlobalHost.ConnectionManager
                          .GetHubContext("Chat");
```

In either case, the methods return an instance of IHubContext, through which we can access the functionalities for sending information and managing groups available in hubs (see Figure 6-4).

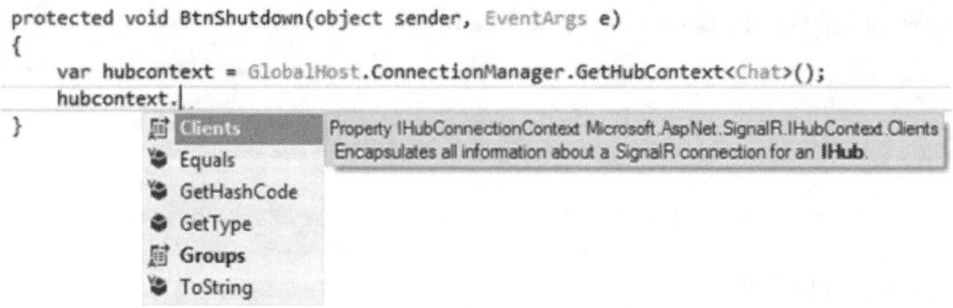

FIGURE 6-4 Members of the IHubContext interface.

As you can easily guess, the Clients property, of the IHubConnectionContext type, is the gateway to recipient selection methods, discussed in Chapter 5, although it is more limited. For example, because we will use this interface from other processes, we will not have properties such as Caller or Others, which make sense only when the code is inside a hub and it is being executed as a consequence of the reception of a message from a client. However, we will find other useful selectors such as All, AllExcept(), Client(), or Group() to specify the recipients of any code invocation on the client side:

```
hubContext.Clients.Group("jedis").Alert(
    "I felt a great disturbance in the force"
);
```

On its part, the Groups property allows managing the members of groups of SignalR clients, through its Add() and Remove() methods.

```
hubcontext.Groups.Add(lukeConnectionId, "jedis");
```

Complete example: Progress bar

To better illustrate the operation and possibilities of external access to hubs or persistent connections, we will present the complete development of a system that notifies the progress of expensive processes in real time, as shown in Figure 6-5.

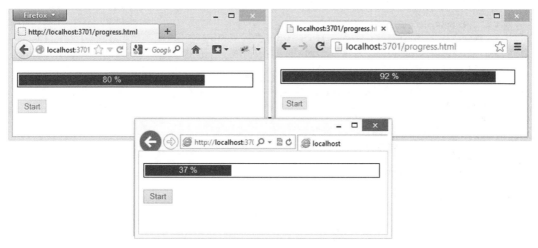

FIGURE 6-5 Progress bars operating.

In this case, we will have a client page from which we will use jQuery to launch an AJAX request to a costly process written inside an ASPX page. There will be notifications of the progress in real time from inside this process, and this will be displayed as a progress bar over the page.

Project creation and setup

For the purpose of creating the application that we will develop over the following pages, it is necessary to first create a project of the "ASP.NET Web Application" type from Visual Studio 2013 and then select the "Empty" template to create a completely empty project[2]. The version of the .NET Framework used must be at least 4.5.

After we have created it, we must install the following package using NuGet:

```
PM> install-package Microsoft.AspNet.SignalR
```

---

[2] In Visual Studio 2012, we can achieve the same goal by creating a project from the template "ASP.NET Empty Web Application."

Implementation on the client side

HTML markup (progress.html)

```html
<!DOCTYPE html>
<html xmlns="http://www.w3.org/1999/xhtml">
<head>
    <title>Progress bar</title>
    <script src="Scripts/jquery-1.6.4.min.js"></script>
    <script src="Scripts/jquery.signalR-2.0.0.min.js"></script>
    <script src="/signalr/js"></script>
    <script src="Scripts/progressbar.js"></script>
    <link rel="stylesheet" href="styles/progressbar.css"/>
</head>
<body>
    <div id="progressBarContainer">
        <div id="progressBar"></div>
    </div>
    <input type="button"
            id="start" value="Start" disabled="disabled" />
    <div id="result" style="display: none;"></div>
</body>
</html>
```

Styles (Styles/ProgressBar.css)

```css
#progressBarContainer {
    width: 400px;
    height: 18px;
    border: 1px solid black;
    padding: 2px;
    margin: 20px 0 20px 0;
}

#progressBar {
    width: 0px;
    height: 18px;
    background-color: blue;
    margin: 0;
    overflow: hidden;
    text-align: center;
    color: white;
    font-family: arial;
    vertical-align: middle;
    font-size: 14px;
}

#result {
    border: 1px solid black;
    background-color: yellow;
    padding: 10px 10px 0 10px;
    margin-top: 10px;
}
```

```
#result p {
    margin: 0 0 10px 0;
}
```

Script (Scripts/ProgressBar.js)

```javascript
$(function () {
    var hub = $.connection.progressBarHub;
    hub.client.update = function (value) {
        $("#progressBar").css("width", value + "%")
                         .text(value + " %");
    };

    $("#start").click(function () {
        $(this).attr("disabled", true);
        $("#result")
            .hide("slow")
            .load("hardprocess.aspx?connId=" + $.connection.hub.id,
                    function () {
                      $(this).slideDown("slow");
                      $("#start").attr("disabled", false);
                    });
    });

    $.connection.hub.start()
        .done(function () {
            $("#start").attr("disabled", false);
        });
});
```

Implementation on the server side

Hub

```csharp
using Microsoft.AspNet.SignalR;

namespace ProgressBar
{
    public class ProgressBarHub : Hub { }
}
```

Note that we do not need any method in the hub, because the information is sent to the clients through the external process, as shown in the following code example.

Expensive process (HardProcess.Aspx)

```aspx
<%@ Page Language="C#"
        Inherits="System.Web.UI.Page" EnableSessionState="false" %>
<%@ Import Namespace="System.Diagnostics" %>
<%@ Import Namespace="System.Threading" %>
<%@ Import Namespace="Microsoft.AspNet.SignalR" %>
<%@ Import Namespace="ProgressBar" %>
<%
```

```
    Response.Expires = -1;
    var connectionId = Request["connId"];
    var hub = GlobalHost.ConnectionManager
                        .GetHubContext<ProgressBarHub>();
    Stopwatch stopWatch = Stopwatch.StartNew();

    // Simulate a very very hard process...
    for (int i = 1; i <= 100; i++)
    {
        hub.Clients.Client(connectionId).update(i);
        Thread.Sleep(150);
    }
%>
<p>The answer to life, the universe and everything is: 42.</p>
<p>
    And it only took <%:stopWatch.ElapsedMilliseconds / 1000 %>
    seconds to find it out.
</p>
```

This page receives the connection identifier as a parameter, which allows it to send the progress data only to the specific client that initiated the process.

Startup code (startup.cs)

```
using Owin;

public class Startup
{
    public void Configuration(IAppBuilder app)
    {
        app.MapSignalR();
    }
}
```

CHAPTER 7

Real-time multiplatform applications

U ntil now, we have focused on explaining the operation and features of SignalR both on the client and the server side, but only in web environments. On the server side, all the examples that we have seen and developed throughout the book worked on IIS and ASP.NET, although thanks to the independence that the Open Web Interface for .NET (OWIN) provides and the abstractions offered by SignalR, we were not using any of the features specifically belonging to either of these components.

And we have used only the JavaScript client too, due to the ubiquity of the web, the facility with which solutions can be implemented in this environment, and the spectacular results that we can produce in this type of scenario, where the traditional pull model of HTTP used to greatly hamper the creation of real-time multiuser systems.

But, as we know, SignalR again goes far beyond this. Hubs or persistent connections can be hosted in practically any type of solution, from console applications to Windows services, not forgetting web-based applications. It is even possible to execute them in environments other than Windows, thanks to independent implementations of the framework, such as the one provided by the Mono project.

Likewise, its services can be consumed from virtually any type of client platform, such as the familiar JavaScript-based web clients, Windows Phone, Silverlight, or WinRT native applications, or any type of system operating on .NET 4.0 or above, and even native platforms not based on Windows.

In this chapter, we will focus on the multiplatform capabilities of SignalR. First we will show how to host services in different types of systems. When finished with the server side, we will jump to the other end and study the different choices that we have for implementing SignalR clients.

Multiplatform SignalR servers

On the server side, we'll look at SignalR hosting in console applications, in a Windows service, and in some platforms other than Windows.

SignalR hosting in non-web applications

Although it might look as if IIS and ASP.NET made up the only environment from which we would want to host SignalR services, this is actually not the case. There are multiple scenarios where it can be a good idea to publish services created with this framework without having to rely on these two elements, including the following:

- Server infrastructures where IIS is not an option due to system policies or other reasons.

- Scenarios where we want to fully control the life cycle of the host processes on which our applications operate.

- Distributed scenarios where we want to simplify and reduce the requirements for the deployment of certain applications.

- Scenarios in which we want to provide highly controlled responses, where because IIS/ASP.NET will not be used, the server will not perform any other processes than those strictly necessary.

- Scenarios where we want to include SignalR in servers of existing applications that already have independent host processes, such as Windows services or Azure worker roles, where it is better to publish the services from that point, to avoid complicating the architecture.

In any case, the decoupling offered by OWIN means that we can host these services in practically any type of system without having to change a single code line of our application on either the server or the client side. We will simply have to enter small modifications regarding the startup of the services so that everything works properly.

SignalR is executed in web applications simply because there is a package called `Microsoft .Owin.Host.SystemWeb`, provided by the Katana project, which acts as a go-between for the middleware and the hosting based on ASP.NET/IIS. In fact, it is the host that is automatically included in our projects when we install the generic package `Microsoft.AspNet.SignalR`.

If we want to publish services from another type of application, we must simply change this component, which acts as Server, substituting it for another one capable of being executed independently.

As we also know, the Katana project provides us with one, `Microsoft.Owin.Host .HttpListener`, on which the possibilities for self-hosting (that is, hosting the services in the OWIN-based systems' own processes) are based.

As you can guess by its name, this component is based on the `HttpListener` class of the .NET Framework, and it can open a port and remain waiting for HTTP requests, passing them to the frameworks, modules, or applications that are found at a higher level in the technology stack.

We will now describe in detail how to perform the installation and startup of hubs or persistent connections on a console application, although these same techniques can be used in any other type of system detached from ASP.NET.

Hosting in a console application

We will now show in detail the necessary process to implement a SignalR service based on hubs on an existing console application.

The first step is to install the `Microsoft.AspNet.SignalR.SelfHost` package, using, as usual, the indispensable NuGet:

```
PM> install-package Microsoft.AspNet.SignalR.SelfHost
```

When this package is installed, all its dependencies will also be entered into the project, thus making the server components of SignalR, OWIN, and the server based on `HttpListener` readily available.

When this process is concluded, a readme.txt file will open automatically; see Figure 7-1. In it, the creators of the package have entered some brief instructions to help us start the services. These instructions highlight the need to map the services to their corresponding access URLs, as well as explaining how to start the web server that will receive the requests.

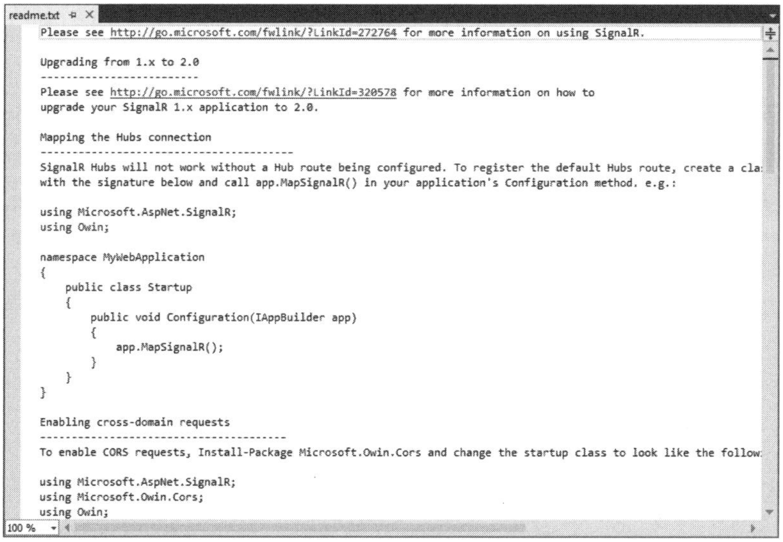

```
readme.txt ↔ X
Please see http://go.microsoft.com/fwlink/?LinkId=272764 for more information on using SignalR.

Upgrading from 1.x to 2.0
-------------------------
Please see http://go.microsoft.com/fwlink/?LinkId=320578 for more information on how to
upgrade your SignalR 1.x application to 2.0.

Mapping the Hubs connection
---------------------------
SignalR Hubs will not work without a Hub route being configured. To register the default Hubs route, create a cla
with the signature below and call app.MapSignalR() in your application's Configuration method. e.g.:

using Microsoft.AspNet.SignalR;
using Owin;

namespace MyWebApplication
{
    public class Startup
    {
        public void Configuration(IAppBuilder app)
        {
            app.MapSignalR();
        }
    }
}

Enabling cross-domain requests
------------------------------
To enable CORS requests, Install-Package Microsoft.Owin.Cors and change the startup class to look like the follow

using Microsoft.AspNet.SignalR;
using Microsoft.Owin.Cors;
using Owin;
100 %
```

FIGURE 7-1 Readme.txt file.

Hubs and persistent connections are created inside the console application just as always, because the package installed also includes references to the SignalR core:

```
public class PingConnection: PersistentConnection
{
    protected override Task OnReceived(
        IRequest request, string connectionId, string data)
    {
        if (data == "Ping")
        {
            Console.WriteLine("[Connection] Ping received");
            return Connection.Send(
```

```
                    connectionId,
                    "Ping received at " + DateTime.Now.ToLongTimeString()
                    );
            }
            return base.OnReceived(request, connectionId, data);
        }
    }
}

public class PingHub: Hub
{
    public Task Ping()
    {
        Console.WriteLine("[Hub] Ping received");
        return Clients.Caller.Message(
            "Ping received at " + DateTime.Now.ToLongTimeString());
    }
}
```

The way to map the URLs to these services is exactly the same as we have seen throughout this book, and it simply consists in specifying the address through which it will be possible to access the different endpoints of SignalR. Remember that this address will be a single one for hubs, whereas in the case of persistent connections, each one must be associated to a different URL.

Therefore, as on other occasions, paths are defined in a startup class, using the extensions offered by SignalR on the IAppBuilder object that receives the Configuration() method of the class as a parameter.

The following code shows a startup class with the mapping definition of a hub and a persistent connection. In the first case, the default route is used, whereas in the second case, it is set explicitly. Note that the code requires you to additionally install the Microsoft.Owin.Cors package:

```
public class Startup
{
    public void Configuration(IAppBuilder app)
    {
        app.UseCors(CorsOptions.AllowAll)
            .MapSignalR<PingConnection>("/ping-connection")
            .MapSignalR("/hub", new HubConfiguration());
    }
}
```

As you can see, the code would be exactly the same as we would use if we created the definition in an ASP.NET/IIS environment instead of self-hosting: we activate CORS to provide support for browsers connecting to the service from other domains, and we create the mappings for the hubs and persistent connections of our system.

After this startup class has been created and the routes to the endpoints have been defined, we still need to do something else: start the web server and tell it where it can find the startup class that we have previously created. We can achieve this with a method such as the following, which we could enter into the `Main()` static method, which works as the starting point of a console application or wherever suits our needs best:

```
using (WebApp.Start("http://localhost:5000"))
{
    Console.WriteLine("Server running at http://localhost:5000/");
    Console.ReadLine();
}
```

The WebApp static class, part of the Katana set of components, offers us the `Start()` method, whose purpose is to start a web server on which to execute the different frameworks, modules, and applications based on OWIN. For example, the preceding call starts the server on port 5000 of localhost, and by convention, it executes the configuration in the `Configuration()` method of the Startup class.

> **Note** If we want to respond to requests that are performed on port 5000 with any host name, we could use *http://*:5000*, although run-time errors might occur if the process is executed for a user without elevated permissions.

However, there are other variants of `Start()` that allow us to customize the way in which this server will be started. In the following code, an overload is used, which allows us to specify via a generic parameter the startup class of our system (`Startup`). Note that we do not need to specify the method to be executed because, by convention, the server will already know that it is `Configuration()`.

```
using (WebApp.Start<Startup>("http://localhost:44444/"))
{
    Console.WriteLine("Server running at http://localhost:44444/");
    Console.ReadLine();
}
```

It is also possible to specify the configuration method and class, as well as some other additional options, using the `StartOptions` class:

```
var options =
    new StartOptions("http://*:44444")
    {
        AppStartup = "Namespace.StartupClass.ConfigurationMethod"
    };

using (WebApp.Start(options))
{
    ...
}
```

In the preceding examples, we have assumed that all the startup, mapping, and server start code is found in the console application itself. However, this is not necessarily the case—we could also have said code in a class library referenced from the console application.

In these scenarios, it is important to take into account that, in the host (in our example, the console application), we must add the following NuGet package to ensure that the host based on HTTP listeners is available:

```
PM> Install-Package Microsoft.Owin.Host.HttpListener
```

SignalR in a Windows service

SignalR hosting inside an operating system service is another case where it is necessary to use self-hosting and where SignalR must be independent from the infrastructure on which it is executed.

Windows services are just executables, as console applications are, but due to their special nature they have to be programmed in a different way to respond to the different events related to the life cycle of this type of component. The implementation of SignalR in a system of this type will therefore be similar to the one we have seen previously, so we'll now show only a quick example.

When a Windows Service project is created in Visual Studio, the basic structure of the service will be generated. As always, we must add the `Microsoft.AspNet.Signalr.SelfHost` package with NuGet and implement the startup class `Startup` to perform mapping and, of course, the hubs or persistent connections that we want to publish from the service.

```
// File: Broadcaster.cs
public class Broadcaster: Hub
{
    public Task Broadcast(string message)
    {
        return Clients.All.Message(message);
    }
    public override Task OnConnected()
    {
        return Clients.All.Message(">> New client arrived");
    }
    public override Task OnDisconnected()
    {
        return Clients.All.Message(">> Client disconnected");

    }
}


// File:Startup.cs.
// Note that you will need to install the NuGet package Microsot.Owin.Cors

public class Startup
{
    public void Configuration(IAppBuilder app)
    {
        app.UseCors(CorsOptions.AllowAll)
            .MapSignalR();
    }
}
```

Again, the only thing that we are doing is enabling CORS, to allow external browser connections, and mapping the hubs to the default address.

Starting the web server is a different process in this case. In the console application, we would simply launch it when execution began and we would keep it active until exiting the application. However, operating system services have a different life cycle: they can be launched, stopped, restarted, and even paused for a time, if we have so allowed in the definition of the service. We should thus take into account these aspects when managing the lifetime of the web server.

Fortunately, the classes in which the services are implemented inherit from `System` `.ServiceProcess.ServiceBase` and include virtual methods that are executed when these events occur and which can be overridden by the descendant classes. Thus when we host SignalR persistent connections or hubs inside a service, we want to take control at the right moments to start or stop the web server that processes the requests.

We can achieve this in a simple way, as shown here:

```
public partial class BroadcasterService : ServiceBase
{
    private IDisposable _webApp;
    public BroadcasterService()
    {
        InitializeComponent();
    }

    protected override void OnStart(string[] args)
    {
        var address = (args != null && args.Length > 0)
                        ? args[0]
                        : "http://localhost:54321";

        _webApp = WebApp.Start<Startup>(address);
    }

    protected override void OnStop()
    {
        _webApp.Dispose();
    }
}
```

In this code, we are making use of the `OnStart()` method, invoked when the service is started, to start the web server, the process that listens to requests using an `HttpListener`. The arguments received, which we can use to introduce some variations in the behavior of the service, can be sent when the service is started manually.

We also take control at the point in which the service stops to stop our server too.

Finally, in the entry point of the application, it is necessary to specify the service that is to be launched:

```
static class Program
{
    /// <summary>
    /// The main entry point for the application.
    /// </summary>
    static void Main()
```

```
    {
        ServiceBase[] ServicesToRun;
        ServicesToRun = new ServiceBase[]
        {
            new BroadcasterService()
        };
        ServiceBase.Run(ServicesToRun);
    }
}
```

In contrast to other types of projects, Windows Services cannot be started from Visual Studio; it is necessary to install them in the system. To do this, we have to perform the following steps:

1. We have to add an installer to our project. This is a special class that stores information about the server and allows us to enter logic to be executed in this installation. We can create it easily by opening the context menu on the design surface of the service class and selecting the Add Installer action, as shown in Figure 7-2.

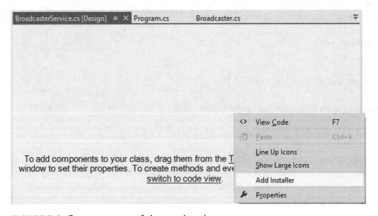

FIGURE 7-2 Context menu of the service class.

2. After we have compiled the project, we open the developer command prompt for Visual Studio 2013. *It is essential that we do this as an administrator,* because we will need permissions to change the configuration of the system. From this window, we go to the binaries folder of the project and we find the executable file for the project.

3. We now execute the following command, which will install the service on Windows:

```
installutil [exeName]
```

where [exeName] is the full name of the executable that we have generated, including its extension. Each time we compile, we will have to repeat this operation, and therefore we could include this task inside the build process of the project.

Depending on the user that we have defined in the properties of the service—or rather, in the properties of the service installer—it might be necessary to specify at this point the credentials of the user to be employed. This is achieved by adding the parameters /username and /password to the preceding command:

```
installutil SignalrService.exe /username=jmaguilar /password=1234
```

However, to uninstall the service from the system, it will suffice to do this:

```
installutil SignalRService.exe /u
```

4. After we have installed it, the server will be available in our system and we will be able to start it by using the Windows Services management console (see Figure 7-3) or from the command line with the familiar net start.

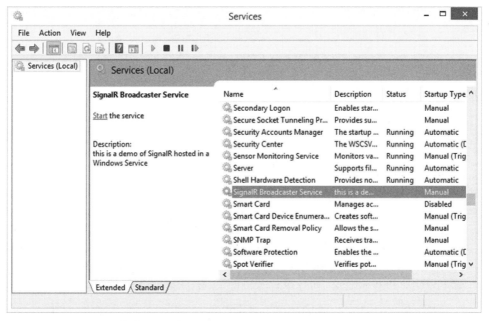

FIGURE 7-3 Service installed on Windows.

We could use the parameters that we previously received in the OnStart() method of the service, sending them to the service when we start it manually, as shown in Figure 7-4.

FIGURE 7-4 Sending parameters to the service.

SignalR hosting in platforms other than Windows

It is a good idea to note that all the infrastructure on which we are building our services is based on open standards, in many cases with implementations distributed under very permissive licenses, which opens the door to the possibility of executing the applications on platforms other than Windows.

If we add this to the availability of multiplatform implementations of the .NET platform, it is possible to take SignalR applications to other popular operating systems where it would *a priori* seem impossible, such as Linux, BSD, or Mac OS X.

The Mono[1] project was begun in 2001 by Ximian, a company started by Miguel de Icaza for the purpose of creating a multiplatform and open source implementation of Microsoft's .NET Framework, based on the ECMA standard of C# and Common Language Runtime (CLR). Currently, Mono provides support, even at binary level, for a large number of features offered by version 4.5 of the .NET Framework, although there is obviously a slight delay in their implementation when it comes to the new features that continue to appear in the new versions of the .NET Framework. In fact, to access the most recent features, it is recommended that you download the source code from its repository at

---

[1] Official website of the Mono project: *http://www.mono-project.com*

GitHub[2] and that you generate the specific binaries for the local computer by following the instructions provided.

At the time of writing, even the SignalR framework itself can be completely compiled on Mono. The Readme.md file that we find on the main page of the repository in GitHub provides instructions to obtain a copy of the source code and compile it using the command line as shown in Figure 7-5.

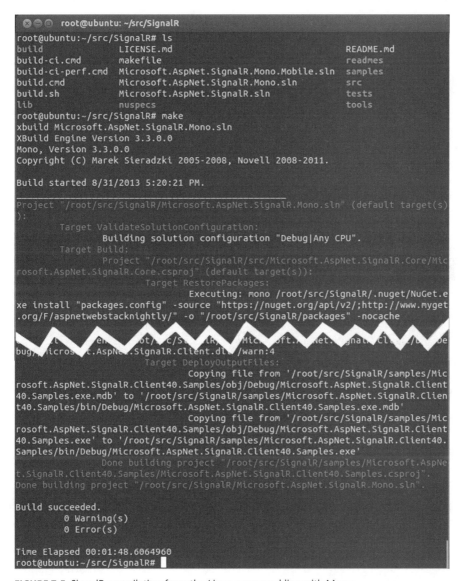

FIGURE 7-5 SignalR compilation from the Linux command line with Mono.

---

[2] Mono Project repository at GitHub: *http://github.com/mono*

It is also possible to debug or make modifications to SignalR by using MonoDevelop[3], a multiplatform integrated development environment also created and distributed under the same open source premises as the Mono ecosystem. For this, in the SignalR source code, a solution file is included (Microsoft.AspNet.Signalr.Mono.Sln), which we can open from this IDE to modify or compile the project, as shown in Figure 7-6. Obviously, projects that are very specific to the Microsoft platform, such as scalability adapters for SQL Server or Windows Azure, are not found in this solution.

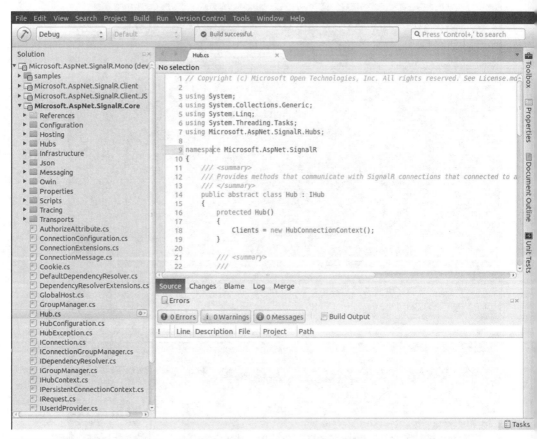

FIGURE 7-6 Compiling SignalR from MonoDevelop.

The SignalR self-hosting server components can be successfully executed on Mono (see Figure 7-7), but the same does not happen with the server based on ASP.NET/IIS, because the implementation of the latest version of the platform is not yet fully supported. Hopefully, this will change in the near future.

---

[3] Official website of the MonoDevelop project: *http://monodevelop.com*

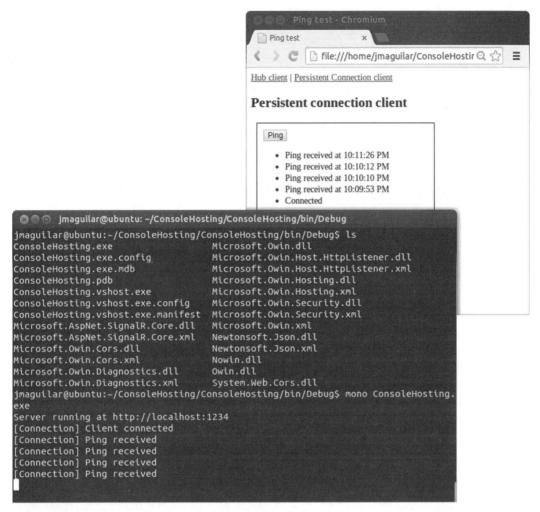

FIGURE 7-7 Self-hosting application operating on Linux and Mono.

Multiplatform SignalR clients

Until now, on the client side, we have focused only on studying the specific JavaScript component. However, this library—whose scope is circumscribed to web environments—is but one among those available.

It is possible to find client components for Windows Phone, Silverlight, WinRT, or .NET generic clients, which broadens the range of SignalR's possibilities as a real-time application development framework in any type of scenario. Table 7-1 lists the client component packages currently available.

TABLE 7-1 SignalR clients

Client technology	Package to be installed
JavaScript	Microsoft.AspNet.SignalR.JS
.NET 4 .NET 4.5 Silverlight 5 WinRT Windows Phone 8	Microsoft.AspNet.SignalR.Client

Note that, with the exception of the client libraries for JavaScript, the rest are found in the same NuGet package. The variety of platforms becomes evident if we observe the folder structure generated in the "packages" directory of the solution after downloading the package from the repository; see Figure 7-8.

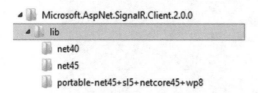

FIGURE 7-8 Contents of the SignalR client NuGet package.

Thus, if we wanted to access a SignalR service as a client from a console application, a Windows forms application, or an operating system service, the specific libraries for .NET 4 or .NET 4.5 would be used, depending on the platform version with which we are working. In the case of a WinRT, Windows Phone, or Silverlight application, the .NET client version designed as a portable class library would be used.

Accessing services from .NET non-web clients

Regardless of the platform on which we work, the libraries included in the `Microsoft.AspNet`
`.SignalR.Client` package share a common API, which is in fact similar to the one we saw when we studied JavaScript clients for persistent connections and hubs, when they did not use the self-generated proxy. Therefore, the concepts and principles that we will deal with are generally common to all platforms.

Creating and opening a persistent connection

From the client side, a persistent connection is created through the instantiation of a `Connection` type object, available in the `Microsoft.AspNet.SignalR.Client` namespace. At this point, we must mandatorily supply the URL where the SignalR server is awaiting connections. The URL provided must include the protocol, host, port (if different to the default port), and the part of the route that has been included in the mapping of the server.

```
// Server side (mapping)
app.MapConnection<EchoConnection>("/echo");
```

```
// Client side (connection)
var connection = new Connection("http://localhost:2713/echo");
```

Optionally, we can use this moment to specify key-value pairs that will travel in the query string of requests. We have two ways to do this. Each will use one overload for the constructor. This is the first way:

```
var connection = new Connection(
                "http://localhost:2713/echo",
                "username=johnsmith&color=red"
            );
```

And this is the other way:

```
var values = new Dictionary<string, string>()
            {
                { "username", "johnsmith"},
                { "color", "red"},
            };
var conn = new Connection("http://localhost:2713/echo", values);
```

The `Connection` object created offers additional methods and properties to customize in detail the information that will travel in the requests made against the server. See Figure 7-9.

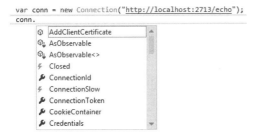

FIGURE 7-9 Members of the `Connection` class.

The most useful members that we can find in the `Connection` class are the following:

- `AddClientCertificate(certificate)`, which allows adding an X509 certificate to a connection made under SSL. The following code shows how it is possible to obtain the certificate from a file and include it in the connection:

  ```
  var connection = new Connection("https://secureserver.com/signalr");
  connection.AddClientCertificate(
                  X509Certificate.CreateFromCertFile("User.cer")
      );
  ```

- `ConnectionId`, which allows obtaining or setting the identifier of the connection.

- `CookieContainer`, which provides access to a container of the `System.Net` `.CookieContainer` type, which can be useful to enter cookies that will travel to the server side. By default, this property contains a null value, so to use the property, we first need to enter an instance of this type in it:

```
var cookie = new Cookie("username", "johnsmith");
connection.CookieContainer = new CookieContainer();
connection.CookieContainer.Add(cookie);
```

- **Credentials**, which allows obtaining or setting the authentication information for the connection. The following example shows how it could be used to include the credentials of the security context where the application is executed:

```
connection.Credentials = CredentialCache.DefaultNetworkCredentials;
```

- **Headers**, of the IDictionary<string,string> type, which allows adding custom headers to the requests made in the context of a connection:

```
connection.Headers["CustomToken"] = "12345";
```

- **Proxy**, which allows defining the proxy that is going to be used to make the connections to the server:

```
connection.Proxy = new WebProxy("http://192.168.1.2:8080")
                    {
                        Credentials = new NetworkCredential(
                                          "proxyuser",
                                          "1234"
                                      )
                    };
```

- **State**, a value of the ConnectionState enumeration that gives the state of the connection at all times.

After we have configured and adapted the connection to our needs, we can begin communication with the server invoking the Start() method. As you can surely guess, this method starts the connection procedure asynchronously. Therefore, it returns a Task object representing this task. We can use this object in different ways to take control upon success or failure of the operation.

Thus it is possible to use the Wait()method. If problems occur in the connection, an exception will be thrown, which can be easily caught:

```
try
{
    connection.Start().Wait();
}
catch (Exception ex)
{
    Console.WriteLine("Error connecting to the server...");
}
```

Or we can also employ the the async/await construct of C# 5 to invoke the asynchronous method in a very clean way:

```
try
{
    await connection.Start();
}
catch (Exception ex)
{
    Console.WriteLine("Error connecting to the server...");
}
```

The `Start()` method also allows specifying a precise transport to be used for the connection, which can be useful if we want to force one of them due to environment needs or simply to perform tests. However, transport objects cannot be reused across multiple connection instances:

```
var connection = new Connection("http://localhost:2713/echo");
connection.Start(new LongPollingTransport());
```

When we do not need a connection anymore, we can close it explicitly by using its `Stop()` method.

Sending and receiving data using persistent connections

Clients of persistent connections can work directly on the `Connection` object to send and receive data to and from the server, as well as to subscribe to the main events relating to the connection.

We will send data as we did with the JavaScript client: using the `Send()` method of the connection. As is usual in asynchronous environments, the `Send()` method returns the `Task` object in charge of sending data in the background.

```
await connection.Send("Hello, world!");
// The message has been sent
```

We can send objects of any type directly. They will be serialized automatically by the framework before sending them to the server side:

```
var message = new ChatMessage()
            {
                Message = "Hello, world!",
                From = "Joe"
            };
connection.Send(message);
```

However, the server side will receive the message as a text string and will have to deserialize it in the form of a CLR object if it wants to work with it in a typed and secure way.

To obtain the data sent from the server to the client, as well as to take control during the main events that take place during the lifetime of the connection, the `Connection` class offers a set of events to which it is possible to subscribe, to take control when they occur using delegates to functions, anonymous functions, or lambda functions. The following example shows how to implement the code to handle message reception by using a lambda function:

```
connection.Received += data =>
                      {
                            Console.WriteLine("Received: " + data);
                      };
```

The main events available are the following:

- **Closed**, which is executed when the connection has been closed by one of the ends. In case of a disconnection made by the server end, the client library will try to reconnect to retrieve the connection, and only if it does not succeed will it launch this event.

- **ConnectionSlow**, which occurs when it is detected that the connection is slow or unstable. We can use this event to notify the user too:

```
connection.ConnectionSlow += () =>
                      Console.WriteLine("Please be patient!");
```

- **Error**, launched when there has been any exception on the connection. The handling code will receive as an argument an **Exception** object with specific information about the error.

- **Received**, which occurs when data is received from the server. The handling code will receive a character string with the information received.

- **Reconnecting, Reconnected**, which are events launched when the client side detects that connection to the server has been lost and it begins the recovery sequence. The first event is launched when the reconnecting process begins, and the second one is launched when it has been successful.

- **StateChanged** occurs when the connection changes state. In the handling code, we will receive an object of the **StateChange** type as an argument, with which we will be able to know both the previous and the current state of the connection.

```
connection.StateChanged += info =>
    Console.WriteLine(
        "Going from " + info.OldState + " to " + info.NewState
    );
```

Creating and opening connections to hubs

Consuming hubs as clients by using .NET libraries is quite similar to what we have seen when handling JavaScript libraries without using a self-generated proxy. To access the services provided by a hub, it is necessary to first start a connection with the server. For this, instead of the **Connection** class that we used with clients of persistent connections, we will now use one of its descendants, the **HubConnection** class.

```
var hubConn = new HubConnection("http://localhost:9638");
```

The URL supplied can include the part of the route where the hubs were mapped at the server or not. There is an optional parameter in the constructor, called `useDefaultUrl`, which specifies whether or not we want to use the default value (automatically adding the string "/SignalR" to the URL provided). By default, the value of this parameter is `true`, and for this reason, we can use a URL such as the one in the preceding example; the framework will add "/SignalR" to it. If we set it to `false`, this suffix will not be added to the URL supplied, and we will have to state the URL specified in the server side exactly.

The following code shows the use of this parameter to open a connection to the system of hubs published at the root of the host stated in the URL:

```
// Server mapping.
// The Hubs will be published directly at http://host/
app.MapSignalR("", new HubConfiguration());

// Client connection
var hubConn = new HubConnection("http://localhost:9638",
                                useDefaultUrl: false);
```

The `HubConnection` class provides features specifically designed to facilitate work with hubs, apart from all the ones inherited from its ancestor, `Connection`, which we have already used: control over the query string, cookies, credentials, headers, proxy configuration, the methods `Start()` and `Stop()`, events such as `Closed` or `StateChanged`, and so on. Because they are inherited, all these aspects are identical to those already described, so we will not go over them again.

To work with a hub, we will need to have a class to represent it at the client and on which we can implement the code for treating the methods invoked from the server, as well as to call it when needed. We can create this proxy by calling the `CreateHubProxy()` method, to which we will send the name of the hub to be used as an argument:

```
var hubConn = new HubConnection("http://localhost:9638/");
var hubProxy = hubConn.CreateHubProxy("Calculator");
... // Other initialization code
hubConn.Start();
```

Finally, after we finish configuring the proxy, we must open the connection by using the `Start()` method of `HubConnection` to start working with the hub. It is important to remember that this method is asynchronous, so the proxy cannot be used right after the call to it. We will have to wait for it to finish or use the promise pattern to continue execution when the connection has been made successfully.

Communication with the server using hubs

To invoke server methods, after the connection is opened, we just need to use the `Invoke()` method of the proxy that we have created for the hub, specifying the name of the server action or method to execute, and the parameters that it needs:

```
... // Initialization code
await hubConn.Start();
hubProxy.Invoke("Broadcast", "john", "Hi, all!");
```

For example, the preceding statement would invoke the following method of the hub referenced by hubProxy:

```
public void Broadcast(string from, string message)
{
    // Code
}
```

The arguments that we send to the remote method are defined as object type parameters, which indicates that we can pass any object type. The SignalR client will automatically take care of serializing it before sending it to the other end of the communication.

Invoke() returns a Task object, which we can use again to take control when its execution completes by using the promise pattern or wait for its completion using Wait() or the async/await construct of the language.

When the server method returns a data type, we can use a generic Invoke<T>() overload, as shown in the following example, and get the result returned by accessing the Result property of the task:

```
// Client code
var result = hubProxy.Invoke<int>("Sum", 2, 3).Result;
// or using an async flavour:
// var result = await hubProxy.Invoke<int>("Sum", 2, 3);
Console.WriteLine("Result: " + result);

// Server code (Hub)
public int Sum(int a, int b)
{
    return a+b;
}
```

We can also receive any object type as a return value, deserialization being fully automatic.

```
var customer = _customerServices.GetById(3);
var provider = _providerServices.GetById(34);
var result = await hubProxy.Invoke<IEnumerable<Invoice>>(
                "GetInvoices",
                customer,
                provider
        );

foreach(var invoice in result)
{
    Console.WriteLine("Invoice: " + invoice.Id);
}
```

Let's see what happens with the opposite direction of the communication—that is, when the server is the one who invokes an action from a client connected to the service. From the point of view of the client, it is a mere subscription to an event. Using its internal protocol, the server sends a command specification that includes the name of the method to be executed and the arguments that need to be supplied to it. For this to occur, on the client side, we will have to previously subscribe to each of the events, or actions, where we want to include handling logic.

To associate an action invoked by the server to a handler, we must use the On() method, an extender defined in the SignalR client library on the IHubProxy interface, which allows us to do this in a very quick and expressive manner:

```
hubProxy.On(
    "message",
    (string msg) => {
                        Console.WriteLine(msg);
                    }
);
```

The first parameter is the name of the method or action, case-insensitive, and the second parameter is a delegate of the Action type, a method with zero or more parameters and no return value, which is where we will enter the handling code. Again, the parameters that the server sends can be of any type, and they are deserialized automatically.

```
hubProxy.On(
    "InvoiceAdded", (Invoice invoice) => {
                        // TODO
                    }
);
```

The handling code will depend to some extent on the platform on which we are executing our application. For example, in WinRT, Windows Phone, WPF, or Silverlight environments, to update the user interface from this code, we will normally use the mechanisms provided by each one of them to securely access the user interface from the thread on which the call to the event is being executed:

```
// WinRT code:
hubProxy.On<Invoice>("InvoiceAdded", invoice =>
    Dispatcher.RunAsync(CoreDispatcherPriority.Normal,
    () => {
        // TODO
    }
));
```

Finally, the client library also allows access to the features of state maintenance between the client and the server, which we studied when we looked at the JavaScript client in Chapter 5, "Hubs." As a very brief reminder, this capability allowed us to define "variables" at the client, which traveled to the server accompanying each message sent to the hub. From the server, their values could be read and even changed, and in this case, the new value traveled back automatically to the client so as to always maintain full and consistent state between both ends.

To add state variables, we will use the hub proxy directly as if it were a dictionary allowing us to set key-value pairs:

```
// Client side
hubProxy["color"] = "red";
hubProxy["username"] = "scott";
```

```
hubProxy["refreshCount"] = 1;
hubProxy.Invoke("refresh").Wait();
Console.WriteLine(hubProxy.GetValue<int>("refreshCount")); // 2


// Server side (Hub)
public Task Refresh()
{
    var userColor = Clients.Caller.color;
    var userName = Clients.Caller.username;
    Clients.Caller.refreshCount++;
    ... // More code
}
```

In this case, the naming of state variables at the client and the server is case-sensitive. Thus we must write them in exactly the same way on both ends.

As we can see in this code, state variables will be accessible from the server directly via Clients.Caller. From the client, we will be able to query their value using the hubProxy .GetValue<T>("varName") extender, which will return it converted to the type that we want.

Logging

The SignalR client includes infrastructure to perform a complete tracing of what is happening in the backstage during and after the connection process. We can also use it to register the application's own events.

First, it offers a Trace() method directly on the Connection or HubConnection object, which is used internally by the client libraries to register events or messages. However, we client application developers can also use it to add our own information, as in the following example:

```
connection.Trace(
    TraceLevels.None,                     // Event type
    "Hello, world! Today is {0}",         // Message
    DateTime.Now.ToLongDateString()       // Message params
);
```

The first argument specifies the event type that will be associated to the message that we are registering, to be chosen among those available in the TraceLevels enumeration provided by SignalR. The value chosen is important because there is another property in the connection that allows restricting the messages that we want to see in the trace: TraceLevel.

We can set the TraceLevel property of the Connection object to one or several of the following values (it is an enumeration of flags):

- **TraceLevels.Messages**   In the trace, we will see only information on the messages received.

- **TraceLevels.Events**   We will see the main events and errors that are occurring during the life of the connection.

- **TraceLevels.StateChanges**   We will see the changes of state of the connection.

- **TraceLevels.None** The trace will contain information not associated to any of the previous elements, such as the code example that we have previously shown.

- **TraceLevels.All** All the messages sent to the trace will be shown, as shown in Figure 7-10.

FIGURE 7-10 Complete trace viewed from the console.

These messages are dumped in a `TextWriter` object, present in the `TraceWriter` property of the connection. For example, the console output shown in Figure 7-10 has been made with the following code:

```
connection.TraceWriter = Console.Out;
```

Likewise, it would be quite easy to create our own `TextWriter` and implement any other output or persistence mechanism for traces. The following example implements a basic writer that shows the trace messages through the debugging console, in a similar way to the implementation that comes out of the box with SignalR:

```
// Custom text writer
class DebugTextWriter: TextWriter
{
    public override void WriteLine(string value)
    {
        Debug.WriteLine(value);
    }

    public override Encoding Encoding
    {
        get { return Encoding.UTF8; }
    }
}

// Set as trace writer
var connection = new Connection("http://localhost:2713/echo");
connection.TraceWriter = new DebugTextWriter();
connection.Start();
```

Example: Console application

We have previously seen the implementation of a shared drawing board using the SignalR JavaScript client. Now we will use the generic .NET client to implement a simplified client of the drawing board that will be executed in a console application.

Our goal is shown in Figure 7-11. The console application is connected to the hub and reproduces the points drawn from the web client on screen.

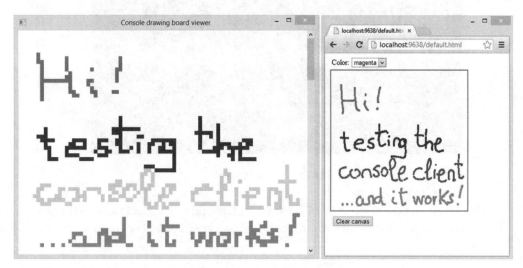

FIGURE 7-11 Console application as a client of the shared drawing board.

After we have created the console type project, it is necessary to download the `Microsoft.AspNet.SignalR.Client` package via NuGet and then create the client as shown in the following code. Because it is a console application, we will simply edit the Program.cs file:

```
using System;
using Microsoft.AspNet.SignalR.Client;

class Program
{
    private static ConsoleColor[]
        _colors = new[]
                {
                    ConsoleColor.Black, ConsoleColor.Red,
                    ConsoleColor.Green, ConsoleColor.Blue,
                    ConsoleColor.Yellow, ConsoleColor.Magenta,
                    ConsoleColor.White
                };

    static void Main(string[] args)
    {
        Console.Title = "Console drawing board viewer";
        Console.SetWindowSize(80, 60);
        Console.BackgroundColor = ConsoleColor.White;
```

```
        Console.ForegroundColor = ConsoleColor.Black;
        Console.Clear();

        var server = "http://localhost:1497/signalr"; // Change to your server's port number
        var hubConn = new HubConnection(server);
        var hubProxy = hubConn.CreateHubProxy("drawingBoard");


        hubProxy.On("clear", () =>
                {
                    Console.BackgroundColor = ConsoleColor.White;
                    Console.Clear();
                }
        );

        hubProxy.On("drawPoint", (int x, int y, int color) =>
                {
                    DrawPoint(x, y, color);
                }
        );

        hubProxy.On("update", (int[,] buffer) =>
            {
                for (int x = 0; x < buffer.GetLength(0); x++)
                {
                    for (int y = 0; y < buffer.GetLength(1); y++)
                    {
                        if (buffer[x, y] != 0)
                            DrawPoint(x, y, buffer[x, y]);
                    }
                }
            }
        );

        hubConn.Start().ContinueWith(t =>
            {
                if (t.IsFaulted)
                {
                    Console.WriteLine("Error connecting to "
                      + server + ". Are you using the right URL?");
                }
            }
        );
        Console.ReadLine();
        hubConn.Stop();
    }

    private static void DrawPoint(int x, int y, int color)
    {
        int translatedx = Console.WindowWidth*x/300;
        int translatedy = Console.WindowHeight*y/300;
        Console.SetCursorPosition(translatedx, translatedy);
        Console.BackgroundColor = _colors[color - 1];
        Console.Write(" ");
    }
}
```

Example: Windows 8/Windows 8.1 application with C#/XAML

When creating SignalR clients, there is really very little difference between platforms, because the concepts, the philosophy, and even the objects that we will handle are identical. To illustrate this, we are going to implement PaintR, a client for Windows 8 and Windows 8.1 of our well-known shared drawing board, using C# and XAML; see Figure 7-12.

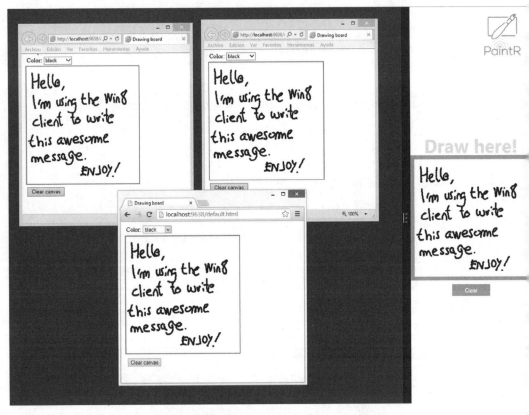

FIGURE 7-12 PaintR in snap view mode (right).

Project creation and setup

For the purpose of creating the application that we will develop over the following pages, it is necessary to first create a project of the "Blank App (XAML)" type from Visual Studio. After we have created it, we must install the following package using NuGet:

```
PM> install-package Microsoft.AspNet.SignalR.Client
```

MainPage.xaml

```
<Page
    x:Class="PaintR.MainPage"
    xmlns="http://schemas.microsoft.com/winfx/2006/xaml/presentation"
    xmlns:x="http://schemas.microsoft.com/winfx/2006/xaml"
```

```
        xmlns:local="using:PaintR"
        xmlns:d="http://schemas.microsoft.com/expression/blend/2008"
        xmlns:mc="http://schemas.openxmlformats.org/markup-compatibility/2006"
        mc:Ignorable="d">


    <Grid Background="White">
        <StackPanel VerticalAlignment="Center" Orientation="Vertical">
            <TextBlock MaxWidth="320" Margin="0,0,0,0"
                        Text="Draw here!" VerticalAlignment="Bottom"
                        FontFamily="Global User Interface" FontSize="48"
                        Foreground="#FFEAEAEA" FontWeight="Bold"
                        TextAlignment="Center" Width="320" Height="49"/>
            <Border Margin="0,0,0,0" BorderThickness="10"  Width="320"
                    Height="320" BorderBrush="#a0a0a0"   >
                <Canvas Name="InkCanvas" Background="white"
                        Margin="0,0,0,0" Width="300" Height="300"
                        MaxWidth="300" MaxHeight="300"
                        HorizontalAlignment="Center"  />
            </Border>
            <Button Content="Clear" Name="ClearButton" Width="100"
                    HorizontalAlignment="Stretch"
                    VerticalAlignment="Stretch"
                    Style="{StaticResource TextButtonStyle}" />
        </StackPanel>
        <Image HorizontalAlignment="Right" VerticalAlignment="Top"
                Source="Assets/Logo.png" Stretch="None"
                Opacity="0.5"></Image>
    </Grid>
    <Page.BottomAppBar>
        <AppBar Padding="10,0,10,0">
            <Grid>
                <StackPanel Orientation="Horizontal"
                            HorizontalAlignment="Left">
                    <Button AutomationProperties.Name="Color"
                            Click="SelectColor"
                            Style="{StaticResource
                                    AppBarButtonStyle}"/>
                </StackPanel>
            </Grid>
        </AppBar>
    </Page.BottomAppBar>
</Page>
```

MainPage.xaml.cs

```
using System;
using Windows.Foundation;
using Windows.UI;
using Windows.UI.Core;
using Windows.UI.Input;
using Windows.UI.Input.Inking;
using Windows.UI.Popups;
using Windows.UI.Xaml;
using Windows.UI.Xaml.Controls;
using Windows.UI.Xaml.Input;
using Windows.UI.Xaml.Media;
```

```csharp
using Windows.UI.Xaml.Navigation;
using Windows.UI.Xaml.Shapes;
using Microsoft.AspNet.SignalR.Client;

namespace PaintR
{
    public sealed partial class MainPage : Page
    {
        private bool _pressed = false;
        private readonly InkManager _mInkManager = new InkManager();
        IHubProxy _drawingBoard;
        HubConnection _hub;

        public MainPage()
        {
            InitializeComponent();
            InkCanvas.PointerPressed += OnCanvasPointerPressed;
            InkCanvas.PointerMoved += OnCanvasPointerMoved;
            InkCanvas.PointerReleased += OnCanvasPointerReleased;
            InkCanvas.PointerExited += OnCanvasPointerReleased;
            ClearButton.Click += OnClearButtonClick;
        }


        /////////////////////////////
        // Startup code
        /////////////////////////////

        protected async override
                void OnNavigatedTo(NavigationEventArgs e)
        {
            base.OnNavigatedTo(e);
            if(_hub != null)        // If the client has already been initialized
                return;             // do not initialize again

            _hub = new HubConnection("http://localhost:9638/");
            _drawingBoard = _hub.CreateHubProxy("DrawingBoard");

            // Define state vars
            _drawingBoard["color"] = 1; // Black by default;

            // Subscribe to Hub events
            _drawingBoard.On<int, int, int>(
                "DrawPoint", (x, y, c) =>
                    Dispatcher.RunAsync(CoreDispatcherPriority.Normal,
                    () =>
                      {
                          DrawPoint(x, y, c);
                      }
            ));

            _drawingBoard.On(
                "Clear", () =>
                    Dispatcher.RunAsync(CoreDispatcherPriority.Normal,
                    () =>
                      {
                          ClearDrawingBoard();
```

```
                }
        ));

        _drawingBoard.On<int[,]>(
            "Update", (int[,] buffer) =>
                Dispatcher.RunAsync(CoreDispatcherPriority.Normal,
                () =>
                    {
                        UpdateDrawingBoard(buffer);
                    }
        ));

        // Go!
        await _hub.Start();
    }


    /////////////////////////
    // Flyout Context Menu
    /////////////////////////

    private Rect GetElementRect(FrameworkElement element)
    {
        GeneralTransform buttonTransform =
                element.TransformToVisual(null);
        Point point = buttonTransform.TransformPoint(new Point());
        return new Rect(point,
                        new Size(
                            element.ActualWidth,
                            element.ActualHeight));
    }

    private async void SelectColor(object sender, RoutedEventArgs e)
    {
        var menu = new PopupMenu();
        menu.Commands.Add(new UICommand("Black", null, 1));
        menu.Commands.Add(new UICommand("Red", null, 2));
        menu.Commands.Add(new UICommand("Green", null, 3));
        menu.Commands.Add(new UICommand("Blue", null, 4));
        menu.Commands.Add(new UICommand("Yellow", null, 5));
        menu.Commands.Add(new UICommand("Magenta", null, 6));

        IUICommand chosenCommand =
            await menu.ShowForSelectionAsync(
                    GetElementRect((FrameworkElement)sender)
            );

        if (chosenCommand != null)
        {
            _drawingBoard["color"] = (int)chosenCommand.Id;
        }
    }


    /////////////////////////
    // Event handlers
    /////////////////////////
```

```
public void OnCanvasPointerReleased(
            object sender, PointerRoutedEventArgs e)
{
    _pressed = false;
}

public void OnCanvasPointerPressed(
            object sender, PointerRoutedEventArgs e)
{
    _pressed = true;
}

private async void OnCanvasPointerMoved(
                object sender, PointerRoutedEventArgs e)
{
    if (!_pressed)
        return;
    PointerPoint pt = e.GetCurrentPoint(InkCanvas);
    var x = Convert.ToInt32(pt.Position.X);
    var y = Convert.ToInt32(pt.Position.Y);
    if (x >= 0 && x < InkCanvas.Width
            && y >= 0 && y < InkCanvas.Height)
    {
        DrawPoint(x, y, (int) (_drawingBoard["color"]));
        await _drawingBoard.Invoke("BroadcastPoint", x, y);
    }
}

async void OnClearButtonClick(object sender, RoutedEventArgs e)
{
    ClearDrawingBoard();
    await _drawingBoard.Invoke("BroadcastClear");
}

////////////////////////////
// Drawing board Helpers
////////////////////////////

private Color[] _colors = new[]
                    {
                        Colors.Black,
                        Colors.Red,
                        Colors.Green,
                        Colors.Blue,
                        Colors.Yellow,
                        Colors.Magenta,
                        Colors.White
                    };

private Color GetColorFromInt(int color)
{
    return (color >0 && color <= _colors.Length)?
            _colors[color-1]
            : Colors.Black;
}

private void DrawPoint(int x, int y, int color)
```

```
{
    if (color == 0) return;
    var brush = new SolidColorBrush(GetColorFromInt(color));
    var circle = new Ellipse()
    {
        Width = 4,
        Height = 4,
        Fill = brush,
        StrokeThickness = 1,
        Stroke = brush
    };
    InkCanvas.Children.Add(circle);
    Canvas.SetLeft(circle, x);
    Canvas.SetTop(circle, y);
}

private void ClearDrawingBoard()
{
    InkCanvas.Children.Clear();
}

private void UpdateDrawingBoard(int[,] buffer)
{
    for (int x = 0; x < buffer.GetLength(0); x++)
    {
        for (int y = 0; y < buffer.GetLength(1); y++)
        {
            DrawPoint(x, y, buffer[x,y]);
        }
    }
}
        }
    }
}
```

> **Note** To avoid compilation errors, we will need to include the namespace PaintR in the project's App.xaml.cs file:
>
> ```
> using PaintR;
> ```

Windows Phone 8 clients

Aside from the obvious differences at platform level, there is nothing in relation to SignalR to differentiate these developments from any other type of client. We can open connections, create proxies, send data, subscribe to the reception of information or invocations made from hubs, and so on, and all this in the same way as we have seen so far.

The only aspect worth noting is a problem that we will often encounter while developing Windows Phone solutions: connectivity with the local host from the device emulator. Keep in mind that it is running on a virtual machine that, for all purposes, is a different computer on the network, so by default it will not have access to SignalR services provided from the local system.

In fact, this problem is not unique to SignalR. The exact same thing happens when trying to connect to REST APIs or to any other service available at "localhost", due to the following reasons:

- The emulator uses a different IP addressing space.

- The server that we use (typically, IIS Express) is usually not configured to receive requests from computers other than the local one.

- There might be security elements (for example, the Windows firewall) that block the requests.

For successful testing, we first have to ensure access to the server that we are using, for which it is important that it is associated to an address that is accessible from the emulator. Normally, we can use the one assigned to the virtual network adapter used by the emulator, which is usually of the 169.254.80.80 type.

Therefore, we must ensure that the server that we are using is capable of responding to requests made to this address, at the port that we are using.

When using IIS Express, as is the usual case, we must perform the following steps:

1. Close IIS Express.

2. Employing a user with elevated privileges, access its configuration file, called applicationhost .config, usually found at "%userprofile%\Documents\IISExpress\config".

3. Look for the specific configuration section of the website that we are using to debug. Such sections look like this:

```
<site name="MySignalrApp" id="304">
    ...
</site>
```

4. Add a binding to make IIS Express respond to requests directed to a new IP address accessible from the emulator. In the following example, we have added the second `<binding>` with the address and port through which the server will be accessed from the emulator:

```
<site name="MySignalrApp" id="304">
    ...
 <bindings>
   <binding protocol="http"
            bindingInformation="*:7890:localhost" />
   <binding protocol="http"
            bindingInformation="169.254.80.80:54321:" />
 </bindings>
</site>
```

Next we just need to start Visual Studio with elevated privileges so that IIS Express can use the specified address, and the service will be available from outside as long as the firewall does not intercept the calls—in which case the ideal thing to do is to add a rule that allows them. (A much worse solution would be to temporarily disable this security feature.)

Finally, it is important to remember that instead of using "localhost" to access the local computer from the client, we must specify the IP address that we have configured.

Consumption of services from other platforms

Both the SignalR team and the user community are developing client implementations that allow consumption of hub or persistent connection services environments other than Windows, and even from those not based on the .NET Framework.

For developers of native applications for Windows, the SignalR team is working on a pure C++ client so that these systems can also benefit from the consumption of real-time services.

The following example shows how to access a persistent connection from a C++ client:

```
auto connection =
        make_shared<MicrosoftAspNetSignalRClientCpp::Connection>(
            U("http://localhost:40476/raw-connection")
        );

connection->SetReceivedCallback([](string_t message)
{
    wcout << message << endl;
});

connection->SetStateChangedCallback([](StateChange stateChange)
{
    wcout <<
        ConnectionStateString::ToString(stateChange.GetOldState())
        << " => "
        << ConnectionStateString::ToString(stateChange.GetNewState())
        << endl;
});
connection->SetErrorCallback([](exception& ex)
{
    wcerr << U("========ERROR==========") << endl;
    wcerr << ex.what() << endl;
    wcerr << U("=======================") << endl;
});
connection->Start().wait();
connection->Send("Hi!").wait();
```

For .NET developers, the easiest option to implement native clients on platforms such as Linux or Mac OS is via the use of Mono and tools such as MonoDevelop, Xamarin Studio[4], or Visual Studio extensions created by the same company. The SignalR .NET client libraries are valid on these platforms.

---

[4] Official Xamarin Studio website: *http://xamarin.com/studio*

It is also possible to create native applications for iOS or Android using the languages to which we are accustomed with the set of multiplatform solutions provided by Xamarin. To access SignalR services from them, we will simply need to use the same client libraries as usual.

There are also unofficial libraries that are being created by the community, for Android and iOS native environments, Java, C++ on QT (Windows and Linux), NodeJS, and others.

CHAPTER 8

Deploying and scaling SignalR

If we had to summarize the deployment process in one sentence, we could say that it is the set of actions that need to be performed to install software in environments where it can be put to use by users, be it during staging or in the production phase. Within the context of SignalR applications, deployment scenarios can vary a lot because of the large number of platforms that we can find on both the client side and the server side and the combinatorial explosion of these platforms. Obviously, deploying SignalR services inside an ASP.NET application executed on IIS is not the same as doing it in an operating system service or in a Windows Azure worker role. Nor is the deployment procedure of a Windows Phone 8 application that uses the SignalR client to access real-time notifications the same as the deployment process of an application for Windows 8 or a simple JavaScript client.

Each of these platforms has its own deployment procedures, which will remain intact with SignalR. That is, including SignalR components in a server-side application has no effect at all on the way in which it has to be deployed, nor does it affect the client side.

For example, in classic web systems, deployment consists of installing the application on the server, usually in the following ways:

- Using publishing tools integrated in the development environment, such as the Visual Studio publishing utility

- In the case of automated processes, using Web Deploy[1] or FTP, for example

- Manually, using any type of transfer protocol allowing us to directly copy the files to the server

However, usually there are no specific actions to facilitate the deployment of components to the client side. They will be distributed on demand when accessing the different pages or features provided, and they will be executed on the user's browser.

In web applications with SignalR, it is exactly the same. In fact, because all the server components of SignalR applications are compiled (hubs, persistent connections, configuration classes, and so on), it is sufficient to follow whatever publishing process we normally use to get our real-time services working on the operation environments. The client components—basically JavaScript files—will be included in the installation package and will be entered into the application as static files.

We frequently encounter ASP.NET applications deployed in this way, with the structure shown in Figure 8-1.

---

[1] *http://www.iis.net/downloads/microsoft/web-deploy*

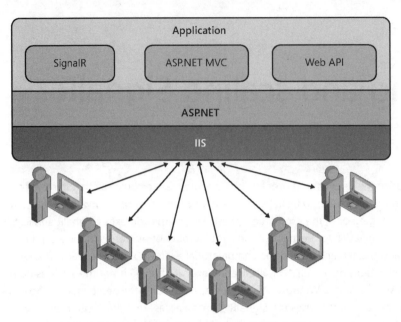

FIGURE 8-1 Usual deployment of web applications with SignalR.

Our application can be written using frameworks such as ASP.NET MVC, ASP.NET Web Forms, or Web API, whose pages load the SignalR client components to consume services provided via the hubs or persistent connections defined in compiled classes inside the application itself. Of course, it could be accompanied by other assemblies, such as visual components, utility functions, model classes, or any type of content, but the schema would still be the same. This is the simplest deployment architecture that we can find.

Growing pains

Well, after endless hours of work, many weeks with virtually no rest and sleepless nights, we have finally launched our revolutionary social system in which, of course, we have employed SignalR to implement spectacular features that use push and real-time communications as mankind has never known before. Now we just have to reveal it to the world and begin to attract users by the hundreds. One might say that our problems are over. (Or you could say that they have just begun.)

From this point, basically two things could happen, intermediate states aside. In the first case, our super application would turn out not to be as necessary as we thought, or perhaps users would not understand its true value, and it would end up being used by no one and ultimately fading into oblivion.

Or we could have the exact opposite case: our application is a real hit. Attracted by the novelty and the promise of finally getting their lifelong-awaited online experiences, users begin registering timidly. Word of mouth and fast spread through social networks causes the number of registrations to grow exponentially after a few weeks. Users begin to number in the hundreds, then thousands, and then come the first complaints of slowness and problems with the service. This effect is often called "death by success," and it is the reason for the demise of many interesting projects. It is a delicate moment, and the survival of our creature will depend largely on our ability to resolve these issues.

It is time to scale—that is, to find ways to provide quality service to a growing number of users.

Fortunately, it is always possible to extend the server that we have rented to host our application, so our first approach in this case is normally to invest there: maximizing RAM, installing as many processors as the board or the virtual machine allows, and improving persistent storage in terms of speed and space. This way of increasing the capacity of our infrastructure to support more users is called *vertical scalability*. (See Figure 8-2.) It requires virtually no software changes or special precautions during development; it simply involves buying or renting more metal or adding more resources to our VM.

> **Note** Scaling using this approach is often called a *scale-up*.

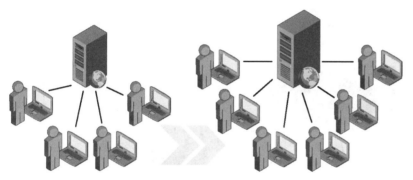

FIGURE 8-2 Vertical scaling of a server.

The more optimistic members of the team might think that this large investment in hardware would overcome the problem. And it would...at least for some amount of time. The problem with vertical scalability is that it is inherently limited: however much we want to extend a server, there will be a point beyond which it is physically impossible to increase its capacity. Here we would switch to a server whose architecture allowed for more expansion, but given the growth rate of our super app, this would serve only to give us some breathing space while we look for a more definitive solution. And we should not forget the cost either: adding memory or CPU to a system tends to be expensive, and normally there is a rather limited return on investment. It is also not a very flexible option. If we know that our users connect primarily in office hours, during the rest of the day all the power and resources of the server will be underused, so we will not be getting the most from our investment.

In short, vertical scalability is valid for closed or tightly controlled environments, such as corporate applications or systems that have a low number of users because of the very nature of the service and its context. After all, we are unlikely to need much more if we are creating a chat application for the die-hard fans of the synchronized swimming infant team of the local neighborhood—opting for more complex solutions in this scenario might be considered oversizing, over-engineering, or just overkill.

When vertical scalability is not enough, the solution comes via a much more powerful approach: *horizontal scalability*. Scaling horizontally consists in increasing the number of servers until they can respond to user demand.

 Note Scaling using this approach is often called a *scale-out*.

In traditional web environments, the ideal solution is to introduce a mechanism to automatically distribute the load among various nodes in a way that is fully transparent to the user, acting for all intents and purposes as if the application worked on a single server, although each request (even those from the same user) can be processed by a different node in the network. These elements, called *load balancers*, are located at the entrance to a server farm and redirect requests to the least busy server to be processed there. See Figure 8-3.

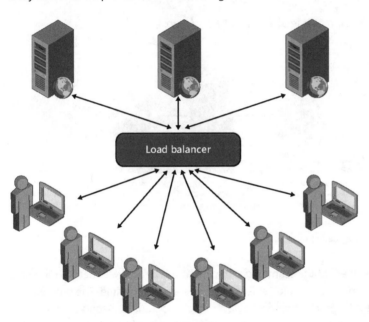

FIGURE 8-3 Transparent horizontal scalability.

And, thanks to currently existing technologies, we could even use cloud services like those provided by Windows Azure[2] to dynamically adapt the number of servers to the actual demand at each time, thus obtaining the assurance that our application will always be available to serve its users, as well as achieving great ease of management of infrastructure and a good level of fault tolerance.

Also, to reduce latency and boost performance, it is possible to bring contents and services closer to the users who consume them, using CDN[3] (Content Delivery Networks) or strategically located servers. The main advantage in comparison to scaling up is that in scale-out there is *a priori* no

---

[2] Windows Azure: *http://www.windowsazure.com*

[3] CDN: Content Delivery Network.

physical limitation: we can always add new servers to withstand a greater load. However, to work on this architecture, applications have to be designed anticipating this possibility, because as each request can be processed by a different server, you cannot use the local resources of the latter (such as the memory or the file system) to store data persistently or to store the state of the application itself.

As a side note, there is an alternative called *session affinity,* which consists in making the load balancer always assign the requests coming from a certain user to the same server, whereby state information could be stored in the servers. Also known as *sticky sessions,* this technique is better than vertical scale-up but worse than the horizontal scale-out with a stateless approach.

Scalability in SignalR

We have explained that in horizontally scaled web environments we should not use local server resources such as the memory or disk. Things get even more complicated when it comes to SignalR applications.

When we looked at state maintenance techniques at the server in Chapter 5, "Hubs," we described the problems of having multiple SignalR servers serving in parallel and we gave some guidelines for solving them. But, as we also explained, SignalR poses a real challenge in horizontally distributed scenarios, especially because each server is aware of only the clients that are connected to it directly. The problem this presents is illustrated in the "minimalist" example shown in Figure 8-4: user A is connected to the SignalR service, and the load balancer allocates it to server #1. Then comes user B and it is allocated to server #2.

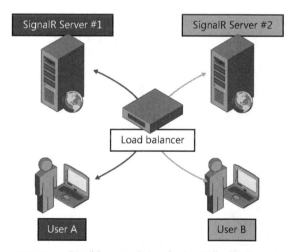

FIGURE 8-4 Possible scenario in a horizontally distributed environment with SignalR.

Although both users would theoretically be connecting to the same persistent connection or hub—there would be only one access URL—the balancer would have delegated its processing to a particular server, a different one in each case. And because each one would be physically connected to a different server, a broadcast message issued by server #1 would be received only by user A, and the same applies to the other server.

In addition, this allocation of clients to servers could change every time a new physical connection opens, generating situations that would be difficult to manage due to roaming. For example, imagine that user A is connected to server #1 and then experiences a time-out due to network problems, reconnects, and is allocated to server #2. From the perspective of server #1, user A has left the application, whereas from server #2, user A would be considered a new user. Moreover, during the time taken for the reconnection process, new messages that merit being sent to the user could have entered the system.

This same effect can take place with parallel connections made by the client to send information to the server in push one-way transports such as server-sent events or long polling. Each one could be processed by a different server, yet the main push connection would remain active and fixed from the start. As you can guess, these problems are not easy to tackle.

To address these scenarios, SignalR comes with a powerful out-of-the-box mechanism allowing the deployment of its server components in horizontally distributed environments through backplanes. As shown in Figure 8-5, a backplane is a component that acts as a messaging system between SignalR nodes, similar to a bus for internal communication between systems. When enabled on a server, all messages generated from it will be sent through the backplane, where the remaining servers will be listening to forward them to their clients.

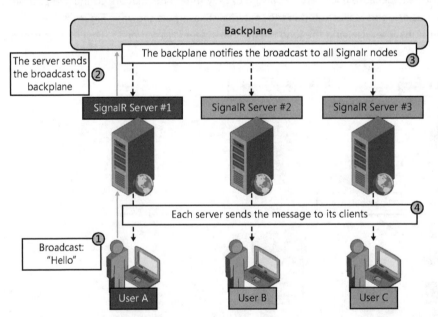

FIGURE 8-5 Operation of SignalR with a backplane.

There exist different backplanes, each using a different technology to manage publications and subscriptions internally used by the messaging system. Currently, SignalR officially offers backplanes for Windows Azure Service Bus, SQL Server, and Redis, but the developer community has provided some additional ones. We will describe each one in detail later on.

Although employing a backplane enables the use of SignalR in a server farm and the distribution of user load among its servers, doing so also has its limitations. The main limitation is that it will inevitably lead to an increase in the time required to send each message and hence to a significant decrease in the number of messages that can move through the system—that is, the throughput. Paradoxically, the same solution used to enable horizontal scalability of SignalR services could become a bottleneck in certain scaled out architectures. In fact, scalability is not synonymous with increased performance in this case.

Therefore, we should not think of backplanes as the ultimate solution to the scalability problems of all kinds of SignalR applications, but only as the mechanism that allows using this framework with balanced server farms, in the event that this were to be the deployment architecture finally chosen for our system.

The use of backplanes is recommended in applications where there is a server broadcasting the same message to several clients or groups of clients. This is because, in SignalR, messages are processed in such a way that sending the same message to many clients would not saturate the bus. Their use is also appropriate when there is a very low frequency of submissions, or where their amount is not directly related to the increase in the number of clients. In all these cases, a backplane could offer good performance and, potentially, at the same time, nearly unlimited scalability.

However, as soon as personalized information needs to be sent to each client or immediacy is critical, we have to resort to other solutions.

When designing a scalability strategy that offers appropriate performance for the type of application in question, there are as many solutions as types of systems and development teams trying to implement them. What would be the best way to design a scalable SignalR application? The best answer we can give is "it depends."

In general, the formula for scaling our systems always consists in distributing the load across multiple servers, but if we want to maintain a good performance in SignalR-based real-time services, we have to design and implement our own solutions. And in this case, they will almost always involve searching for techniques for partitioning or distributing users following logical criteria that are specific to the domain of the application that we are developing, to group them into the same server. If all the users with whom we want to communicate as a group are found on the same server, submissions will be direct and we will avoid intermediaries that might introduce latency, such as when using backplanes. We will also achieve efficiency, and we will be able to scale out as much as the grouping strategy that we have chosen allows us, although usually at the cost of increased development effort.

The simplest and most basic approach could arise if we knew in advance and with certainty what users we are dealing with and their distribution, because we would be able to define a static architecture for them. We would just have to prepare an infrastructure of servers configured and adapted to the initial needs of the system, as shown in Figure 8-6, and adapt it according to the evolution of demand.

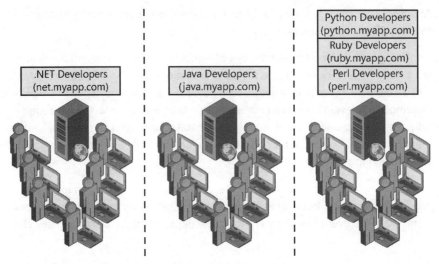

FIGURE 8-6 Horizontal partitions of a social network for developers.

In this example, we could create new chat services as new technologies emerged in the future and host those services on servers with spare capacity or add new servers. However, to make this option possible, due to the very nature of the service, we should ensure that none of the partitions will grow beyond what has been assumed when planning the size of the infrastructure.

We can also take a more dynamic and flexible approach, which would be advisable in most scenarios. Conceptually, this would mean creating a "smart" balanced system, sensitive to the domain of the application, which could consist of a front service able to redirect clients to the appropriate server, based on certain criteria.

For example, in a collaborative text editing service, a user-grouping criterion could be the document itself. If a user entered the application and decided to open a document, a SignalR server could be assigned to them on the fly—the least busy server in a set of available servers. This mapping would be stored in a centralized persistence system, and the user would be redirected to said server so that she could start working on the document. If some other user accessed the same document later, the application would know that there is already a real-time server assigned to it and would redirect this new user to it. In this case, the criterion for partitioning or distributing users would be the document.

We could find another use in an internal messaging system on a multitenant ERP distributed as SaaS[4]. In this case, the criterion for allocating users could be the tenant itself—that is, the company using the services—because each of them would be completely independent of the others and, therefore, real-time services could be provided in separate servers.

Note that a similar approach is currently used in many applications. For example, there are many online games where users have a usable area to find opponents or to perform other activities, but at the time of starting the game, an existing server is assigned and all users associated with the same game are redirected to it. In this case, the partitioning criterion would be the game.

---

[4] SaaS: Software as a Service.

It would also be unfeasible to use backplanes in systems where it is essential to have real-time communications with a fixed frequency of updates per second, such as in a multiplayer shooter. This scenario, probably the most extreme one that we might face when developing a real-time application, can be approached in the same way: making all users involved in the action or game connect to the same server to be able to send their messages directly and without any middlemen.

Another possibility we might consider when using backplanes is trying to optimize the traffic generated in the messaging bus based on the needs of our application. For example, it would be possible to create a system to keep the subscriptions users should receive updated on every node, and implement a filtering system preventing messages that a node is not going to need from reaching that node through the backplane.

Of course, we can combine several of these techniques or devise new strategies that fit the exact needs of each application, but unlike with backplanes, we will have to implement our own solution.

Scaling on backplanes

The SignalR team has managed to make the activation of a backplane completely trivial. All that we have to do is install the specific package of the backplane using NuGet and insert a line of code to provide the basic configuration information that it needs. Now we will see how to configure and start the official backplanes available today: Windows Azure Service Bus, SQL Server, and Redis.

Windows Azure Service Bus

The Windows Azure bus is a scalable infrastructure for cloud messaging that offers various features for efficient communication of applications such as queues, topics (for publish/subscribe—pub/sub—schemes), relay, or push notifications, among other things. The backplane for SignalR uses topics to convey messages to the nodes connected to it.

This is a paid service, charged by the number of messages sent. Each call to a method of the hub enters a message into the bus, as do internal notifications of user connections or disconnections. However, the cost is not unreasonable. At the time of writing, you can send a million messages, or even more if you opt for an annual subscription, for one dollar.

Configuring the service

The bus service is created and configured through the Windows Azure management portal by accessing Service Bus in the main menu; see Figure 8-7.

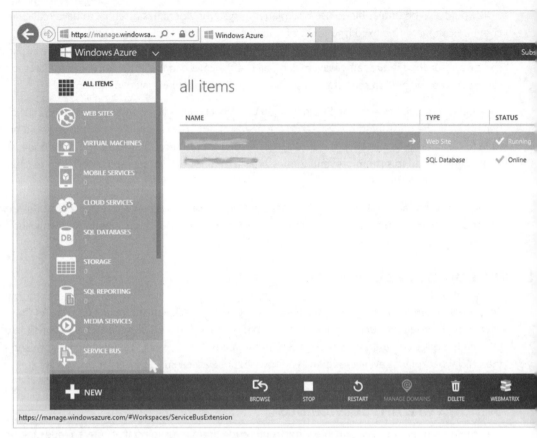

FIGURE 8-7 Accessing the Service Bus from the Azure management console.

If we have not used this feature before, a screen will appear, as shown in Figure 8-8, telling us that no namespace has been created and inviting us to create one. A namespace is a name used to identify the Service Bus when we reference it—for example, to connect from client applications.

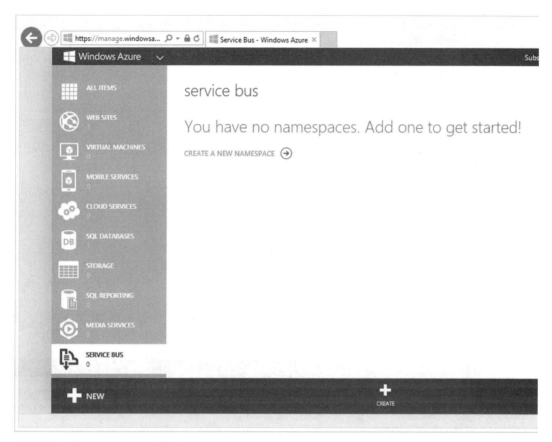

FIGURE 8-8 No namespaces defined.

After clicking any of the various links available to create the namespace, we will just have to fill out a short form—see Figure 8-9—and it will be ready. We need to provide the following data:

- The name of the bus that we are creating, which will serve to compose the URL to access it. The suffix *.servicebus.windows.net* will be automatically added to it, and it must be unique.

- The region where the servers that will use the bus are located. The closer they are geographically, the more efficient the communication between them will be.

After the form is completed, the system will inform us that the namespace has been created correctly, and we will be able to use it from our application. See Figure 8-10.

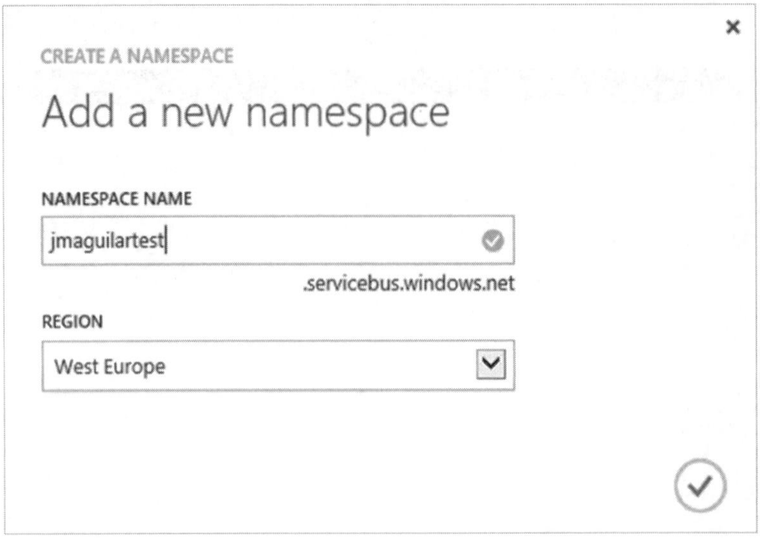

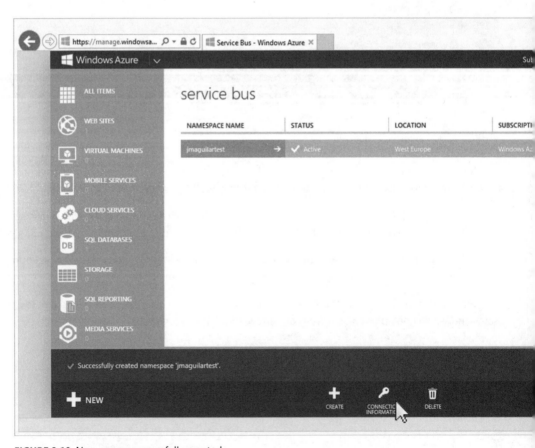

FIGURE 8-9 Adding a new service bus namespace.

FIGURE 8-10 Namespace successfully created.

Notice the Connection Information link at the bottom of the figure. We can use this link to get the connection string, which we will use later on when configuring the backplane in the SignalR application.

Activating the backplane

Thanks to the pluggable architecture with which SignalR has been designed, activation of the backplane is insultingly simple, as we will see now. For any SignalR application to use Service Bus as a backplane, first we have to install the following NuGet package:

```
PM> Install-Package microsoft.aspnet.signalr.ServiceBus
```

Next we have to tell SignalR that it must use said backplane, supplying it certain configuration parameters. This code must be found at a point that is executed during application startup, such as the Startup class:

```
public class Startup
{
    public void Configuration(IAppBuilder app)
    {
        var connectionString =
            "Endpoint=sb://jmaguilartest.servicebus.windows.net/;"
            + "SharedSecretIssuer=owner;"
            + "SharedSecretValue=YOURSECRETVALUEHERE>";
        GlobalHost.DependencyResolver.UseServiceBus(
            connectionString: connectionString,
            topicPrefix: "Broadcaster"
        );
        // ...
        app.MapSignalR();
    }
}
```

The first parameter of UseServiceBus() is the connection string to the server that we previously obtained from the Azure Management Tool. The second one is usually the name of the application, and it is used only to discriminate and group messages inside the bus. All SignalR nodes must use the same name so that they can share information, and it must be different than the name used by other applications that share the bus service.

This is all that we need to provide horizontal scalability to our SignalR application. From this moment on, we can run two instances of the same site on different servers and both will be communicated in a transparent way; see Figure 8-11.

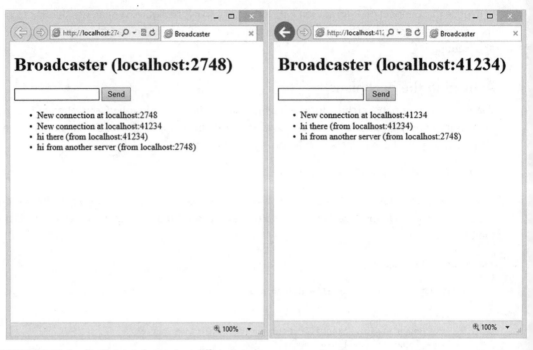

FIGURE 8-11 Application running on two different nodes.

We can provide additional configuration information to the backplane through a ServiceBusScaleoutConfiguration type object. For example, in the following code, in addition to the connection string and topic prefix, we are setting the message life span to five seconds:

```
var config = new ServiceBusScaleoutConfiguration(
                        connectionString, "Broadcaster")
            {
                TimeToLive = TimeSpan.FromSeconds(5)
            };
GlobalHost.DependencyResolver.UseServiceBus(config);
```

Additionally, it is worth noting that for the purpose of functional testing of web applications distributed across multiple nodes, a good way to do it is to launch additional IIS Express instances from the command line, as shown in the following example:

```
"c:\Program Files (x86)\IIS Express\iisexpress.exe" /port:5456
 /path:d:\signalrdemos\servicebusdemo
```

Obviously, both the port chosen and the path to the application must be adapted to the needs in each case. This way, we can have multiple instances of the server application on the local computer, each one running on a different port.

SQL Server

The Microsoft database engine is another option that we can use to horizontally scale our SignalR applications. As in the previous case, we shall see that the implementation is completely trivial.

Configuring the database

The SQL Server–based backplane uses tables to store message queues circulating through the system and, optionally, the internal messaging broker for the optimized management of publications and subscriptions. It supports any version of SQL Server from 2005 onwards, both in the Express and server editions.

Creating the data structure is automatic. It will be done by the adapter when it detects that the tables and items that it needs do not exist in the database whose connection string we will supply at application startup.

Therefore, all that we have to do is create a database and ensure that the accessing user has permissions to create schemas and tables on it. After this is done, when we run the application for the first time, we will see that the structure has been generated, as shown in Figure 8-12.

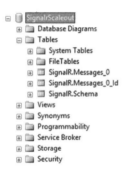

FIGURE 8-12 Database schema automatically created by SignalR.

To improve performance, it is recommended that we check that the service broker is enabled on the database that we will use. This is easy to query using the following statement:

```
SELECT name, is_broker_enabled FROM master.sys.databases
    WHERE name='YOUR_DB_NAME_HERE'
```

The result could be something close to what is shown in the following screen shot of SQL Server Management Studio, where you can see that, as it often happens by default, the broker is not enabled for new databases. In this case, as you can see in Figure 8-13, we have named our database SignalrScaleout.

FIGURE 8-13 Disabled broker.

If this is the case, we can enable it just as easily:

```
ALTER DATABASE SignalrScaleout SET SINGLE_USER WITH ROLLBACK IMMEDIATE
ALTER DATABASE SignalrScaleout SET ENABLE_BROKER
ALTER DATABASE SignalrScaleout SET MULTI_USER
```

The second line of code is what enables the broker on the specified database. The first and last lines just ensure that no other users are connected when we modify the database, which would cause a concurrency deadlock. After the script is executed, if we execute the preceding query, we get the result shown in Figure 8-14.

FIGURE 8-14 Broker enabled.

Activating the backplane

For SignalR to make use of the infrastructure created on SQL Server, we must configure and activate the corresponding backplane. For this, we will first obtain the following package via NuGet:

```
PM> Install-package Microsoft.AspNet.SignalR.SqlServer
```

When the package is installed, we would just need to enter the following configuration code, with the information on the connection with SQL Server adapted to our execution environment:

```
public class Startup
{
    public void Configuration(IAppBuilder app)
    {
        var connectionString =
                @"server=.\SQLExpress;database=DB_NAME;"
                +"Trusted_Connection=yes";

        GlobalHost.DependencyResolver.UseSqlServer(connectionString);
        // ...
        app.MapSignalR();
    }
}
```

If the connection string is not valid, if the user cannot log in, or if she is not allowed to create either schemas or tables in the database, an exception will be raised each time a client connection to the SignalR service is attempted.

We can also use a configuration object, which is useful for providing additional information. For example, the following code indicates that five tables must be created to store messages, which can improve performance by reducing contention caused by table locks in concurrent accesses. (The table structure is shown in Figure 8-15.)

```
var connectionString = @"..."; // Put your connection string here
var config = new SqlScaleoutConfiguration(connectionString)
            {
                TableCount = 5
            };
GlobalHost.DependencyResolver.UseSqlServer(config);
```

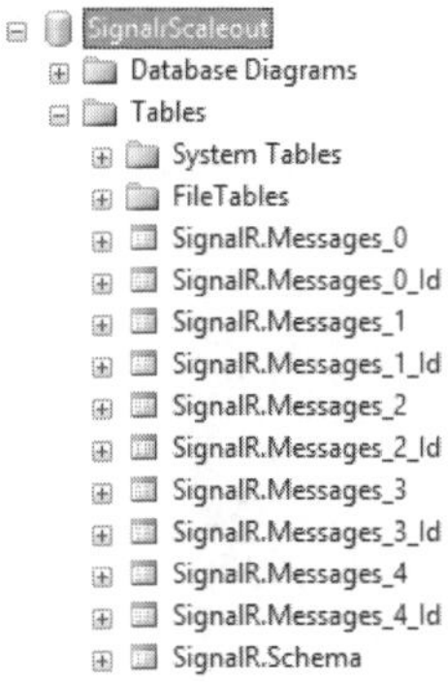

FIGURE 8-15 Table structure.

Redis

Redis[5] is a key-value open source storage system (with BSD license) that is popular in non-Microsoft environments and that has been ported to Windows by Microsoft Open Technologies.[6] Its main advantage is that it provides native mechanisms to publish and subscribe (pub/sub) on an in-memory store, which offers unmatched performance in systems that use this approach and require great immediacy, such as SignalR.

Installing Redis

From the point of view of the SignalR server, there is no difference between using Redis installed on Linux or another operating system and doing so on Windows. Therefore, the choice of server to install this software is determined by the preferences or infrastructure requirements of the system to be rolled out.

If we choose to install it on Linux (as shown in Figure 8-16), we can download the source code from the repository used and build it on the server itself:

```
$ wget http://redis.googlecode.com/files/redis-2.6.14.tar.gz
$ tar xzf redis-2.6.14.tar.gz
$ cd redis-2.6.14
$ make
```

---

[5] Official Redis website: *http://redis.io*

[6] Official Microsoft Open Technologies website: *http://msopentech.com/*

But if we want something simpler, we can also download the software from the repository of the distribution used. For example, in systems running on Ubuntu, the following statements would install and execute the server, putting it to listen on port 54321:

```
$ sudo apt-get install redis-server
[...]

$ redis-server --port 54321
```

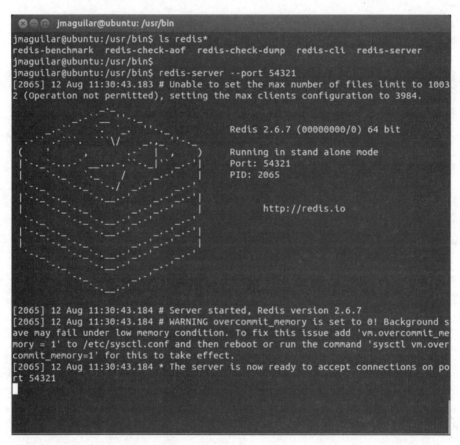

FIGURE 8-16 Redis running on Linux.

To execute it on Windows, we also have several alternatives. One is to download the source code from its GitHub repository[7] and build it using Visual Studio. Another (see Figure 8-17) is to use NuGet to get the executable file and launch it directly from the console:

```
PM> Install-Package Redis-64
Installing 'Redis-64 2.6.12.1'.
Successfully installed 'Redis-64 2.6.12.1'.

PM> start redis-server.exe
```

[7] Redis for Windows in GitHub: *https://github.com/MSOpenTech/redis*

> **Note** It is possible to use the Redis-32 package for 32-bit computers.

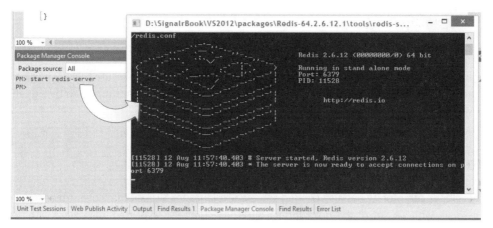

FIGURE 8-17 Launching Redis for Windows from the NuGet console.

In either case, we could begin to connect clients to these instances of Redis openly. If we prefer to specify a particular port or a password for all the clients who will use them, we can do so at command-line level:

```
PM> start redis-server "--requirepass YOUR_PASSWORD --port 54321"
```

Better yet, we can enter this password in the configuration file of the component, redis.conf. However, in both cases, it is recommended that the password be very strong, because due to the high performance of Redis, it would be possible to perform an attack by brute force, testing tens of thousands of keys per second, and the more obvious or direct passwords would be discovered very quickly.

Activating the backplane

As in the rest of backplanes, the first thing to do is to download and install the appropriate component in the project:

```
PM> Install-package Microsoft.AspNet.SignalR.Redis
```

After that, as always, we specify at application startup that we will use Redis as support for horizontal scaling. The simplest way is by specifying the basic data of the Redis server: the host, port, password, and unique string that will be used to separate messages if the server is being used by more than one application.

```
public class Startup
{
    public void Configuration(IAppBuilder app)
    {
        GlobalHost.DependencyResolver.UseRedis(
```

```
        server: "localhost",
        port: 54321,
        password: "12345",
        eventKey: "Broadcaster"
    );
    app.MapSignalR();
    }
}
```

Again, this is all that we need to run our services on Redis. When we execute them, we will also see that the difference in performance compared to the other two mechanisms provided by SignalR is quite significant.

Custom backplanes

The developer community has also created some backplanes for SignalR that cover other serial technologies without out-of-the-box support, and their number is expected to increase with time. We must take into account the short age of the project and, more specifically, of scale-out mechanisms.

Obviously, in these cases, Microsoft does not provide official support, but these backplanes might be quite useful in scenarios not initially covered, such as those that use components such as NServiceBus or RabbitMQ.

If we have specific needs, nothing stops us from creating our own backplane. Although its creation is not overly complex, right now it is not very well documented and learning relies heavily on observing the code of existing adapters and trying to replicate them, adding the necessary customizations.

Very broadly speaking, the process consists of at least the following steps:

- Creating a messaging bus inheriting from the `ScaleoutMessageBus` class provided by SignalR.

- Implementing the `Send()` method, which will be invoked by SignalR when sending data to the backplane from the current node. In it, we should contact our bus and enter in it the message that are received. This bus will be queried by all nodes connected to the server farm.

- Creating a process to retrieve the messages sent from persistence and entering them into the message flow of the local node. This can be a background process, or it can be code written in the event handler that receives data from the system used for persistence.

- At application startup, telling SignalR that the messaging bus to be used must be the class that we created earlier.

The following code shows a backplane that uses the file system as persistence. Obviously, it is pointless outside the local computer and its sole purpose is to give an example of the smallest messaging bus that would allow sharing messages between nodes within the same computer. Therefore, it must not be used in real environments.

```
// File: FilesystemMessageBus.cs
public class FileSystemMessageBus : ScaleoutMessageBus
{
    // Uses the folder %temp%/backplane
    private readonly string BasePath =
                Path.Combine(Path.GetTempPath(), "Backplane");
    private FileSystemWatcher _watcher;

    public FileSystemMessageBus(IDependencyResolver resolver,
                             ScaleoutConfiguration configuration)
        : base(resolver, configuration)
    {
        Open(0); // Use only one stream
        if (Directory.Exists(BasePath))
        {
            var files = new DirectoryInfo(BasePath).GetFiles();
            foreach (var file in files)
            {
                file.Delete();
            }
        }
        else Directory.CreateDirectory(BasePath);

        _watcher = new FileSystemWatcher(BasePath, "*.txt")
        {
            IncludeSubdirectories = false,
            EnableRaisingEvents = true
        };
        _watcher.Created += FileCreated;
    }

    // Process messages sent from the backplane to the server
    private void FileCreated(object sender, FileSystemEventArgs e)
    {
        byte[] bytes;
        while (true)
        {
            try
            {
                bytes = File.ReadAllBytes(e.FullPath);
                break;
            }
            catch                 // The file is still in use
            {
                Thread.Sleep(10); // Let's wait for a short while
            }                     // and try again
        }
        var scaleoutMessage = ScaleoutMessage.FromBytes(bytes);
        ulong id;
        string fileName = Path.GetFileNameWithoutExtension(e.Name);
        ulong.TryParse(fileName, out id);
        foreach (var message in scaleoutMessage.Messages)
        {
            OnReceived(0, id,
                new ScaleoutMessage(new[] { message }));
        }
```

```
    }

    // Send messages from the server to the backplane
    protected override Task Send(int streamIndex,
                                    IList<Message> messages)
    {
        return Task.Factory.StartNew(() =>
        {
            var bytes = new ScaleoutMessage(messages).ToBytes();
            var filePath = BasePath + "\\" +
                            DateTime.Now.Ticks + ".txt";

            File.WriteAllBytes(filePath, bytes);
        });
    }

    protected override void Dispose(bool disposing)
    {
        if (disposing)
        {
            _watcher.Dispose();
        }
        base.Dispose(disposing);
    }
}
```

As you can see, sending messages to the backplane is done just with the Send() method, serializing the message to a file in the "%temp%\Backplane" folder.

To detect new messages from the backplane, we are using a FileSystemWatcher object on this same folder. When it detects new files—messages—the FileCreated() method is executed, which gets the new file, deserializes it, and enters it into the flow of messages of the current node.

To inform SignalR that it is the message bus to be used, we would just need to execute the following code during startup:

```
// File: Startup.cs

var bus = new Lazy<FileSystemMessageBus>(
            () => new FileSystemMessageBus(
                    GlobalHost.DependencyResolver,
                    new ScaleoutConfiguration())
);
GlobalHost.DependencyResolver.Register(
            typeof(IMessageBus),
            () => (object)bus.Value
);
```

In Chapter 9, "Advanced topics," we will learn what the Dependency Resolver is, and we will fully understand what we are doing with this code. For now, it will suffice to know that we are setting the object to be used internally when any component of SignalR needs to access the messaging bus.

Improving performance in SignalR services

In all applications, we have to be careful and prudent in the use of resources to ensure that the host they run on can work at its full potential, and even more so in SignalR applications, where real-time and immediacy are essential features. Moreover, sometimes this is purely a matter of survival, because these are applications that can keep hundreds of active sessions with thousands of messages circulating. A small mistake or neglect is significantly amplified and can be fatal.

The following are general recommendations to be carefully taken into account when developing systems using SignalR if we want to achieve the best performance and application stability:

- Never use blocking calls, especially those that use external resources such as an invocation of a web service or a heavy query to a database. Use asynchrony whenever possible, as well as ASP.NET 4.5, to make better use of these features.

- Do not send messages that are too long. A message several tens or hundreds of KB in size and distributed to thousands of clients adds a load in terms of memory and bandwidth that can hardly be supported on the server side. Minimize submissions as much as possible, and meticulously optimize the data structures used to reduce size. For example, we can modify the way messages are serialized so as to minimize their additional load:

```
public class MyMessage
{
    [JsonProperty("a")]
    public double Address { get; set; }

    [JsonProperty("n")]
    public double FullName { get; set; }

    [JsonIgnore] // Don't serialize this property
    public string OtherProperty { get; set; }
}
```

- Minimize the number of messages circulating through the network. In certain scenarios, it is possible to group messages and send them all at once or to send them with a certain frequency and make the other end interpolate the intermediate states. For example, if we want to inform thousands of clients that an object is being moved across the screen in a multiuser game, it is not necessary to inform them of each pixel of movement so that they refresh their interface. Sending the information periodically each time the displacement reaches a certain number of pixels is enough, because the clients could infer the intermediate path given the old and new locations.

  Also, it is sometimes possible to perform buffering, or server clustering, and send clients the result of actions performed only from time to time. For example, if there are several clients moving various objects across the screen, the changes could be stored at the server but only notified to the other clients connected every n seconds so that they could update their interfaces. Thus we could get a fixed ratio of state update submissions per second, regardless of the number of actions performed between each update, which could be useful for real-time high frequency scenarios, as in a multiplayer shooter.

 Note The SignalR team does not recommend frequencies above 25 updates per second.

- Prevent memory leaks that in the medium term might bring the server to its knees. We must be always scrupulous with the release of resources used.

- Never use session variables. Although this tool is widely used in other web applications, it involves serializing concurrent requests from the same user, which automatically involves the loss of SignalR's high-performance ability to process in parallel. To maintain state, we must use other mechanisms, such as cookies, state via roundtrips in hubs, client storage, databases, or any other non-blocking systems.

- Simplify as much as possible the processes that are performed at the server—for example, by moving as much logic as possible to the client side. Thus the processing load becomes distributed among all users, freeing the server from tasks that do not need to be performed on it.

- Be aware of the transports used. Some consume more resources than others and are less efficient. WebSockets are by far the most efficient transport, making it convenient to execute systems in production on infrastructure that will support them, such as IIS 8 and ASP.NET 4.5.

- Do not use the server edition of IIS on client computers such as those running Windows 7 or Windows 8, because they include a hard limit of 10 concurrent connections. In these cases, it is better to use IIS Express, but remember that the Express editions should not be used in production environments.

Server configuration

Following the preceding recommendations will certainly result in improved performance and robustness of services, but it is also possible to configure IIS and ASP.NET to optimize their use in SignalR applications. Normally, they are configured for scenarios very much oriented to the traditional web, whose operation is primarily based on the processing of short requests, rather than the long-lived connections that take place during the lifetime of a SignalR client.

In the case of IIS, we can increase the number of concurrent requests that this server can handle, which can be very useful in the case of long-lived connections. To do this, we simply have to open a command console with administrator privileges, go to the %windir%\system32\inetsrv folder, and run the following:

```
appcmd.exe set config /section:system.webserver/serverRuntime /appConcurrentRequestLimit:50000
```

The default value for this parameter is 5,000 for IIS 7 and above, which might be on the short side for certain types of SignalR applications.

However, by default, ASP.NET limits the number of concurrent connections that it can handle. In version 4.0 of this framework, this maximum number is set by default to 5,000 for every CPU available in the system. To increase this value, we can go to the aspnet.config file present in the folder of the .NET Framework version with which we are working and enter the new value:

```xml
<?xml version="1.0" encoding="UTF-8" ?>
<configuration>
    ...
    <system.web>
        <applicationPool maxConcurrentRequestsPerCPU="10000" />
    </system.web>
</configuration>
```

> **Note** In 64-bit environments, .NET 4 is found inside the system folder %windir% \Microsoft.NET\Framework\v4.0.30319.

When the maximum number of connections has been exceeded, ASP.NET enters new connections into a queue, where they wait for the ones already in use to be freed. The default size of this queue is 5,000 connections. After the size is exceeded, the users begin to receive HTTP 503 errors indicating that it is not possible to deal with them.

The size of this queue can be controlled by tweaking the machine.config file, also present in the .NET Framework folder:

```xml
<?xml version="1.0"?>
<configuration>
  ...
  <system.web>
    ...
    <processModel enable="true" requestQueueLimit="15000" />
    ...
  </system.web>
</configuration>
```

Monitoring performance

One of the main tools that we can use to monitor the performance of SignalR applications is the Windows Performance Monitor (Perfmon.exe). In addition to the performance counters that we regularly use in web and ASP.NET applications, we can also install on it a set of counters specific to SignalR that will help us get a precise view of what is happening inside our system.

To install these counters, we must use the Signalr.exe utility that we already employed to generate a static JavaScript proxy based on a hub. As we saw then, we can bring this tool to our computer by using NuGet:

```
PM> Install-package Microsoft.AspNet.SignalR.Utils
```

Upon completion of the download, the signalr.exe executable file is entered into the packages folder of our project under the name Microsoft.AspNet.SignalR.Utils-2.0.0\Tools. To install the performance counters, we just need to execute the following command from a console with administrator permissions:

```
Signalr.exe ipc
```

The letters "ipc" stand for "install performance counters." Likewise, we can uninstall them using the sequence "upc" ("uninstall performance counters").

After the installation process has completed, we will have new counters available in the performance monitor that we can add to the monitoring session by clicking the "Add" button pointed to in Figure 8-18 (and also accessible via Ctrl+N).

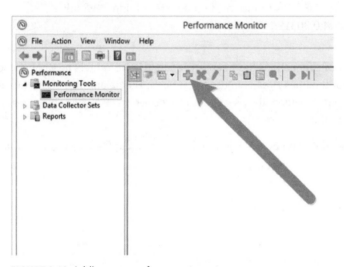

FIGURE 8-18 Adding new performance counters.

Next we will get the Add Counters dialog box, like the one shown in Figure 8-19, in which we must select the counters that we want to query, as well as the specific application instances that are using them. The counters installed are found grouped under the name SignalR. After selecting them, we can also select the instances to be monitored, in the lower left of the dialog box.

After the counters to be included have been selected and we have clicked OK, we will be able to query their values in real time. See Figure 8-20.

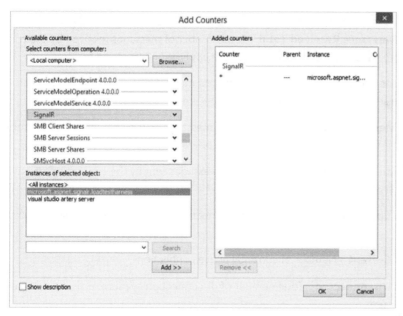

FIGURE 8-19 Selecting counters and instances to monitor.

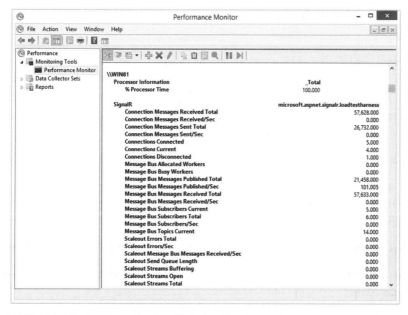

FIGURE 8-20 Performance Monitor displaying SignalR counters.

The meaning of SignalR-specific performance counters is described in the following four sections.

Connection activity

- **Connection Messages Received Total**   Total number of messages received by the connections (sent from the server to the client) since the application was started

- **Connection Messages Received/Sec**   Number of messages received by the connections (sent from the server to the client) per second

- **Connection Messages Sent Total**   Number of messages sent by the connections (from the client to the server) since the application started operating

- **Connection Messages Sent/Sec**   Number of messages sent by the connections (from the client to the server) per second

- **Connections Connected**   Total number of connections made since the application was started

- **Connections Current**   Number of currently active connections

- **Connections Disconnected**   Total number of disconnection events executed since the application was started

- **Connections Reconnected**   Total number of reconnection events that have occurred since the application was started

Errors

- **Errors: All Total**   Total number of errors generated since the application was started

- **Errors: All/Sec**   Number of errors generated per second

- **Errors: Hub Invocation Total**   Total number of errors of any type that have occurred during the invocation of hubs since the application was started

- **Errors: Hub Invocation/Sec**   Number of errors occurring per second during the invocation of hubs

- **Errors: Hub Resolution Total**   Number of hub name resolution errors that have occurred since the application was started

- **Errors: Hub Resolution/Sec**   Number of errors relative to hub name resolution per second

- **Errors: Transport Total**   Total number of errors that have occurred in transports since the application was started

- **Errors: Transport/Sec**   Number of errors relative to transports occurred per second

Activity in the messaging bus

- **Message Bus Allocated Workers**   Number of processes in charge of managing the submissions created on the bus

- **Message Bus Busy Workers**   Number of such processes that are currently making submissions on the bus

- **Message Bus Messages Published Total**   Total number of messages that have been published on the messaging bus since the application started operating

- **Message Bus Messages Published/Sec**   Number of messages that are being published on the bus per second

- **Message Bus Messages Received Total**   Total number of messages received by subscribers since the application was started

- **Message Bus Messages Received/Sec**   Number of messages that are being received by the subscribers per second

- **Message Bus Subscribers Current**   Current number of connections subscribed to the messaging bus

- **Message Bus Subscribers Total**   Total number of subscribers to the messaging bus since the application was started

- **Message Bus Subscribers/Sec**   Number of new subscriptions made to the bus per second

- **Message Bus Topics Current**   Number of topics currently defined on the messaging bus

Scale-out providers

- **Scaleout Errors Total**   Total number of errors that have occurred in the scale-out system since the application was started

- **Scaleout Errors/Sec**   Number of errors relative to the scale-out provider that are occurring per second

- **Scaleout Message Bus Messages Received/Sec**   Number of messages per second that subscribers are receiving from the messaging bus of the scale-out provider

- **Scaleout Send Queue Length**   Current size of the submission queue of the scale-out provider

- **Scaleout Streams Buffering**   Number of streams that are currently entering information into the buffer

- **Scaleout Streams Open**   Total number of streams configured on the bus that are currently open

- **Scaleout Streams Total**   Total number of streams—logical channels—currently configured on the provider's messaging bus

Other useful performance counters

Besides SignalR's own counters, which we have already mentioned, many other counters provide useful information about the state of our applications and help us detect problems. For example, it is usually crucial to know the CPU load that the computer is currently bearing. We can query it by adding the counter Processor information / % Processor time to our monitoring data.

It is also useful to know the evolution of memory footprint. For this, we have several counters grouped inside the Memory category. For example, the Available KBytes (or Available MBytes) counter can illustrate the situation quite plainly. We can also query .NET CLR Memory#bytes in all heaps on the execution process of the application to get the memory footprint in garbage collection heaps. Continual surveillance of these values can reveal memory leaks or other problems.

In the .NET CLR LocksAndThreads category we find counters that display information about the execution threads associated with the application. For example, # of current logical Threads gives the current number of threads managed by the CLR, while # of current physical Threads gives the number of threads actually in use at operating system level. Monitoring these counters could help us detect problems related to an excess of active threads and take actions such as modifying server parameters.

In the ASP.NET category we also find counters that provide a lot of valuable information. In particular, knowing the number of requests that are being processed and how many could not be processed (queued or rejected) due to saturation of the server can give us insight in many scenarios. We can obtain this information from the counters Requests Current, Requests Queued, and Requests Rejected.

The comprehensive reference of available performance counters can be reviewed at the following MSDN page: *http://msdn.microsoft.com/en-us/library/w8f5kw2e.aspx*.

CHAPTER 9

Advanced topics

In this chapter, we'll look at some of the more advanced aspects you might want to consider in your SignalR implementation.

Authorization in SignalR

It is very common to find scenarios in which we want SignalR services to be consumed only by users who have been authenticated by the system. This affects how we build our applications, because at every possible entry point to the server, we have to check that the requestor is authorized to access, and from the client side we also have to make the credentials reach the other end.

SignalR does not include any mechanism to authenticate clients, because this is something that depends on the application and the platform. For example, in a web application, authentication will normally be performed using a credential entry form or using third parties (such as Google, Facebook, Live ID, and so on) to which this responsibility is delegated. In a desktop application, authentication perhaps will have been delegated to Active Directory Domain Services (AD DS) for the company.

What we do have in SignalR are tools to know which user is accessing these resources—basically, by examining the information available in the request—and to determine whether the user has permission to do so.

Access control in persistent connections

As we know, in all the methods of the `PersistentConnection` class that allow us to take control when an important event takes place (connection, disconnection, data arrival, and so on) we have an `IRequest` type parameter available that allows us to obtain information from the request, where, among other things, we can get the authenticated user.

Therefore, a possibility when controlling access to specific functions within a persistent connection would be to query this information and act accordingly.

```
protected override Task OnReceived(IRequest request,
                                   string connectionId, string data)
{
    if (request.User==null || !request.User.Identity.IsAuthenticated)
        throw new NotAuthorizedException();
    ...
}
```

When this code is common to all operations relative to the `PersistentConnection` class that we are implementing, it is recommended that we override the `AuthorizeRequest` method that will be invoked by SignalR before passing control to the other events. This method receives a parameter of the `IRequest` type with information about the incoming request and returns a simple Boolean indicating whether access is allowed or not:

```
protected override bool AuthorizeRequest(IRequest request)
{
    return (request.User!=null &&
            request.User.Identity.IsAuthenticated);
}
```

Obviously, the access criteria can be more complex—for example, requiring the checking of other information included in the request, access times, role membership, or whatever we need for our application.

Access control in hubs

In this case, we can control access to specific actions or complete hubs by using a mechanism that is similar to the one we already have in other ASP.NET technologies: the `Authorize` attribute.

A hub method decorated with this attribute causes it to be accessible only to users authenticated in the application:

```
[Authorize]
public Task SecureBroadcast(string message)
{
    return Clients.All.Message(message);
}
```

Likewise, if we want to apply this control to all methods of the hub, we just have to apply it at class level:

```
[Authorize]
public class SecureEchoHub : Hub
{
    ...
}
```

It is very important to take into account that this is a different attribute than the one we use in Web API or in ASP.NET MVC, so we must be careful not to include incorrect namespaces when we are using it. If we apply the Web API [Authorize] attribute (defined in `System.Web.Http`) on a hub it will simply not take effect. In Figure 9-1, we can see that when [Authorize] is included, Visual Studio suggests the inclusion of three different namespaces, where attributes with this name are defined.

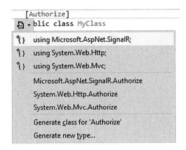

FIGURE 9-1 Namespaces available when including the `Authorize` attribute in our applications.

If we want this check to be performed on all the hubs of our application, we can set it globally during system initialization:

```
// Inserts an AuthorizeModule in the pipeline
GlobalHost.HubPipeline.RequireAuthentication();
```

When decorating our actions or hubs, we can be more explicit and not leave it at a mere check of user authentication status. The following code shows how to allow access to the method to specific users of the system:

```
[Authorize(Users="fmercury,mjackson,fsinatra")]
public void Sing(string song)
{
    // ...
}
```

We also have the ability to restrict it to certain application roles:

```
[Authorize(Roles= "greatsingers")]
public void Sing(string song)
{
    // ...
}
```

Unlike its Web API and MVC counterparts, the SignalR `Authorize` attribute has an additional parameter that makes sense only when applied at hub level:

```
[Authorize(RequireOutgoing=false, Roles="admin")]
public class SecureEchoHub : Hub
{
    ...
    public Task SecureBroadcast(string message)
    {
        return Clients.All.Message(message);
    }
}
```

In the preceding example, only authenticated users belonging to the "admin" role can invoke hub methods such as `SecureBroadcast()`, but by setting the `RequireOutgoing` parameter to false, we are indicating that no authorization is required to connect to the hub and receive messages sent from it. Therefore, thanks to this mechanism, we can have hubs to which anonymous clients connect in "passive mode" only to receive messages, whereas other privileged users would be able to invoke their methods.

We can also extend the `Authorize` attribute to implement our own authorization logic. For example, the following attribute is used to allow passage to users whose name contains the character "a":

```
public class OnlyIfUsernameContainsAAttribute: AuthorizeAttribute
{
    protected override bool UserAuthorized(IPrincipal user)
    {
        return base.UserAuthorized(user)
                && user.Identity.Name.ToLowerInvariant().Contains("a");
    }
}

// Usage in a Hub method:
[OnlyIfUsernameContainsA]
public void DoSomething()
{
    ...
}
```

Or we could ensure that the connection is made using SSL, as in the following example:

```
public class OnlySslAttribute: AuthorizeAttribute
{
    public override bool AuthorizeHubConnection(
            HubDescriptor hubDescriptor, IRequest request)
    {
        return request.Url.Scheme == "https"
            && base.AuthorizeHubConnection(hubDescriptor, request);
    }
}
```

Client authentication

We have seen how to protect access to persistent connections or to methods and hubs on the server side using diverse techniques, but basically, all of them rely on the assumption that the execution context will contain information about the connected user. That is, we assume that some component previously executed in the pipeline will have correctly set the `User` property of the context of the request, that information such as `User.Identity.Name` or `User.Identity.IsAuthenticated` will be available, and that we will be able to determine their role membership with the familiar `User.IsInRole()` method.

Although at first it might seem as though the SignalR framework itself is the one in charge of establishing identity in its requests to ensure that information about the active user reaches the application, this is not the case; the ones that do this dirty work are found further down the technology stack—see Figure 9-2—at OWIN middleware level.

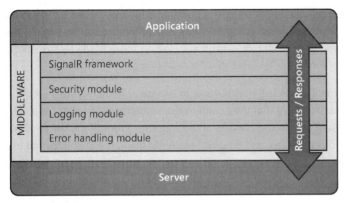

FIGURE 9-2 The architecture of OWIN systems.

This way, these modules are completely reusable across projects and systems. For example, the module responsible for managing authorization through cookies is the same one for SignalR and Web API, Nancy, or FubuMVC. In fact, the implementation of authentication and authorization management middleware modules is not even found in the SignalR project, but in Katana.

Currently, the Katana project includes the following modules, although more are expected to come in the future:

- **Microsoft.Owin.Security.ActiveDirectory** Implements authentication based on AD DS—either on-premise or on Windows Azure—integrated into the OWIN pipeline.

- **Microsoft.Owin.Security.Cookies** Implements cookie-based authentication, similar to standard ASP.NET mechanisms and authentication via forms.

- **Microsoft.Owin.Security.Facebook** Implements the Facebook OAuth authentication process in the pipeline.

- **Microsoft.Owin.Security.Google** Implements Google authentication based on OpenID.

- **Microsoft.Owin.Security.Jwt** Middleware that allows you to protect and validate JSON Web Tokens.

- **Microsoft.Owin.Security.MicrosoftAccount** Middleware specifically designed to support authentication with Microsoft (Windows Live) accounts.

- **Microsoft.Owin.Security.OAuth** Enables an application to support any standard OAuth 2.0 workflow, both on the client side and the server.

- **Microsoft.Owin.Security.Twitter** Allows supporting the Twitter OAuth 2.0 authentication protocol on an OWIN pipeline.

When we are in a pure web environment, the way authentication information reaches the server side and our hubs is quite straightforward, because we are normally in the same application.

For example, if we are using traditional cookie-based security and have accessed a page to log in to the website, those same cookies that it sends us upon successful authentication and which keep our session open on the server will travel in all requests to it, including those made by SignalR to open the virtual connection.

The `Microsoft.Owin.Security.Cookies` middleware, in charge of managing this security mechanism, will capture the requests, verify that they contain the authentication token, and set the user information obtained from said user in the context of the requests. From there, the request will continue to rise through the various modules, and when it reaches SignalR, the user information will be available and ready to be used.

However, when it comes to clients that are external to the server runtime environment, such as .NET generic clients or WinRT applications, we need to use other alternatives based on the mechanisms that SignalR client libraries offer to append information to requests, such as cookies or HTTP headers, to send data about the user. Obviously, in this case, the server side should implement the corresponding code to obtain this information and convert it to processable authentication information. For example, the following code adds an authentication token to the connection in the form of cookie:

```
var connection = new HubConnection("http://localhost:3421");

string token = GetAuthToken();    // Gets an auth token
                                  // from anywhere

// Attach the token to the connection
connection.CookieContainer = new CookieContainer();
connection.CookieContainer.Add(new Cookie("Token", token));
```

After we have generated the token and attached the cookie with it to the connection to the hub, all requests made in that context will be accompanied by said cookie.

In fact, a frequently implemented technique is to get the token via a previous call to the server, which returns it in a cookie. When we obtain the cookie, we would use it for the SignalR connections as shown in Figure 9-3.

Applying this technique is quite simple, because all we need is the web service that we would invoke from the client side. This web service would check whether the supplied credentials are valid and, if so, return the cookie proving that the user was authenticated successfully.

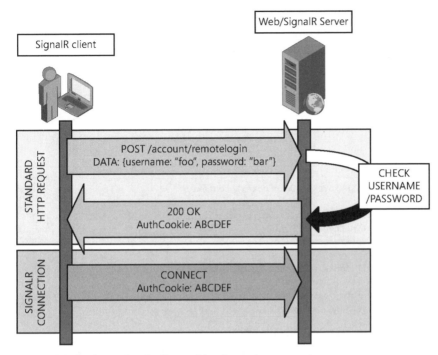

FIGURE 9-3 Getting authentication cookies via previous request.

Now we will see an example implementation of this authentication based on the cookie-based security module of the Katana project: `Microsoft.Owin.Security.Cookies`. Thus, the first thing we would have to do is install the package containing the module on our server:

```
PM> install-package Microsoft.Owin.Security.Cookies
```

Next we would include it in the OWIN process flow during application startup:

```
public class Startup
{
    public void Configuration(IAppBuilder app)
    {
        ...
        var options = new CookieAuthenticationOptions()
        {
            CookieName = "Token"
        };
        app.UseCookieAuthentication(options);
        ...
    }
}
```

The `UseCookieAuthentication()` extender enters the middleware into the OWIN pipeline, supplying it a configuration object, which, in this case, we use only to tell the module the name of the cookie where it must enter the authentication information. This name is important because we will need to recover the information from the client side.

At this point, our system is ready both to generate authentication cookies and to process them in every call, modifying the user of the request context based on the information in the token. Now we are going to implement the web service that will receive the user's credentials and, based on them, return the corresponding cookie:

```
public class CustomLoginMiddleware : OwinMiddleware
{
    public CustomLoginMiddleware(OwinMiddleware next)
        : base(next)
    {
    }

    public override async Task Invoke(IOwinContext context)
    {
        var path = context.Request.Path.Value.ToLower();
        if (context.Request.Method == "POST"
            && path.EndsWith("/account/remotelogin"))
        {
            var form = await context.Request.ReadFormAsync();
            var userName = form["username"];
            var password = form["password"];
            if (validate(userName, password))
            {
                var identity = new ClaimsIdentity(
                    CookieAuthenticationDefaults.AuthenticationType
                );
                identity.AddClaim(
                    new Claim(ClaimTypes.Name, userName)
                );
                identity.AddClaim(
                    new Claim(ClaimTypes.Role, "user")
                );
                context.Authentication.SignIn(identity);
                context.Response.StatusCode = 200;
                context.Response.ReasonPhrase = "Authorized";
            }
            else
            {
                context.Response.StatusCode = 401;
                context.Response.ReasonPhrase = "Unauthorized";
            }
            return;
        }
        await Next.Invoke(context);
    }
    private bool validate(string username, string password)
    {
        return true; // Just for brevity
    }
}
```

As usual in custom middleware modules, the class inherits from `OwinMiddleware`, which basically imposes the following two obligations on us:

- To create a constructor that takes as a parameter the next middleware module available in the pipeline, and which we must invoke if we want to continue the process of the request.

- To create the asynchronous method `Invoke()` with the processing logic of the request. This method takes request context information as an argument and can terminate the application process by managing the output directly (as it happens inside the main `if` block) or can continue executing the pipeline by invoking the next middleware module available.

Inside the module, the only thing that is done is the checking of the validity of the credentials (it is very simplified in this case) and, if they are valid, invoking the `Authentication.SignIn()` method of the context, supplying it a `ClaimsIdentity` object with user information, generating the cookie that will accompany the response to the request.

This module would be installed on the startup code and also in the pipeline. We already include the complete code of the `Configuration()` method, where you can see the SignalR mapping at the end:

```
public class Startup
{
    public void Configuration(IAppBuilder app)
    {
        var options = new CookieAuthenticationOptions()
        {
            CookieName = "Token"
        };
        app.UseCookieAuthentication(options);
        app.Use<CustomLoginMiddleware>();
        app.MapSignalR();
    }
}
```

After we have done this, our server will be able to respond to POST requests directed to the URL /account/remotelogin. Let's now see how we can invoke this service from the client side to get the cookie and attach it to the SignalR connection.

First, let's look at a possible implementation of a method that takes as arguments the URL of the authentication service and the credentials and that is used to obtain and return the value of the cookie called "Token" (note that this name is the one that we previously set on the server side):

```
private static async Task<Cookie> GetAuthCookie(
        string loginUrl, string user, string pass)
{
    var postData = string.Format(
                        "username={0}&password={1}",
                        user, pass
    );
    var httpHandler = new HttpClientHandler();
    httpHandler.CookieContainer = new CookieContainer();
    using (var httpClient = new HttpClient(httpHandler))
```

```
    {
        var response = await httpClient.PostAsync(
            loginUrl,
            new StringContent(postData, Encoding.UTF8,
                    "application/x-www-form-urlencoded"
            )
        );
        var cookies = httpHandler.CookieContainer
                                .GetCookies(new Uri(loginUrl));
        return cookies["Token"];
    }
}
```

With appropriate adaptations, this method could be consumed from any type of .NET system. The following example demonstrates its use from a console application that acts as a SignalR client. In the code, you can see how the cookie is obtained with the authentication token from the server and is attached to the hub connection:

```
var host = "http://localhost:5432";
var loginUrl = "/account/remotelogin";
var authCookie = GetAuthCookie(loginUrl, username, password).Result;
if (authCookie == null)
{
    Console.WriteLine("Impossible to get the auth token.");
    return;
}
var connection = new HubConnection(host);
connection.CookieContainer = new CookieContainer();
connection.CookieContainer.Add(authCookie);
var proxy = connection.CreateHubProxy("EchoHub");
...
connection.Start().Wait();
proxy.Invoke("SendPrivateMessage", "Hi, I'm authenticated!");
...
```

The same authentication middleware, being ultimately a service, can also be invoked from a web client—for example, by an AJAX call in JavaScript, or even (with some modifications in the component) as a destination for a login form. The following code shows how to deliver the cookie to the client by using AJAX. All subsequent requests to the service will include this cookie:

```
$("#login").click(function () {
    var u = $("#username").val();
    var p = $("#password").val();
    $.post("/account/login", { username: u, password: p })
        .done(function () {
            // The auth cookie will be attached
            // to the following request so I'll be authenticated
            location.href = "/chat/index";
        });
    return true;
});
```

An extensible framework

Internally, SignalR is designed in a completely modular form, where each component has its particular mission and clear-cut responsibilities, fitting with the other elements as if they were pieces of a jigsaw puzzle. One of the main advantages of its architecture is that it is designed for extensibility. Almost any element of the framework can be removed and easily replaced by another that fits in its place, making it possible to achieve great customization of the internal behavior of the framework itself. This is because SignalR components are quite decoupled from each other thanks to the intensive use of interfaces when creating references between classes, and to the application of design patterns such as Service Locator and Dependency Injection[1].

Thus, when a SignalR component needs to use another one, instead of referring to it directly, it usually does it through the abstractions that the interfaces allow so that both components are not bound by rigid links and so that they can maintain a high degree of independence from each other. In fact, the only thing that a component knows about another one is its interface—the contract defining its operations. This is precisely one of the secrets of customizing SignalR's internal behaviors: if we want to modify a component, we just need to know what interfaces it presents to its consumers, create a class that implements them, and replace the piece in the jigsaw puzzle.

At the time of replacing the piece, the Dependency Resolver comes on stage. This is a component included in SignalR and, indeed, in other products such as Web API or ASP.NET MVC, and it acts as a "parts supplier" for the other framework components. Its mission is simple: to provide instances of classes that implement a particular interface.

> **Note** For all purposes, the Dependency Resolver is an implementation of the Service Locator pattern.

When SignalR needs to instantiate a component of the framework that implements a particular interface, it does not do it directly. Instead, it calls the Dependency Resolver to see whether it can provide an instance. If the Dependency Resolver can indeed provide an instance, it will return it to the requestor so that the latter can use it for the purpose intended. Otherwise, the Dependency Resolver will execute the default logic, which usually consists in instantiating a class defined by default. Normally, to maintain low cohesion between components, the requestor will ask the Dependency Resolver for an instance that implements a particular interface, although specific classes can also be requested.

Note that, when obtaining instances using an external component rather than creating them when needed, we are reversing the normal execution flow of a program. This technique is often called *Inversion of Control*, or *IoC*.

---

[1] Dependency Injection & Service Locator: *http://martinfowler.com/articles/injection.html*

Let's look at an example. The following piece of code is the initialization method of the SignalR `PersistentConnection` class:

```
public virtual void Initialize(IDependencyResolver resolver)
{
    ... // Code omitted

    MessageBus = resolver.Resolve<IMessageBus>();
    JsonSerializer = resolver.Resolve<JsonSerializer>();
    TraceManager = resolver.Resolve<ITraceManager>();
    Counters = resolver.Resolve<IPerformanceCounterManager>();
    AckHandler = resolver.Resolve<IAckHandler>();
    ProtectedData = resolver.Resolve<IProtectedData>();
    UserIdProvider = resolver.Resolve<IUserIdProvider>();

    ... // Code omitted
}
```

As you can see, the method receives an instance that implements the `IDependencyResolver` interface. Basically, it is a reference to the dependency resolution component that will be in charge of providing us with all the objects that this persistent connection needs: a messaging bus, a JSON serializer, a trace manager, and so on. These are the dependencies of `PersistentConnection`—the components that it depends on to be able to perform the task entrusted to it. Certainly, the creators of SignalR could have instantiated these objects directly from the `Initialize()` method, but then the `PersistentConnection` class would be strongly coupled with them and the framework would be less flexible.

In the code, you can see that, for every dependency, the `Resolve()` method of the Dependency Resolver[2] is invoked. Basically, we are asking it (for example, in one case) something like, "Hey, have you got an instance of something that implements the `IMessageBus` interface?" And it will respond with a valid instance capable of complying with the contract imposed by the requested interface.

We can find the Dependency Resolver used by the system in the `GlobalHost` `.DependencyResolver` property. `GlobalHost` is a publicly accessible static object that contains configuration information of the SignalR application. Its `DependencyResolver` property, of the `IDependencyResolver` type, contains, by default, an object of the `DefaultDependencyResolver` class, which is the basic implementation of this component. Of course, we can (and shall!) replace this component with another one that allows us to take control over this dependency resolution process.

For example, we might be curious to observe the requests that are made to the Dependency Resolver internally during the normal execution of a SignalR application. To query it easily, we can create a class inheriting from `DefaultDependencyResolver` like this:

```
public class MyDependencyResolver : DefaultDependencyResolver
{
    public override object GetService(Type serviceType)
    {
```

---

[2] Actually, `Resolve()` is an extender of the `IDependencyResolver` interface, which uses its `GetService()` method internally to obtain the instances.

```
        var result = base.GetService(serviceType);
        var msg = string.Format(
            "*** Requested type {0}, provided: {1}",
            serviceType.Name,
            result == null ? "null" : result.GetType().Name
        );
        Debug.WriteLine(msg);
        return result;
    }

    public override IEnumerable<object> GetServices(Type serviceType)
    {
        var results = base.GetServices(serviceType);
        var msg = string.Format(
            "*** Requested type {0}, provided: {1}",
            serviceType.Name,
            string.Join(",",
                        results.Select(o => o.GetType().Name))
        );
        Debug.WriteLine(msg);
        return results;
    }
}
```

As we can guess, the GetService() method is invoked by the components when they need a single instance that implements an interface, while GetServices() is used when the result can be more than one instance.

Now we will set our MyDependencyResolver class at application startup as a dependency resolution component of the system, something that we can do by setting the Resolver property in the configuration of the hub or persistent connection:

```
public class Startup
{
    public void Configuration(IAppBuilder app)
    {
        app.MapSignalR(new HubConfiguration() {
            Resolver = new MyDependencyResolver()
        });
    }
}
```

In this case, we would be modifying the Dependency Resolver exclusively for the hubs in our system. If we wanted to make a global modification, we would simply replace the instance in GlobalHost.DependencyResolver at system initialization:

```
public class Startup
{
    public void Configuration(IAppBuilder app)
    {
        GlobalHost.DependencyResolver = new MyDependencyResolver();
        ... // Other initialization code
    }
}
```

The result obtained by the debug output when executing a SignalR application that uses a persistent connection is the following (duplicates removed):

```
*** Requested type ITraceManager, provided: TraceManager
*** Requested type IPerformanceCounterManager, provided: PerformanceCounterManager
*** Requested type MyEchoConnection, provided: null
*** Requested type IStringMinifier, provided: StringMinifier
*** Requested type IConfigurationManager, provided: DefaultConfigurationManager
*** Requested type IMessageBus, provided: MessageBus
*** Requested type JsonSerializer, provided: JsonSerializer
*** Requested type IAckHandler, provided: AckHandler
*** Requested type IProtectedData, provided: DataProtectionProviderProtectedData
*** Requested type ITransportManager, provided: TransportManager
*** Requested type IServerIdManager, provided: ServerIdManager
*** Requested type IServerCommandHandler, provided: ServerCommandHandler
*** Requested type ITransportHeartbeat, provided: TransportHeartbeat
```

When we display the trace, this time executing an application that uses a hub, we obtain the following result. We can see that many components are the same as in the previous case, but the use of hubs means that other different ones also come into play:

```
*** Requested type ITraceManager, provided: TraceManager
*** Requested type IPerformanceCounterManager, provided: PerformanceCounterManager
*** Requested type IHubDescriptorProvider, provided: ReflectedHubDescriptorProvider
*** Requested type IMethodDescriptorProvider, provided: ReflectedMethodDescriptorProvider
*** Requested type IHubActivator, provided: DefaultHubActivator
*** Requested type IHubManager, provided: DefaultHubManager
*** Requested type IJavaScriptMinifier, provided: null
*** Requested type IJavaScriptProxyGenerator, provided: DefaultJavaScriptProxyGenerator
*** Requested type IParameterResolver, provided: DefaultParameterResolver
*** Requested type IHubRequestParser, provided: HubRequestParser
*** Requested type JsonSerializer, provided: JsonSerializer
*** Requested type IHubPipelineInvoker, provided: HubPipeline
*** Requested type IStringMinifier, provided: StringMinifier
*** Requested type IConfigurationManager, provided: DefaultConfigurationManager
*** Requested type IMessageBus, provided: MessageBus
*** Requested type IAckHandler, provided: AckHandler
*** Requested type IProtectedData, provided: DataProtectionProviderProtectedData
*** Requested type ITransportManager, provided: TransportManager
*** Requested type IServerIdManager, provided: ServerIdManager
*** Requested type IServerCommandHandler, provided: ServerCommandHandler
*** Requested type IAssemblyLocator, provided: EnumerableOfAssemblyLocator
*** Requested type ITransportHeartbeat, provided: TransportHeartbeat
*** Requested type MyEchoHub, provided: null
```

Both cases clearly show which pieces are requested throughout the execution of the applications and with which specific classes they are answered. However, a question arises: how does the Dependency Resolver know the specific class with which it must respond to a request?

To resolve dependencies, the Dependency Resolver keeps an internal register where requested data types are mapped to actions for obtaining instances of them. That is, during application startup, associations are stored in the register of the Dependency Resolver in the form "when you are requesting an object that implements the interface I, execute the action A, which will return an instance of that type to you." At code level, this is accomplished in a similar way to the following example:

```
GlobalHost.DependencyResolver.Register(
  typeof(IExample),              // Type requested
   () => new ExampleClass()  // Action returning an object of this type
);
```

To be able to associate more than one specific instance to the registered type, the Register() method has an overload that also allows us to specify a set of actions for obtaining instances so that they can be obtained later by calling the GetServices() method.

Let's look at a practical example. The following code registers the IJavaScriptProxyGenerator interface in the system's Dependency Resolver. This interface must implement the component that generates the dynamic proxy of hubs. The interface is then associated to a custom builder class that enters some comments into the file footer:

```
// Initialization code
GlobalHost.DependencyResolver.Register(
    typeof(IJavaScriptProxyGenerator),
    () => new CustomProxyGenerator()
);

// Custom generator
public class CustomProxyGenerator: IJavaScriptProxyGenerator
{
    private DefaultJavaScriptProxyGenerator _generator;

    public CustomProxyGenerator()
    {
        _generator = new DefaultJavaScriptProxyGenerator(
            GlobalHost.DependencyResolver
        );
    }

    public new string GenerateProxy(string serviceUrl)
    {
        var proxy = _generator.GenerateProxy(serviceUrl);
        proxy += "\n\n"
                +"// Please don't use this code from the dark side";
        return proxy;
    }
}
```

When we want the instance returned from the Dependency Resolver to be the same for all requests made to it, we can implement this at register level in the form of a singleton object with lazy initialization using the Lazy<T> type available in the .NET Framework:

```
var generator = new Lazy<CustomProxyGenerator>(
                    () => new CustomProxyGenerator()
                );
GlobalHost.DependencyResolver.Register(
```

```
        typeof(IJavaScriptProxyGenerator),
        () => generator.Value
);
```

The lists that we saw earlier with the calls made to the Dependency Resolver requesting components can serve as a guide to know which parts of the framework can be replaced simply by modifying the register in the way that we have already seen.

Another example: when we looked at hubs, we remarked that the minimization and compaction of
the dynamically generated proxy did not come implemented out of the box, but it had been struc-
turally provided for. This can also be seen in the list of calls to `GetService()` from the Dependency
Resolver that we looked at earlier. There is a request for an `IJavaScriptMinifier` object, and a null
value is returned, so SignalR assumes that the proxy will not be minimized.

Again, we can modify the register so that it will return an object in whose `Minify()` method it
will receive a script in the form of a character string, and it must return the result of the minimization
process. Thus, if we install the AjaxMin package with NuGet, we could automatically minimize the
generated proxy as follows:

```
// Initialization code
var minifier = new Lazy<MyJavascriptMinifier>(
                () => new MyJavascriptMinifier()
            );
GlobalHost.DependencyResolver.Register(
    typeof(IJavaScriptMinifier),
    () => minifier.Value
);

// Custom minifier
public class MyJavascriptMinifier : IJavaScriptMinifier
{
    public string Minify(string source)
    {
        return new Minifier().MinifyJavaScript(source);
    }
}
```

Dependency Injection

Dependency Injection (DI) is a design pattern that describes a set of techniques whose purpose is to
achieve less cohesion between the components of our applications. Although it shares objectives with
the Service Locator—the pattern implemented by the SignalR Dependency Resolver—it uses a different approach regarding the way in which each component obtains the dependencies—other components—that it needs to operate.

Thus, whereas the Service Locator advocates an active schema—that is, it is the component itself
that uses the Dependency Resolver to request from it the required dependencies—with Dependency
Injection, these dependencies are satisfied externally, even achieving total decoupling from the
Dependency Resolver, while favoring the creation of classes with very explicit dependencies at code

level. In practice, this means that our classes will be cleaner, simpler, more independent, reusable, easily testable with unit testing, and highly maintainable.

Let's look at it with a piece of code. As you can see, the following hub is strongly coupled to other components of the system:

```
public class CustomerHub: Hub
{
    ...
    public void Create(Customer customer)
    {
        var repo = new CustomerRepository();
        repo.Save(customer);
        var mailer = new MailManager();
        mailer.Send(customer.Email, "Welcome!");
    }
}
```

The code suggests that, to operate, the CustomerHub class needs the services provided by another two classes, CustomerRepository and MailManager. That is, in the code that we observe, CustomerHub has these two dependencies and is strongly coupled to them. Because they are being instantiated directly, there would be no way to change the classes used without modifying this code and all the points in the system where the same thing is done.

Using interfaces and the Dependency Resolver would improve this situation, because instead of directly creating the instances, we could request them from this component:

```
public class CustomerHub: Hub
{
    IDependencyResolver resolver = GlobalHost.DependencyResolver;
    ...
    public void Create(Customer customer)
    {
        var repo = resolver.Resolve<ICustomerRepository>();
        repo.Save(customer);
        var mailer = resolver.Resolve<IMailManager>();
        mailer.Send(customer.Email, "Welcome!");
    }
}
```

In the body of the method, there would no longer be any reference to the specific classes on which we depend—only to the interfaces or contracts with which they must comply. Thus, the Dependency Resolver will be in charge of providing them.

However, there are still the following problems with this code:

■ First, we have introduced a dependency to the Service Locator used—in this case, the SignalR Dependency Resolver. This limits the possibilities for use and makes the classes less reusable.

■ Second, the code of Create(), whose main objective should be to store a Customer object in the repository and send it a welcome email, has too much noise due to the pipework—obtaining dependencies—that it is forced to do.

- Third, there is an additional, more subtle problem that has been carried on from the start: the dependencies of the class are neither clear nor explicit. Although there are tools to show class dependencies, even graphically, the ideal situation would be that the simple quick view of a component would give us a clear idea of what other elements it needs to function. However, in this case, we would have to review the whole class to see at what points we are using the Dependency Resolver.

Dependency Injection can help with this last point. Although there are several ways to use this principle, the most popular one is to make our classes receive the components they need—their dependencies—as parameters of their constructor, and always using abstractions provided by interfaces.

Applying this concept to the preceding example, our portion of the hub would be as follows:

```
public class CustomerHub : Hub
{
    private ICustomerRepository _customerRepository;
    private IMailManager _mailManager;
    public CustomerHub(ICustomerRepository customerRepository,
                       IMailManager mailManager)
    {
        _customerRepository = customerRepository;
        _mailManager = mailManager;
    }
    public void Create(Customer customer)
    {
        _customerRepository.Save(customer);
        _mailManager.Send(customer.Email, "Welcome!");
    }
    ...
}
```

Note that the size of the Create() method has decreased significantly, because now it has to focus only on performing its principal task. In addition, we need only a quick look at the constructor method of the class to know that it depends on two components, and although we do not know exactly which ones they are, we do know what contracts they are required to fulfill.

Above all, we have completely decoupled our hub from the other components, with the advantages that that entails.

Manual dependency injection

If we tried to connect to a hub such as the preceding one, we would get at best a 500 error indicating that there is no constructor without parameters for the hub. This is only natural, because for all this to work, we need someone to supply the dependencies to the hub constructor. Who better than the Dependency Resolver to take care of that?

Remember that a few pages ago we were checking the calls that were internally made to the Dependency Resolver, and when we obtained the ones corresponding to the execution of a hub, we could see that SignalR asked the Dependency Resolver for an instance of the hub class, but a null value was returned:

```
...
*** Requested type IServerCommandHandler, provided: ServerCommandHandler
*** Requested type IAssemblyLocator, provided: EnumerableOfAssemblyLocator
*** Requested type ITransportHeartbeat, provided: TransportHeartbeat
*** Requested type CustomerHub, provided: null
```

All that we would need would be to register in the Dependency Resolver an association between the data type requested (`CustomerHub`) and the action that would create the instance. This action is the point from which the constructor would be invoked, supplying it the required dependencies.

The code to enter in the application startup would be the following:

```
GlobalHost.DependencyResolver.Register(
    typeof(CustomerHub),
    () => new CustomerHub(
            new CustomerRepository(),
            new MailManager()
        )
);
```

This way, every time SignalR needs a `CustomerHub` type object—which will happen on every call or client interaction—it will request it from the Dependency Resolver, which will execute the lambda function and return the created instance.

If we work with persistent connections instead of hubs, we can get exactly the same result by applying the same techniques. These objects, of types descending from `PersistentConnection`, are also requested from the Dependency Resolver, so we can capture that moment and supply an object with the dependencies already satisfied:

```
// Configuration:
GlobalHost.DependencyResolver.Register(
    typeof(MyConnection),
    () => new MyConnection(
            new MyDependency()
        )
);

// Persistent Connection
public class MyConnection: PersistentConnection
{
    private IMyDependency _dependency;
    public MyConnection(IMyDependency dependency)
    {
        _dependency = dependency;
    }
    ...
}
```

However, the latter case is not quite recommended, and we must be very careful with its use, because the life of a `PersistentConnection` can be long (depending on the transport used, the instance could even be active throughout the whole time the user is connected), and if we create dependencies that use valuable resources, these might be unavailable for other uses. In these cases, it is better to opt for a close control of the lifetime of such dependencies—for example, by obtaining them through the Service Locator and delimiting their use with a `using` block to ensure their release when they are no longer needed.

Releasing dependencies

Sometimes dependencies use external resources that have to be released. For example, a hub could use an Entity Framework data context to persist information in the database, and we should always ensure that both it and (hence) the underlying connection it uses have been closed and released.

Currently, SignalR provides no mechanism to automatically release dependencies (or, for example, those that implement `IDisposable`), so developers are responsible for ensuring that this happens. Generally, a good place to do this is in the implementation of the `Dispose()` method of hubs:

```
public class CustomerHub : Hub
{
    ...

    protected override void Dispose(bool disposing)
    {
        if (disposing)
        {
            _customerRepository.Dispose();
            _mailManager.Dispose();
        }
    }
}
```

It would be necessary to do this at least with direct dependencies of the hub that implement `IDisposable`. If these depend in turn on other components, the latter could be released here or from their respective `Dispose()` methods. In any case, it is also a task that must be performed with extreme caution, because there might be components shared between instances whose early release could cause problems.

Inversion of Control containers

With the techniques seen before, we now know how to inject dependencies in hubs by simply changing the content of the Dependency Resolver register, although this task can be really laborious if we have complex dependency graphs. For example, if our hub depends on an instance that implements the `IService` interface, the specific class to be used needs an instance of `IRepository`, and in turn this instance requires an `IDataStore` object. We can find ourselves with quite convoluted registers, because we have to manage these relationships ourselves:

```
GlobalHost.DependencyResolver.Register(
    typeof (MyHub),
```

```
() => new MyHub(new MyService(new MyRepository(new MyDataStore()))))
);
```

A concept that frequently appears hand-in-hand with Dependency Injection is that of Inversion of Control containers (IoC containers). These are components specializing in managing instances, life cycles, and dependencies between objects, something like Dependency Resolvers on steroids. Not only can they act as powerful Service Locators, but they also tend to be much more flexible when registering services, specifying instantiation modes (for example, deciding which objects will be created as singletons and which will be instantiated upon request), and solving dependencies between components automatically.

Going back to our previous example, where we had a dependency graph, if we were to request an instance of MyHub from the IoC container, the latter would be able to analyze its constructor and determine that it needs an instance of IService. Thanks to its register, it would know that IService must be resolved to the MyService class, but also that the latter, in turn, requires an IRepository object in its constructor, so it would check its register again to see what class would satisfy the dependency, and so on until completing the dependency graph.

Obviously, this way of managing dependencies is much more convenient and productive than doing it manually.

There are many IoC containers on the market, although we could point out Unity, Ninject, Autofac, StructureMap, or Windsor Castle, and others, for their great popularity. Virtually all are open source products, basically very similar in concept and operation, and even quite similar to the operation of the Dependency Resolver that we have previously seen:

- Application startup is used to register in the container associations between requested types and returned types, the way they are obtained, and other aspects.

- At run time, when an instance of some type is needed by the application, the container is called to obtain it.

IoC containers are normally integrated with SignalR through the standard mechanism of dependency resolution, because this is the point already established for obtaining component instances. Usually, the default Dependency Resolver is replaced with a custom one, which uses an IoC container in the backstage to obtain the dependencies making use of the latter's power.

Now we will see how to use dependency injection with two of these containers: Unity and Ninject. The dependency graph that we will use is the following:

```
Broadcaster <requires> IMessageFormatter
MessageFormatter <implements> IMessageFormatter <requires> IClock
```

The Broadcaster hub requires in its constructor an instance of IMessageFormatter, which materializes in the MessageFormatter class and whose constructor, in turn, requires an instance of IClock. In all cases, the interfaces are a true reflection of the signature of the classes, so we will omit their code for the sake of brevity.

```
public class Broadcaster: Hub
{
```

```
        private IMessageFormatter _formatter;

        public Broadcaster(IMessageFormatter formatter)
        {
            _formatter = formatter;
        }
        public Task Broadcast(string message)
        {
            var formattedMsg = _formatter.Format(message);
            return Clients.All.Message(formattedMsg);
        }
    }
}

public class MessageFormatter : IMessageFormatter
{
    private IClock _clock;

    public MessageFormatter(IClock clock)
    {
        _clock = clock;
    }
    public string Format(string message)
    {
        return _clock.GetCurrentDateTime() + " > " + message;
    }
}

public class Clock : IClock
{
    public string GetCurrentDateTime()
    {
        return DateTime.Now.ToString("F");
    }
}
```

SignalR with Unity

Unity[3] is a powerful IoC container promoted by Microsoft Patterns & Practices. Like others, it can be installed very easily on our SignalR application via NuGet:

```
PM> Install-package Unity
```

Now we will create a Dependency Resolver inheriting from the class that SignalR provides: DefaultDependencyResolver. We take control in the methods used to obtain instances (GetService and GetServices), and we enter logic to search first in the IoC container and then, if appropriate, in the default register:

```
public class UnityDependencyResolver : DefaultDependencyResolver
{
    private UnityContainer _container;
    public UnityDependencyResolver(UnityContainer container)
    {
```

---

[3] http://unity.codeplex.com

202 CHAPTER 9 Advanced topics

```
            _container = container;
    }
    public override object GetService(Type serviceType)
    {
        if (_container.IsRegistered(serviceType))
        {
            return _container.Resolve(serviceType);
        }
        return base.GetService(serviceType);
    }
    public override IEnumerable<object> GetServices(Type serviceType)
    {
        return _container.ResolveAll(serviceType)
            .Concat(base.GetServices(serviceType));
    }
}
```

We can now set this component as a dependency resolution mechanism for the application, sending an instance in the initial configuration object. Note that to instantiate it we need to have created a Unity container, which we will also use to register the components that the IoC container will be in charge of creating:

```
public void Configuration(IAppBuilder app)
{
    var container = new UnityContainer();
    container.RegisterType<IClock, Clock>();
    container.RegisterType<IMessageFormatter, MessageFormatter>();
    container.RegisterType<Broadcaster>();

    app.MapSignalR(new HubConfiguration()
        {
            Resolver = new UnityDependencyResolver(container)
        });
}
```

> **Note** Although in this example we are including the container configuration code directly on the `Configuration()` method, it would be much more appropriate to move all operations relating to the IoC to an independent class and, for example, enter them into an `IocConfig.Setup()` method, which would be invoked from this point.

In this case, the instances that will be created for all components through Unity will be single-use. Whenever a component is requested, a new instance of it will be created. If for any reason, such as performance, we want a specific component to be managed in singleton mode, we can specify this at the moment of registration. For example, the instances of `IClock` in our previous example could be the same for the entire application, so the register could be as follows:

```
container.RegisterType<IClock, Clock>(
            new ContainerControlledLifetimeManager()
);
```

Thus, all calls made to the container requesting IClock type components will be answered with the same instance of Clock.

For more information about using Unity, you can review the official product documentation available at *http://msdn.microsoft.com/en-us/library/dn170416.aspx*.

SignalR with Ninject

Besides having a great name, Ninject is a powerful open source IoC container, created with simplicity and ease of use in mind from the beginning. Installation on a project, as usual, can be performed through NuGet:

```
PM> Install-package Ninject
```

As we did before with Unity, the next step is to create our Dependency Resolver to replace the one provided by SignalR by default:

```
public class NinjectDependencyResolver : DefaultDependencyResolver
{
    private IKernel _kernel;
    public NinjectDependencyResolver(IKernel kernel)
    {
        _kernel = kernel;
    }

    public override object GetService(Type serviceType)
    {
        return _kernel.TryGet(serviceType)
                ?? base.GetService(serviceType);
    }

    public override IEnumerable<object> GetServices(Type serviceType)
    {
        return _kernel.GetAll(serviceType)
            .Concat(base.GetServices(serviceType));
    }
}
```

As you can see, it is almost identical to the one we had with Unity, the main difference perhaps being that in Ninject dialect the container is called a "kernel." The creation and initialization of the kernel is also done during application startup:

```
public void Configuration(IAppBuilder app)
{
    var kernel = new StandardKernel();

    kernel.Bind<IClock>().To<Clock>().InSingletonScope();
    kernel.Bind<IMessageFormatter>().To<MessageFormatter>();

    app.MapSignalR(new HubConfiguration()
            {
                Resolver = new NinjectDependencyResolver(kernel)
            });
}
```

The code speaks for itself. `IClock` instances will be resolved as singletons at application level, whereas `IMessageFormatter` objects will be instantiated for each request. Moreover, in this case, it is not necessary to register the hub because, by default, when asked for a specific class, Ninject will be in charge of automatically creating instances of it without needing prior registration.

For more information about the use of this component, you can review the official product documentation available at *http://www.ninject.org/learn.html*.

Unit testing with SignalR

The full extent of unit testing is beyond the scope of this book, but we will do a quick overview of it for those readers who are not yet acquainted with it so that they can at least get an idea of what we will be looking at in the following pages.

Basically, unit tests are small pieces of code whose mission is to ensure the proper functioning of other parts of the code. In a periodical and automated way, they ensure that each component works as we expected it to work when it was implemented, so they add great robustness and maintainability to our applications.

For example, if in the future someone decides to implement new features, we could detect with unit tests whether the changes introduced have unwanted side effects on existing components. Or, if we need to modify the implementation of one of those components, unit testing would allow us to see whether everything still works as before after applying the changes. In large and complex applications, with a long life and where many developers participate, unit testing provides invaluable safety and soundness.

Let's look at a quick example. Imagine the following method, which returns a number based on another one that we send to it as an argument, applying an algorithm that an expert in the domain of our application has given us:

```
public int GetNumber(int a)
{
    if (a > 10) return a*10;
    if (a < 5) return -a;
    return a*2;
}
```

If this method were to be used from hundreds of points of our application, any change in its logic could have a great impact on our system. Therefore, we would want to implement unit tests to ensure throughout the life of our software that this method will always do what all the components that consume it expect it to do.

The following code shows unit tests performed on the preceding code. Note that these are simple methods that use the code tested, sending it different arguments and checking that it reacts as expected. The tests are written using the framework integrated in all Visual Studio editions[4], and they cover all possible paths that can be followed in the execution of the function (100 percent coverage of the code to be checked):

```csharp
[TestClass]
public class DomainGetNumberTests
{
    [TestMethod]
    public void GetNumber_Returns_10xA_if_A_is_greater_than_10()
    {
        // Arrange
        var domain = new Domain();
        var value = 12;
        var expected = 120;

        // Act
        var result = domain.GetNumber(value);

        // Assert
        Assert.AreEqual(expected, result);
    }

    [TestMethod]
    public void GetNumber_Returns_Minus_A_if_A_is_less_than_5()
    {
        // Arrange
        var domain = new Domain();
        var value = 4;
        var expected = -4;

        // Act
        var result = domain.GetNumber(value);

        // Assert
        Assert.AreEqual(expected, result);
    }

    [TestMethod]
    public void GetNumber_Returns_2xA_If_A_Is_In_Range_5_To_10()
    {
        // Arrange
        var domain = new Domain();
        var value = 5;
        var expected = 10;

        // Act
        var result = domain.GetNumber(value);

        // Assert
        Assert.AreEqual(expected, result);
    }
}
```

---

[4] There are other testing frameworks, such as XUnit, NUnit, or MbUnit, which even have total integration with Visual Studio. Although they are different in some details, all the concepts that we will see here can be applied to any of them.

The classes containing tests are marked with the [TestClass] attribute, and test methods are decorated using [TestMethod]. Each one tests a different aspect of the component, and they often have long and very descriptive names. For example, in the preceding code we see three different tests, one for each of the possible paths that execution could take in the method that we are testing.

Obviously, they could be more exhaustive and check more values in each case, but these tests could be a good starting point.

Unit tests are typically created as independent projects, exclusively entrusted with this task. Thus, we will not mix the code of the original project with its testing code.

Another detail that can be observed in the preceding code is that its implementation follows the structure "AAA" (Arrange, Act, Assert), which refers to the encoding preparations, the execution of the test itself, and the verification of the results.

When running tests from Visual Studio, we obtain a satisfactory result, as shown in Figure 9-4. We can perform these tests manually at any time or automate them within the build process of the application.

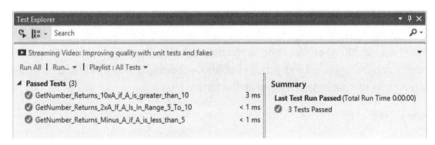

FIGURE 9-4 Satisfactory result of unit testing.

Now let's imagine that, due to a new need of our application, a developer tweaks the method, slightly modifying its behavior in this way:

```
public int GetNumber(int a)
{
    if (a > 10)
        return a * 10;
    if (a < 5)
        return -a;
    return a * 5;  // Changed!
}
```

If we have configured Visual Studio to do so, when the project was built, unit tests would be executed and compilation would fail because one of these tests would not be passed—the one which ensured that for inputs between 5 and 10 the return should be the argument multiplied by two. See Figure 9-5.

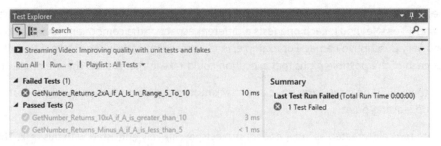

FIGURE 9-5 Incorrect result in unit tests.

At this point, the developer who made the change might realize that her small modification can affect many more points than she had previously estimated, and so rethink it or explore other alternatives. This is the security that unit tests provide: if anything changes from what we had expected at the time of building, the alarms go off.

One of the advantages of unit tests, which often turns into a problem, is that they must check a single component of the system (hence the "unit" in the name), and this is more complicated if the code to be tested uses external dependencies—that is, other components.

Consider the following code, which in the previous case we could check in a very direct way. If any test failed, we knew exactly where we needed to correct it. However, this time, a unit test failure could be either due to an incorrect implementation of the GetNumber() method or to an error in the Calculator class—or, in turn, in a dependence of the latter:

```
public int GetNumber(int a)
{
    var calc = new Calculator();
    if (a > 10)
        return calc.Multiply(a, 10);
    if (a < 5)
        return calc.Multiply(a, -1);
    return calc.Multiply(a, 2);
}
```

The preceding test would be performing a check on not only the GetNumber() method but also its dependencies. Such tests are called "integration tests" because they test how the individual components are integrated with each other, and they are usually a step taken after unit tests are performed.

Therefore, to perform correct unit tests, we should ideally not use dependencies or, if we need to, at least not have coupling as strong as the one shown in the preceding example, where the Calculator object was instantiated directly from the method tested. Forget coupling; that was more like welding.

We have already discussed the techniques that we use to decouple components, so we will not go over them again. Just keep in mind that to perform unit tests easily, low cohesion will always be a great ally. Thus, applying these techniques, we could have implemented our component without any coupling:

```
public class Domain
{
    private ICalculator _calculator;
    public Domain(ICalculator calculator)
    {
        _calculator = calculator;
    }
    public int GetNumber(int a)
    {
        if (a > 10)
            return _calculator.Multiply(a, 10);
        if (a < 5)
            return _calculator.Multiply(a, -1);
        return _calculator.Multiply(a, 2);
    }
}
```

When freed from the instance of `Calculator`, what we use is an abstraction that isolates us from the specific implementation of the calculator that we are going to use. From unit tests, we can properly supply appropriately prepared dependencies to help us check the operation of the `GetNumber()` method exclusively, which is what the test is about, without having the result affected by the operation of `Calculator`, as was previously the case.

To supply these dependencies, mock objects are often used—minimal implementations of the contracts, whose behavior is defined by the tests themselves. That is, they are classes that will implement the interfaces required by the components to be tested, but their code will be exclusively dedicated to facilitate testing. Sometimes, we will find empty implementations; at other times they will emulate production environments (for example, a database emulated in memory for testing). We might find partial implementations oriented only to the test being performed, and sometimes we will predefine the behavior of classes dynamically.

There are frameworks designed exclusively to create and prepare the behavior of these mock objects, such as Moq, Rhino Mocks, Fakes, JustMock, FakeItEasy, TypeMock, and others. Moq is, by far, the one most used for its simplicity and power.

The best way to understand how to work with these tools is to look at some code. The following method uses Moq to dynamically create an object that implements the `ICalculator` interface and to set the behavior that we want for its `Multiply()` method. Note that this is about configuring only the behavior that we need to pass the tests that we will perform on the `GetNumber()` method. It is also not necessary (nor desirable!) to replicate the logic of the original method in this configuration; we simply need to make it so that the desired result is obtained for given input arguments:

```
using Moq; // Requires NuGet package "Moq"
...
[TestMethod]
public void GetNumber_Returns_10xA_if_A_is_greater_than_10()
{
```

```
    // Arrange
    var mock = new Mock<ICalculator>();
    mock.Setup(c => c.Multiply(It.IsAny<int>(), It.IsAny<int>()))
        .Returns((int a, int b) => a * b);
    var fakeCalculator = mock.Object;

    var domain = new Domain(fakeCalculator);
    var value = 12;
    var expected = 120;

    // Act
    var result = domain.GetNumber(value);

    // Assert
    Assert.AreEqual(expected, result);
}
```

When configuring the mock object, we indicate that the result for calls to the `Multiply()` method using any integers as inputs will be the product of both. We could have also set results for specific inputs, or even ranges of inputs, and defined constant returns or returns with any value.

This mock object created and configured with Moq is injected into the constructor of the `Domain` class instance, so it will be the calculator used internally from its `GetNumber()` method. Thus, because we are controlling the behavior of dependencies with this test, we can ensure that if something goes wrong, it will mean that the `GetNumber()` method is the one that is incorrectly implemented.

Moq, like the other frameworks, has a good set of tools to configure the behavior of these mock objects as well as to check that they have been properly used. For example, the following code allows ensuring at the end of the test that the `Multiply()` method of the dependency has been called exactly once when invoking `domain.GetNumber()`:

```
using Moq;
...
// Act
var result = domain.GetNumber(value);

// Assert
Assert.AreEqual(expected, result);
mock.Verify(
        calc => calc.Multiply(It.IsAny<int>(), It.IsAny<int>()),
        Times.Once()
);
```

In the Moq project wiki[5], you can view the syntax for setting up mock objects as well as many examples of their use. It is highly recommended reading for beginners in the use of this framework.

---

[5] Moq wiki: *http://code.google.com/p/moq/wiki/QuickStart*

Unit testing of hubs

Hubs are normal classes and, as such, they can be instantiated and fed with the dependencies they need, so we can decouple them from the remaining components of our application very easily and therefore subject them to unit tests without too much trouble with the techniques and tools that we have been looking at.

Furthermore, SignalR was designed from the outset with decoupling, dependency injection, and unit testing in mind, so it will facilitate performing unit testing of our applications. Virtually all communication that we can have between a hub and the components of the framework is done using abstractions (interfaces) that allow their replacement by mock objects that make unit testing easier.

For example, look at the following code of a hub, where we can see several interactions with the platform. The first one is to get the value of the header variable "Host", the second one is to get the connection identifier, and the third one is to send an information message to all connected clients:

```
public class Broadcaster: Hub
{
    ...
    public override Task OnConnected()
    {
        var host = Context.Headers["host"];
        var id = Context.ConnectionId;
        var message = "New connection " + id + " at " + host;
        return Clients.All.Message(message);
    }
}
```

Thanks to the abstractions used by the SignalR hub class and the magic of mocking frameworks such as Moq, we can create a complete dependency infrastructure whose behavior will be set up in advance so that we can focus on checking that in this method the Message method is invoked in all connected clients, sending them the exact message that we expect.

The verification code for the OnConnected() method of the hub would be as follows. Below we will go over it step by step:

```
[TestMethod]
public void On_Connected_sends_a_broadcast_with_a_specific_message()
{
    // 1) ARRANGE
    var hub = new Broadcaster();
    var connId = "1234";
    var host = "myhost";
    var expectedMessage = "New connection "+connId+" at "+host;

    // 1.a) Set up headers
    var mockRequest = new Mock<IRequest>();
    var mockHeaders = new Mock<INameValueCollection>();
    mockHeaders.Setup(h => h["host"]).Returns(host);
    mockRequest.Setup(r => r.Headers).Returns(mockHeaders.Object);

    // 1.b) Set up context & connection id
```

```
hub.Context = new HubCallerContext(mockRequest.Object, connId);

// 1.c) Set up capture of client method call
var clientMethodInvoked = false;
var messageSent = "";

dynamic all = new ExpandoObject();
all.Message = new Func<string, Task>((string message) =>
{
    clientMethodInvoked = true;
    messageSent = message;
    return Task.FromResult(true);
});

var mockClients = new Mock<IHubCallerConnectionContext>();
mockClients.Setup(c => c.All).Returns((ExpandoObject)all);
hub.Clients = mockClients.Object;

// 2) ACT
hub.OnConnected().Wait();

// 3) ASSERT
Assert.IsTrue(clientMethodInvoked, "No client methods invoked.");
Assert.AreEqual(expectedMessage, messageSent);
}
```

Note how, little by little, we are creating the scaffolding needed to execute the method to be tested, to ensure that it can retrieve the information from its environment, and to capture the calls to the client side:

1. We first create the instance of the hub on which we will perform our tests. If its constructor received dependencies as parameters, we supply them to it at this point too. Next, we create variables to store environment values that we will use later, and we already define the message that we hope will be sent to all connected clients.

   a. We prepare the request headers to be read from the hub. A mock object is created that implements the IRequest interface, and we configure its Headers property so that a query for the "host" key returns the value that we want.

   b. Because the method to be checked needs to obtain the connection identifier, we create a HubCallerContext object to which we supply the aforementioned IRequest interface, as well as a connection identifier representing the client whose call we will simulate. This object is entered into the Context property of the hub, from which it will be possible to access the ConnectionId.

   c. We create a dynamic object called all, in which we implement the Message() method to simulate the invocation to the client side. Inside it, we simply set values in local variables indicating that this method was invoked from the hub. Next, we replace the Clients object of the hub with a new mock object whose All property is set with the all object that we created earlier. Thus, when Clients.All.Message() is called from the hub, the method that will really be invoked will be the one implemented in the lambda.

4. We invoke the `OnConnected()` method. Because it returns a background task represented by a Task, we wait for it to end.

5. We check the value of the variables where we have stored the marks indicating that the method was invoked correctly and with the desired values.

Because preparing this entire infrastructure is sometimes rather tedious, it is often included in helper methods so that all tests can quickly obtain an instance of the hub to be checked, but already configured and ready for us to focus directly on implementing the various tests:

```
[TestClass]
public class BroadcasterTests
{
    // Helper method
    private Broadcaster GetConfiguredHub()
    {
        var hub = new Broadcaster();
        var connId = "1234";
        var host = "myhost";

        // Set up headers
        var mockRequest = new Mock<IRequest>();
        var mockHeaders = new Mock<INameValueCollection>();
        mockHeaders.Setup(h => h["host"]).Returns(host);
        mockRequest.Setup(r => r.Headers)
                    .Returns(mockHeaders.Object);

        // Set up user
        var identity = new GenericPrincipal(
            new GenericIdentity("jmaguilar"), new[] { "admin" });
        mockRequest.Setup(r => r.User).Returns(identity);

        // Set up context & connection id
        hub.Context = new HubCallerContext(mockRequest.Object,
                                            connId);

        return hub;

    }
    [TestMethod]
    public void Test1()
    {
        // Arrange
        var hub = GetConfiguredHub();

        ...// Test hub

    }
    [TestMethod]
    public void Test2()
    {
        // Arrange
        var hub = GetConfiguredHub();

        ... // Test hub
```

```
        }
}
```

Let's look at one more example to show how to resolve other common scenarios when performing this type of testing. The hub method to be tested will be the following:

```
[Authorize]
public Task PrivateMessage(string destConnectionId, string text)
{
    var sender = Context.User.Identity.Name;
    var message = new Message() { Sender = sender, Text = text };

    return Clients.Client(destConnectionId).PrivateMessage(message);
}
```

In this case, we will first need to inject information about the active user into the instance of the hub. To do this, we preset the request context so that when its User property is accessed, a generic identity is returned. The code is similar to the example that we have recently seen:

```
var mockRequest = new Mock<IRequest>();
var identity = new GenericPrincipal(
        new GenericIdentity("jmaguilar"), new[] { "admin" });
mockRequest.Setup(r => r.User).Returns(identity);
...

// Set up context & connection id
hub.Context = new HubCallerContext(mockRequest.Object, connId);
...
```

We must also capture the call to the PrivateMessage method of the dynamic object returned by the call to Clients.Client(connectionId), which can be achieved in very much the same way as we did earlier:

```
[TestMethod]
public void PrivateMessage_Sends_A_Private_Mesage()
{
    // Arrange
    var hub = GetConfiguredHub();
    var destinationId = "666";
    var user = hub.Context.User.Identity.Name;
    var text = "Hi there!";

    var mockClients = new Mock<IHubCallerConnectionContext>();
    Message messageSent = null;

    dynamic client = new ExpandoObject();
    client.PrivateMessage = new Func<Message, Task>((Message data) =>
                            {
                                messageSent = data;
                                return Task.FromResult(true);
                            });

    mockClients.Setup(c => c.Client(destinationId))
            .Returns((ExpandoObject)client);
```

```
    hub.Clients = mockClients.Object;

    // Act
    hub.PrivateMessage(destinationId, text).Wait();

    // Assert
    Assert.IsNotNull(messageSent, "Message not sent");
    Assert.AreEqual(user, messageSent.Sender);
    Assert.AreEqual(text, messageSent.Text);
}
```

Another possibility that we have for capturing calls to client-side methods is to use a mock inter-face with the operations that are allowed and to configure a callback function on the call, to retrieve the information sent. The main section of the setup code would be as follows:

```
...
var mockClients = new Mock<IHubCallerConnectionContext>();
var mockClientOperations = new Mock<IClientOperations>();
mockClientOperations
    .Setup(c => c.PrivateMessage(It.IsAny<Message>()))
    .Returns(Task.FromResult(true))
    .Callback<Message>(msg =>
                    {
                        messageSent = msg;
                    });

mockClients.Setup(c => c.Client(destinationId))
            .Returns(mockClientOperations.Object);
hub.Clients = mockClients.Object;
...
```

The definition of the interface, used only to configure the behavior of the `PrivateMessage()` method with Moq, would be as follows:

```
public interface IClientOperations
{
    Task PrivateMessage(Message msg);
}
```

Unit testing persistent connections

We have seen that performing unit tests on hubs need not be especially complicated if we master a mocking framework, which, incidentally, is absolutely recommended. If the class has been built without rigid dependencies, we will always find a way to perform isolated tests on the aspects that we want. The SignalR architecture itself also makes it very easy for us, because we work on abstractions of components that can be easily replaced with other ones.

With persistent connections, things change a bit, because SignalR does not offer so much flex-ibility anymore. From its base, testing this type of component is a little more difficult because the custom code is implemented on protected methods inherited from their parent class, `PersistentConnection`. Thus, any attempt to invoke one of the overridable methods such as

OnReceived or OnConnected from the outside—for example, from a unit test—will generate a compilation error because they are not visible from outside the base class or its descendants:

```
// Arrange
var connection = new MyConnection();
...

// Act
connection.OnReceived(mockRequest.Object, connId, data); // Error
...
```

The solution to this problem is really simple: we just need to create in the test project a new class inherited from the connection that we want to test and create public methods in it that function as "bridges" to the methods of the base class. We would do the tests on these new methods because they would be visible from the test classes:

```
public class MyTestableConnection : MyConnection
{
    public new Task OnReceived(IRequest request,
                               string connectionId, string data)
    {
        return base.OnReceived(request, connectionId, data);
    }
}
```

Note that, in the constructor of this new class, we would also have to include the dependencies that the original persistent connection requires, if any.

However, when this obstacle is overcome, as soon as we begin testing the code, we will see that there are members that we would like to replace so as to take control in tests, but there is no way to do it. Perhaps the most evident case is found in the Connection property that we use from persistent connections to make direct submissions or broadcasts to clients; its setter is private, and it is set internally in the class. The process is unable to be intercepted or altered from any point.

Therefore, the recommendation regarding unit testing on this type of component is to remove as much code as possible from the methods to be tested (OnConnected, OnReceived, and so on), especially code related to Connection or other non-replaceable components, taking them to points where we *can* control them, using dependencies, inheritance or any other mechanism that can provide alternative implementations.

To illustrate these problems and how to solve them, we are going to implement some tests on the following persistent connection. Note that we have omitted all references to the Connection property of PersistentConnection, and to make submissions, we are using a custom abstraction, which we have named IConnectionWrapper, whose code we will look at later on:

```
public class EchoConnection : PersistentConnection
{
    private IConnectionWrapper _connection;

    public EchoConnection()
    {
```

```
        _connection = new ConnectionWrapper(this);
    }

    public EchoConnection(IConnectionWrapper connection)
    {
        _connection = connection;
    }

    protected override Task OnConnected(IRequest request,
                                       string connectionId)
    {
        var newConnMsg = "New connection " + connectionId + "!";
        return _connection.Send(connectionId, "Howdy!")
                        .ContinueWith(_ =>
                            _connection.Broadcast(newConnMsg)
                    );
    }
}
```

That is, we are replacing the references to this.Connection, rigid and difficult to control from unit tests, with others with no coupling whatsoever. We also define two constructors: the first one will be the one normally used at run time, whereas the second one is prepared to be able to inject the dependencies from the tests.

The abstractions that we have used are the following:

```
public interface IConnectionWrapper
{
    Task Send(string connectionId, object value);
    Task Broadcast(object value, params string[] exclude);
}

public class ConnectionWrapper: IConnectionWrapper
{
    private PersistentConnection _connection;
    public ConnectionWrapper(PersistentConnection connection)
    {
        _connection = connection;
    }

    public Task Send(string connectionId, object value)
    {
        return _connection.Connection.Send(connectionId, value);
    }

    public Task Broadcast(object value, params string[] exclude)
    {
        return _connection.Connection.Broadcast(value, exclude);
    }
}
```

From the testing project, we cannot use the EchoConnection class directly because its members have protected visibility, so we must now create the wrapper that will serve as a gateway to said class:

```
public class TestableEchoConnection : EchoConnection
{
```

```
public TestableEchoConnection(IConnectionWrapper connWrapper)
    : base(connWrapper) { }

public new Task OnReceived(IRequest req, string id, string data)
{
    return base.OnReceived(req, id, data);
}
public new Task OnConnected(IRequest req, string id)
{
    return base.OnConnected(req, id);
}
}
```

Now we can finally implement our unit test, where we verify that when the OnConnected method of the persistent connection is invoked, a submission using Send() and another one using Broadcast() are made:

```
[TestMethod]
public void On_Connected_Sends_Private_And_Broadcast_Messages()
{
    // Arrange
    var mockConnection = new Mock<IConnectionWrapper>();
    mockConnection
        .Setup(c => c.Send(It.IsAny<string>(), It.IsAny<object>()))
        .Returns(Task.FromResult(true))
        .Verifiable();

    mockConnection
        .Setup(c => c.Broadcast(It.IsAny<object>()))
        .Returns(Task.FromResult(true))
        .Verifiable();

    var echo = new TestableEchoConnection(mockConnection.Object);
    var myConnId = "1234";

    var mockRequest = new Mock<IRequest>();

    //Act
    echo.OnConnected(mockRequest.Object, myConnId).Wait();

    // Assert
    mockConnection.Verify(); // Verify expectations
}
```

Intercepting messages in hubs

SignalR comes with an out-of-the-box mechanism that is very similar to Web API delegating handlers or even to the middleware components proposed by OWIN, enabling us to enter small software modules into the execution pipeline of hubs, allowing interception tasks to be performed, as well as pre-processing and post-processing of the messages that enter and exit them.

These modules are classes that implement the `IHubPipelineModule` interface. They are added to the pipeline at application startup using the `AddModule()` method of the `HubPipeline` property present in the `GlobalHost` global object. Internally, what is done is the storing of the module in a stack:

```
GlobalHost.HubPipeline.AddModule(new MyModule());
```

> **Note** It is important that this register is made before the pipeline of the hub is executed for the first time.

The `IHubPipelineModule` interface is defined in the `Microsoft.AspNet.SignalR.Hubs` namespace as follows:

```
public interface IHubPipelineModule
{
    Func<IHubIncomingInvokerContext, Task<object>> BuildIncoming(
            Func<IHubIncomingInvokerContext, Task<object>> invoke
    );
    Func<IHubOutgoingInvokerContext, Task> BuildOutgoing(
            Func<IHubOutgoingInvokerContext, Task> send
    );
    Func<IHub, Task> BuildConnect(Func<IHub, Task> connect);
    Func<IHub, Task> BuildReconnect(Func<IHub, Task> reconnect);
    Func<IHub, Task> BuildDisconnect(Func<IHub, Task> disconnect);
    Func<HubDescriptor, IRequest, bool> BuildAuthorizeConnect(
        Func<HubDescriptor, IRequest, bool> authorizeConnect
    );
    Func<HubDescriptor, IRequest, IList<string>, IList<string>>
        BuildRejoiningGroups(
            Func<HubDescriptor, IRequest, IList<string>,
            IList<string>> rejoiningGroups
    );
}
```

Although it might look rather cryptic, the underlying concept is quite simple. Note that there is a method in the interface that represents each of the main events that occur throughout the lifetime of a hub: connections, disconnections, message sending, and so on. The mission of these methods is to serve as factories, returning delegates to functions to be executed when these events occur. These methods will be invoked by the framework only once to obtain said delegates.

The first time that a connection to a hub is made, the `HubPipeline` inner class is instantiated. This class is in charge of iterating the modules registered during setup several times, invoking all the methods defined in the interface and composing a chain of calls with the return obtained from each of them.

When an event such as a new user connection occurs, the chain of functions obtained in the preceding operation is executed, giving each module the option to enter logic before or after the process, or even to short-circuit it.

The following code shows an implementation of the `BuildOutgoing()` method, which composes the function to be executed when a client method is executed from the server. Note that, in this case, our function displays messages before and after continuing the invocation chain, executing the function that it takes as an argument:

```
public class LoggerModule: IHubPipelineModule
{
    ...
    public Func<IHubOutgoingInvokerContext, Task>
        BuildOutgoing(Func<IHubOutgoingInvokerContext, Task> send)
    {
        return async context =>
            {
                var invocation = context.Invocation;
                Debug.WriteLine(string.Format(
                    "Invoking client method '{0}' with args:",
                    invocation.Method
                ));
                foreach (var arg in invocation.Args)
                {
                    Debug.WriteLine(string.Format(
                            "    ({0}): {1}",
                            arg.GetType().Name,
                            arg.ToString()
                    ));
                }
                await send(context);
                Debug.WriteLine(string.Format(
                    "Client method '{0}' invoked",
                    context.Invocation.Method
                ));
            };
    }
}
```

Thus, as long as we have entered this module into the pipeline, we would see the following result through the debug window of Visual Studio when client-side methods are invoked from the hubs:

```
// Hub code
Clients.All.Message("Hi, everybody!");
Clients.All.Sum(3,5);

// Output result:
Invoking client method 'Message' with args:
    (String): Hi, everybody!
Client method 'Message' invoked

Invoking client method 'Sum' with args:
    (Int32): 3
    (Int32): 5
Client method 'Sum' invoked
```

To simplify the implementation of modules, SignalR developers have created the base class `HubPipeline`, on which we can build them much more efficiently and with a more intelligible code. This abstract class provides a default implementation for the methods defined in the `IHubPipeline` contract. In said implementation, it calls overridable methods that allow us to take control before and after the principal events of the hub take place. All that we have to do is create a descendant class and override the methods that we need:

- `OnAfterConnect`

- `OnAfterDisconnect`

- `OnAfterIncoming`

- `OnAfterOutgoing`

- `OnAfterReconnect`

- `OnBeforeAuthorizeConnect`

- `OnBeforeConnect`

- `OnBeforeDisconnect`

- `OnBeforeIncoming`

- `OnBeforeOutgoing`

- `OnBeforeReconnect`

- `OnIncomingError`

All `OnBefore` methods return a Boolean value. If the value returned is `true`, execution of the pipeline modules will continue, whereas if it is `false`, execution will be cancelled at that point.

To further clarify all these concepts, we will implement a simple example. The aim of this development will be to have an attribute, which we will call `OnlyOn`, which will allow us to specify which days of the week the methods of a hub are accessible, as follows:

```
public class Broadcaster: Hub
{
    ...
    [OnlyOn(Weekday.Friday | Weekday.Saturday | Weekday.Sunday)]
    public Task WeekendMessage(string message)
    {
        return Clients.All.Message(message + ". Let's party!");
    }
}
```

The days of the week are created as an enumeration of flags so that they can be combined with each other as in the preceding code:

```
[Flags]
public enum Weekday
{
    Sunday = 1, Monday = 2, Tuesday = 4, Wednesday = 8,
    Thursday = 16, Friday = 32, Saturday = 64
}
```

The code of the OnlyOn attribute is as follows:

```
[AttributeUsage(AttributeTargets.Method, AllowMultiple = false)]
public class OnlyOnAttribute : Attribute
{
    private Weekday _weekdays;
    public OnlyOnAttribute(Weekday weekdays)
    {
        _weekdays = weekdays;
    }

    public Weekday Weekdays
    {
        get { return _weekdays; }
    }
}
```

So far, it is a normal attribute, and the fact that it is used to decorate a method of the hub does not indicate that it will be taken into account during its execution. This is the time to harness the power of modules in the pipeline to bring it to life. We will take control before executing the method of the hub, we will look for its potential [OnlyOn] attribute, and if it is found, we will compare the days of permitted access with the current day, returning false if they do not match:

```
public class WeekdayControlModule : HubPipelineModule
{
    protected override bool OnBeforeIncoming(
                IHubIncomingInvokerContext context)
    {
        var onlyAttr = context.MethodDescriptor
                            .Attributes.OfType<OnlyOnAttribute>()
                            .FirstOrDefault();
        if (onlyAttr != null)
        {
            var today = DateTime.Today.DayOfWeek;
            var match = onlyAttr.Weekdays
                        & (Weekday)(1 << (int)today);
            return match != 0;;
        }
        return true;
    }
}
```

Finally, we have only to add the module to the pipeline:

```
GlobalHost.HubPipeline.AddModule(new WeekdayControlModule());
```

Integration with other frameworks

In many scenarios, we will need SignalR to work side by side with other development technologies in an integrated way. Now we will see some possible integrations with popular frameworks, both at client and server level.

Web API

When we studied the possibilities that existed for communicating other threads with the clients connected to a SignalR service, we anticipated the possibility of having a service façade to act as a gateway between external systems and hubs or persistent connections of our application, as shown in Figure 9-6.

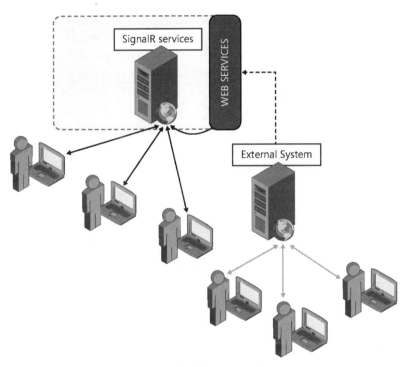

FIGURE 9-6 Access to real-time services from external systems.

This possibility can come in handy when we have external systems from which we need to send messages to a SignalR application for the latter to process them and, where applicable, inform the connected users in real time. For example, we could have a SignalR-based instant messaging service for corporate users, and we could have other applications of the company, such as its ERP or CRM system, send notifications of interest through said service in real time.

Such external systems, which could be created in any language or technology, would send their notifications to the messaging service by using an RPC mechanism toward a façade located on the

SignalR application. From this façade, the messages could be sent to the users concerned, using the techniques already seen to access hubs or persistent connections from other threads.

There are several technologies with which we could write a similar facade, from traditional SOAP/XML-based Web Services to the latest Web API framework. Due to the latter's popularity and growing usage trend, we will dedicate this section to it.

From Web API actions, it is very easy to access the clients connected to a SignalR service. We have already seen how to achieve it by using the `ConnectionManager` property of the `GlobalHost` object, through which we can obtain the context of a hub or persistent connection and send messages to its connected clients or manage its groups:

```
var ctx = GlobalHost.ConnectionManager.GetHubContext<Chat>();
ctx.Clients.All.SendMessage("The system is shutting down now!");
```

This possibility alone would allow us to obtain a reasonable integration of SignalR in our Web API–based services, but we still have other options to achieve it in a more efficient and productive way. For example, it would be quite easy to create a base controller for Web API specifically designed to facilitate access to hubs. Such a controller could be like the following:

```
using System.Web.Http;
using Microsoft.AspNet.SignalR;
using Microsoft.AspNet.SignalR.Hubs;

public abstract class ApiHubController<T> : ApiController
    where T : Hub
{
    protected IHubConnectionContext Clients { get; private set; }
    protected IGroupManager Groups { get; private set; }

    protected ApiHubController()
    {
        var ctx = GlobalHost.ConnectionManager.GetHubContext<T>();
        Clients = ctx.Clients;
        Groups = ctx.Groups;
    }
}
```

As you can see in the preceding code, we are defining the `ApiHubController` class with a generic type parameter T, where T is a Hub of SignalR. As it inherits from `ApiController`, we can safely use this class as a base for our Web API controllers, as follows:

```
public class MyChatController: ApiHubController<Chat>
{
    // Actions
}
```

The implementation of our Web API controllers will be the same as always. The only difference is that, when accessing the hub, the base class offers shortcuts to its features via controller properties instead of doing so via `GlobalHost.ConnectionManager`. These properties are as follows:

- `Clients`, of the `IHubConnectionContext` type, which allows us to access the recipient pickers and send them messages.

```
public class ChatController: ApiHubController<Chat> {
    ...
    public async Task<bool> PostMessage(string message)
    {
        await Clients.All.SendMessage(message);
        var user = User.Identity.Name;
        var ok = await _chatStorage.Save(user, message);
        return ok;
    }
}
```

- `Groups`, of the `IGroupManager` type, which allows us to add or eliminate connections of a group.

```
public async Task<bool> AddToGroup(string connId, string groupName)
{
    await Groups.Add(connId, groupName);
    var ok = await Clients.Group(groupName).SendMessage(message);
    return ok;
}
```

In the source code repository of the Web API framework on CodePlex, we can find a project called System.Web.Http.SignalR[6] with an implementation of base controllers that is conceptually similar to the one we have seen in this section, only broader.

Obviously, we could use the same technique to create Web API controllers oriented to facilitating the use of persistent connections instead of hubs. It could be very similar to the one previously shown:

```
using System.Web.Http;
using Microsoft.AspNet.SignalR;

public abstract class ApiConnectionController<T> : ApiController
        where T : PersistentConnection
{
    protected IConnectionGroupManager Groups { get; private set; }
    protected IConnection Connection { get; private set; }
    protected ApiConnectionController()
    {
        var ctx = GlobalHost.ConnectionManager.GetConnectionContext<T>();
        Connection = ctx.Connection;
        Groups = ctx.Groups;
    }
}
```

---

6 Source code of System.Web.Http.Signalr on CodePlex: *https://aspnetwebstack.codeplex.com/SourceControl/latest#src /System.Web.Http.SignalR/*

ASP.NET MVC

ASP.NET MVC, the popular framework for creating web applications, does not have any component o adapter for integration with SignalR to facilitate the use of hubs or persistent connections.

Thus, basic integration with MVC controllers should be achieved by obtaining the context of the persistent connection or hub at the point from which we want to invoke their functions:

```
public class HomeController: Controller
{
    public async Task<ActionResult> ShutDown()
    {
        var ctx = GlobalHost.ConnectionManager.GetHubContext<Chat>();
        await ctx.Clients.All.SendMessage("System shutting down!");
        return RedirectToAction("ClientsNotified");
    }
}
```

However, we could also easily achieve a similar result to the one previously obtained with Web API if we use the same idea to create controller classes specific for using hubs or persistent connections from the MVC framework. The following could be an example:

```
using System.Web.Mvc;
using Microsoft.AspNet.SignalR;
using Microsoft.AspNet.SignalR.Hubs;

public abstract class HubController<T> : Controller
    where T : Hub
{
    protected IHubConnectionContext Clients { get; private set; }
    protected IGroupManager Groups { get; private set; }
    protected HubController()
    {
        var ctx = GlobalHost.ConnectionManager.GetHubContext<T>();
        Clients = ctx.Clients;
        Groups = ctx.Groups;
    }
}
```

Notice that the only difference with the Web API controller is that, in this case, we inherit from System.Web.Mvc.Controller. Thus, we could easily use it as a base for our MVC controllers:

```
public class ChatController : HubController<EchoHub>
{
    ...
    [HttpPost]
    public async Task<ActionResult> Broadcast(string message)
    {
        await Clients.All.Message(message);
        return Json(new {success = true});
    }
}
```

Knockout

Now, on the client side, we are going to see how we could integrate a SignalR client with Knockout[7], the open source framework based on the popular presentation layer design pattern MVVM[8].

In this framework, there is a complete separation between the presentation elements, the logic that is responsible for managing presentation, and the data it uses. Thus, we will define the interface on the one hand (basically an HTML template with some special features) and the View-Model object on the other hand (which contains the data that feed said template and the logic to manage interactions).

For example, the following code could correspond to the markup of a page that uses Knockout to show a small text submission form and a list of messages received just below. Note that there is no reference to SignalR, only the Knockout binding system's own attributes that indicate different aspects of the behavior and display of the elements of the interface:

```
...
<h1>Knockout Broadcaster</h1>
<div>
    <input type="text" data-bind="value: text, enable: ready" />
    <button data-bind="click: send, enable: ready">Send</button>
</div>
<p data-bind="visible: !ready()">Connecting...</p>
<ul data-bind="foreach: messages, visible: ready">
    <li data-bind="text: $data"></li>
</ul>
...
```

At run time, when connected to SignalR (we will see how to do this later on), the result displayed on screen would look like what you see in Figure 9-7.

---

[7] Knockout official website: *http://knockoutjs.com/*

[8] Model-View-ViewModel

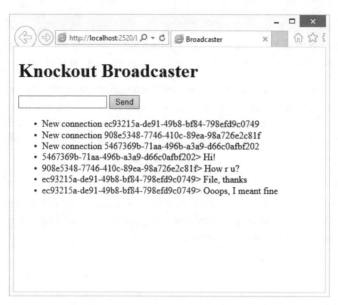

FIGURE 9-7 Knockout and SignalR executing.

In the preceding HTML code, we see the attributes that indicate binding rules of each element of interest with members of the View-Model object, which in Knockout are always called `data-bind`. One step at a time:

- The `<input>` tag bindings indicate that the value of this text box will be backed by a field named `text` in the View-Model object. In addition, the field will be enabled depending on the content of the `ready` field of the same object: if it is `false`, the text box will appear disabled, and if not, it will be enabled. In the following listing, we will initialize `ready` as `false`, and it will become `true` after we have managed to connect to SignalR.

- The button will also be enabled depending on the `ready` field of the View-Model, and clicking it will invoke the `send()` method available in the same object.

- Next we have a static message ("Connecting...") that will be visible only while `ready` is `false`.

- Finally, we have a visible list whose contents depend on an array called `messages` available in the View-Model.

The binding system uses observables in both directions. Thanks to the Knockout dependency management system, if any property of the View-Model changes, the interface will be automatically updated according to the binding rules set, and the same applies in the opposite direction: any update to the data entry fields will be immediately reflected in the properties of the View-Model.

The following code could be the View-Model class for the preceding example. It could be found in a separate script file referenced from the page or on the page itself:

```
var BroadcasterViewModel = function (hub) {
    var self = this;
```

```
self.ready = ko.observable(false);
self.text = ko.observable("");
self.send = function () {
    if (self.ready()) {
        hub.server.broadcast(self.text()).done(function() {
            self.text("");
        });
    }
};
self.messages = ko.observableArray();
self.start = function() {
    $.connection.hub.start().done(function() {
        self.ready(true);
    });
};
hub.client.message = function(msg) {
    self.messages.push(msg);
};
};
```

The class constructor takes as an argument a reference to the hub on which it will act, and as we can see, the members who were referenced from the bindings are defined on the object itself. The properties are set and queried using ko.observable()[9] objects, which are the ones that provide automatic dependency management. For example, the ready property is initially set to false, and it is set to true only when the connection to the hub is completed, whereupon all controls depending on it will automatically update their states, enabling and showing themselves.

The methods are declared directly on the class, and they can use the internal properties to perform their tasks.

The code that would initialize the page would be the one shown in the following example. All that we would need to do in this case is to instantiate the View-Model and supply it the hub on which it will operate, tell Knockout that it must use this instance as a reference for the bindings, and finally, invoke the method that we have prepared in the View-Model to start the connection to the Hub:

```
$(function () {
    var vm = new BroadcasterViewModel($.connection.broadcaster);
    ko.applyBindings(vm);
    vm.start(); // Starts the connection
});
```

Finally, the hub on which we have been working is shown here:

```
public class Broadcaster: Hub
{
    public override Task OnConnected()
    {
        return Clients.All
                .Message("New connection " + Context.ConnectionId);
    }
    public Task Broadcast(string message)
```

---

[9] ko is the principal object of Knockout. As a simplistic parallelism, ko is to Knockout as $ is to jQuery.

```
    {
        return Clients.All
                .Message(Context.ConnectionId +"> " + message);
    }
}
```

AngularJS

Of course, we can also easily integrate a SignalR client into applications built with AngularJS[10], the popular SPA[11] framework based on the MVC pattern.

In AngularJS, views are also defined independently of the other components, and as we saw with Knockout, attributes (directives, in Angular slang) are used to specify the behavior of DOM elements. The following HTML code shows the view portion of an application similar to the one we saw in the preceding section:

```
<body ng-app="angularDemo" ng-controller="BroadcasterController"
                          ng-init="start()">

    <h1>AngularJS Broadcaster</h1>
    <div>
        <input type="text" ng-model="text" ng-disabled="!ready" />
        <button ng-click="send()" ng-disabled="!ready">Send</button>
    </div>
    <p ng-hide="ready">Connecting...</p>
    <ul ng-show="ready">
        <li ng-repeat="msg in messages">{{msg}}</li>
    </ul>
</body>
```

In the <body> tag, we are specifying the name of the application ("angularDemo"), the name of the controller class (BroadcasterController), and the latter's method to be executed when the application starts. We will use this moment to start the connection to SignalR, as we will see later on.

Next we encounter the following:

- The <input> tag, where we specify that it will be bound to the text property of the controller class and that it will be disabled when its ready property, which indicates whether we have established a connection to SignalR, becomes true.

- The button will be disabled in the same way as the text box, and clicking it will cause the execution of the send() method of the controller class.

- Next, we encounter the message "Connecting...", which will be visible only while the connection has not been made.

- Finally, there is a list of messages. All the elements of the messages property—of the array type and defined in the controller class—will appear on this list.

---

[10] AngularJS official website: *http://angularjs.org/*

[11] Single Page Applications

Note that, despite the differences in syntax, the concepts are very similar to those seen with Knockout. To get a graphical idea, the running result of the AngularJS application that we are building would be what's shown in Figure 9-8.

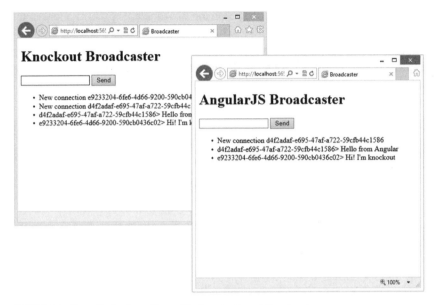

FIGURE 9-8 SignalR clients written with AngularJS and Knockout.

We will now look at the code of the controller class. This class is created automatically by AngularJS—its name is stated in the markup code—and in its constructor, it receives an argument called $scope that references the instance of the model class that is used and on which we must define the properties and methods that we need to use from our application. We have previously referenced the following properties and methods: ready, text, messages, send(), and start():

```
function BroadcasterController($scope, hub) {
    $scope.ready = false;
    $scope.text = "";
    $scope.messages = [];
    $scope.send = function () {
        if ($scope.ready) {
            hub.broadcast($scope.text);
            $scope.text = "";
        }
    };
    $scope.start = function () {
        hub.start(function () {
            $scope.$apply(function () {
                $scope.ready = true;
            });
        });
    };
    hub.messageReceived(function (msg) {
        $scope.$apply(function () {
```

```
        $scope.messages.push(msg);
    });
});
}
```

An important aspect to keep in mind when programming on AngularJS is that changes in the properties of the controller that do not come directly from events or actions managed by this framework will not be detected automatically, so the user interface will not be updated at times. In our example, this happens when we receive data from the SignalR server (implemented in the callback defined in hub.messageReceived) or when we are notified that the connection was successful. In both cases, we must use $scope.$apply() to inform Angular that changes occurred and to force its evaluation to refresh the user interface when necessary.

However, AngularJS is equipped with a magnificent out-of-the-box dependency injection system that makes it quite easy to implement controllers decoupled from the other components, allowing us to create better structured applications that are simpler and easier to maintain, as well as allowing us to perform unit tests on these classes.

In fact, you can see in the preceding code that there are no direct references to $.connection nor to any of its elements, because a service class is received as a dependency and it implements the functionalities that we need from the hub. Thus, from a unit test, we could instantiate the controller class and supply it mock objects, useful to check in an isolated manner that the operation of this component is correct.

The service class is defined as follows on the main module of the application. The name "hub" with which we created the class is used by Angular to perform automatic dependency injection; when it finds a parameter in the controller class with that name, it will search to see whether there is a factory for it in the module and use the value returned by it:

```
angular.module('angularDemo', [])
    .factory('hub', function () {
        return {
            start: function (successCallback) {
                $.connection.hub.start().done(successCallback);
            },
            broadcast: function (msg) {
                $.connection.broadcaster.server.broadcast(msg);
            },
            messageReceived: function (callback) {
                $.connection.broadcaster.client.message = callback;
            }
        };
    });
```

In this class are the three features that we need from the SignalR client for this application and that are used from the controller class: start(), to start the connection; broadcast(), to send a message to the server; and messageReceived(), which allows defining the callback to receive messages.

ndex

A

AAA acronym, 207
access control
  in hubs, 182–184
  in persistent connections, 181–182
actions, receiving and processing, 15
Active Directory Domain Services (AD DS), 181, 185
AD DS (Active Directory Domain Services), 181, 185
adaptive intervals, 8
Add Counters dialog box, 176–177
AJAX (Asynchronous JavaScript And XML), 6, 190
AJAX push, 12
AjaxMin package, 196
Android platform, 150
AngularJS framework, 230–232
API Event Source (Server-Sent Events)
  additional techniques supporting, 15
  described, 11–12
  forever frame and, 14
  push and, 12–15
  transport negotiation, 48
ApiController class, 224
appcmd.exe tool, 174
AppFunc (application delegate), 23
application delegate (AppFunc), 23
ArraySegment type, 34
ASP.NET. *See also* MVC framework
  Authorize attribute, 182–184
  performance counters, 180
  server configuration, 174–175
ASP.NET stack, 17
async/await construct (C#)
  asynchronous event processing, 35
  communicating with server using hubs, 136
  creating and opening persistent connections, 133

  receiving messages, 63
  sending messages to clients, 67
asynchronous communication
  AJAX operations, 6
  event processing, 34–35
  hub methods, 63
  recommendations, 173
Asynchronous JavaScript And XML (AJAX), 6, 190
authentication
  client, 184–190
  cookie-based, 46, 185
  OAuth 2.0, 185
  in SignalR, 181–190
authentication tokens, 186
authorization in SignalR, 181–190
Authorize attribute, 182–184
Autofac IoC container, 201
automatic proxies, 79, 83
Available KBytes performance counter, 180
Available MBytes performance counter, 180
Azure Management Tool, 163

B

backplanes
  custom, 170–172
  described, 156–157
  operation with, 156
  Redis storage system, 157, 167–170
  scaling on, 159–170
  SQL Server, 157, 165–167
  Windows Azure, 157, 159–164
Browser Link feature, 18
browsers
  cookie-based authentication, 46
  JSON parser and, 41

X

About the author

 JOSÉ M. AGUILAR is a technical computer systems engineer. For more than 20 years he has been working in the world of software development, mainly with Microsoft technologies. He has worked as a programmer, analyst, head of computer systems in the area of strategic consulting, and technical director of a development company. He is currently a freelancer, providing technical consulting, training, and development services.

He is a recognized expert and periodically writes about subjects related to software development in his blog in English (*http://www.campusmvp.net/blog /author/jose-m-aguilar*) and on Twitter (@jmaguilar). He has been recognized as a Microsoft MVP in ASP.NET/IIS every year since 2011.